# MERCIES REMEMBERED

## Reflections and Reminiscences
## of a Parish Priest

*Blessings in the merciful Lord,*

*Fr. Matthew R. Mauriello*

**by: Rev. Matthew R. Mauriello, S.T.L.**
*President, North American Congress on Mercy*

XULON PRESS

Copyright © 2010 by Rev. Matthew R. Mauriello

*Mercies Remembered*
*Reflections and Reminiscences of a Parish Priest*
by Rev. Matthew R. Mauriello

Printed in the United States of America

ISBN 9781612150048

All rights reserved solely by the author. The author guarantees all contents are original and do not infringe upon the legal rights of any other person or work. No part of this book may be reproduced in any form without the permission of the author. The views expressed in this book are not necessarily those of the publisher.

Unless otherwise indicated, Bible quotations are taken from The *New American Bible with Revised New Testament and Revised Psalms*. Copyright © 1991, 1986, 1970 by Confraternity of Christian Doctrine. Used by permission.

*Diary of St. Maria Faustina Kowalska: Divine Mercy in My Soul.* Copyright © 1987 by Marian Fathers of the Immaculate Conception, Stockbridge, MA 01263. Used with permission.

Cover design and photo by the author.

www.xulonpress.com

# Dedication

To the Blessed Virgin Mary,
*Mater Mea, Fiducia Mea*
My Mother, My Confidence.
May I echo the words of the Venerable Pope Pius XII,
who, on the occasion of his visit to Lourdes in April 1935
prior to his election to the Papacy, said,
"If I have done anything good in my Priesthood,
I owe it all to the Virgin Mary."

# PART ONE: REMINISCENCES

## Section 1. Early Blessings

Chapter

## Section 2. The Villalba Years

## Section 3. The Danbury Years

## Section 4. The Stamford Years

## Section 5. The Bridgeport Years

## Section 6. The Mercy Congress

# PART TWO: REFLECTIONS

## Section 7. Living One's Faith

## Section 8. J.M.J.L.

## Section 9. Our Life of Grace

## Section 10. Thoughts on Christian Living

## Section 11. Closing Reflections

# FOREWARD

C ardinal Newman insists that a preacher should preach first to himself, hoping he is normal enough that others need to hear what he presents. A preacher doesn't preach because he has arrived, but because he needs to challenge himself, along with his hearers. And, to ensure his authentic message, he does it as *he* does things. St. Teresa of Avila claims the most she did for God was to be herself.

I first met Fr. Mauriello when I was preaching to him and his brother priests of the Diocese of Bridgeport, CT in October 2002. Since then, we have shared views and approaches on how life needs to find help from God's inspired and challenging Word. The Word needs to find further expression in what we call "homilizing." A homily is to bring the message from that time down to this time: from the lips of Jesus to our own concrete circumstances. In this, Fr. Mauriello's first book, he shares what he has shared with himself and his hearers over the span of his 22 years as a priest. He does it his way, as he should, for that approach is the only door to authenticity.

His background studies have fortified him with a B.A., M.A. and an S.T.L. in the Theology of Mary. And so, the teaching of the church buttresses his message. His experience as pastor and a member of the Executive Committee of the World Apostolic Congress on Mercy practicalizes his presentations. He presents his thoughts so simply that their profundity resonates with the challenge to any willing hearer or reader.

"Whatever is received is received after the manner of the receiver." What we get is meant to coalesce with what we bring. Our life experiences meet, sometimes match, what Providence uniquely offers us in our every day journey toward our final goal, heaven. And so, let us read on and then revisit the veritable treasure paged out before us. If we do – as I see it – we will be helped spiritually, now laughing, now lifting the eyebrow, but regularly finding what Cardinal Newman calls, "heart speaking to heart." It's an honor for me to offer these thoughts to *Mercies Remembered: Reflections and Reminiscences of a Parish Priest.*

> \+ Lambert Reilly, O.S.B.
> Archabbot Emeritus
> St. Meinrad, IN 47577

# In Appreciation

F irst and foremost, my deep gratitude to Our Lord, for the many blessings He has so generously bestowed upon me, more than I could ever have imagined or deserved. "The Almighty has done great things for me; holy is His Name" (Lk. 1:49). I thank Our Blessed Mother Mary, under whose loving and maternal care, I have entrusted my priesthood.

My sincere thanks also go to His Excellency, Bishop Arthur J. Serratelli of the Paterson, NJ Diocese, who has been my Spiritual Director since 1977. His excellent homilies over the years, and in particular at my First Mass of Thanksgiving, have always inspired me. There are others who have spoken movingly from their hearts and have also been a source of inspiration to me. These include: His Eminence, Edward Cardinal Egan, His Excellency, Bishop William E. Lori, Archabbot Lambert Reilly, O.S.B., Rev. John M. Vaccaro, Sr. Carmel Livolsi, O.P., Sr. Carol Marie Collins, O.P., Rev. Msgr. John F. Davis, Rev. Anthony C. Dandry, Fr. Benedict J. Groeschel, C.F.R., Rev. Msgr. Thomas W. Powers, Rev. Msgr. James M. Cafone, Rev. Michael A. Merlucci and Rev. Michael J. Roach.

A special word of thanks also goes to all of those dear parishioners, friends and family who have encouraged me to write this book. Over the years, I had mentioned to them, my long time desire to put my experiences of the goodness and mercy of the Lord into a book. Their encouragement has given me a big push in the right direction. I am particularly grateful to Mrs. Judy Natale, Mrs. Debra Wortman and my brother, Dr. Anthony J. Mauriello, Jr., for their kind assistance in proofreading.

Finally, I wish to extend my appreciation and love to my dear parents who have been supportive of all my endeavors over the years, as well as my sister, Suzanne, her husband and family and my brother, Anthony. I consider myself indeed blessed, to have been raised in a loving family, and part of a wonderful extended family. My gratitude and love also goes to those whom I have had the privilege of serving in the Lord's Name over the years, and for their encouragement and friendship, many of them are mentioned in the pages that follow.

Rev. Matthew R. Mauriello, S.T.L.
May 31 in the Year for Priests 2010
Feast of the Visitation

# Introduction

P raised be Jesus Christ today and always!
Over the past more than twenty years, since my Ordination to the Priesthood, on January 11, in the Marian Year 1988, I can make the words of the psalmist my own, "How good the Lord has been to me" (Ps. 13:6). In my own way, I have tried my best to be good to Him in return. There is an expression that some people see life through "Rose-colored glasses." I have been seeing my experiences over these past two decades of my priesthood, and in fact, the past five decades of my life, through the "Mercy-colored glasses."

It has been my desire to write these pages with a sense of humility and appreciation for the blessings and the mercies that I have received, and tried to live, in my own life. Although this book has some autobiographical elements, hopefully you will see that it is not just about me, but about the goodness and mercy of the Lord that I have experienced, and by serving as His priest, have been able to bring to others.

As St. Paul wrote, quoting the Prophet Jeremiah, "As it is written, 'whoever boasts, should boast in the Lord' " (I Cor. 1:31). The mercies of which I have written are threefold: the mercy of God given to others which I have witnessed, or about which I have learned, the mercy of God which I have received, and lastly, my priestly ministry as an instrument of bringing the mercy of God to others.

In recent years, there has occasionally been sad news in the press about the actions of some priests. Every time I read about those things, I think to myself, "What about the rest of us, the vast majority, who are trying to do good?" Many priests are trying their best to follow St. Paul's advice, "Rejoice in hope, be patient in tribulations, and steadfast in prayer" (Rom. 12:12). This book is a product of my own looking back over the years, as I have tried to serve the Lord Jesus Christ and His Church to the best of my ability, complete with my faults and imperfections, as "Another Christ," a great honor given to me and every priest on the day of our Ordination.

My deep appreciation goes to our dear Holy Father, Pope Benedict XVI, for his words on his visit to the United States of America. In his homily, during the celebration of Holy Mass at Nationals Stadium, on Thursday, April 17, 2008, he told the thousands of those attending and all of us, who were watching, "Love your priests, affirm them in the excellent work that they do." May this suggestion of our beloved Holy Father come to pass in the parishes throughout the land, and in the Universal Church. Hopefully, many of the faithful will come to realize that we priests, although limited human beings, are trying to live our lives in faithful service, and bring the love and mercy of the Lord to those entrusted to our care.

Since May 2007, I have had the great privilege of serving as the North American Coordinator for the First World Apostolic Congress on Mercy, which was held at the Basilica of St. John in the Lateran in Rome, Italy in April, 2008. The Congress was the realization of the desire of the Venerable Pope John Paul II that the message of the Lord's Mercy be brought to the whole world. During a pastoral visit to Cracow, Poland, in 2002, the Holy Father stated, "Apart from God's Mercy, there is no other source of hope for mankind."

After the Mercy Congress, it has been our hope that the spark of that "Message of Mercy," which was initiated at the Congress, would be brought to the various continents and nations throughout the world. The North American Congress followed the World Apostolic Congress on Mercy, and was held in November 2009 in Washington, DC. With God's help, the next World Apostolic Congress on Mercy will be held in Cracow in October 2011.

With my involvement in the preparatory work for the Mercy Congress, I have had the "crash course" in mercy. This has given me the opportunity to learn about the Lord's mercy throughout Sacred Scripture, and I have incorporated the theme of His great mercy for all of us, much more in my spiritual life and preaching. Consequently, I have looked back at many experiences throughout my life, even before my Ordination, as the hand of the merciful Lord at work. In the same way that I can see the goodness of the Lord throughout my life, I am sure that each one of us can do the same.

You will read about a variety of interesting experiences and people in these pages. Although the majority of my priestly ministry has been with the flock entrusted to my care, I have had wonderful opportunities to meet so many great people along life's journey, some of them even famous. By the Lord's grace, I was present with Pope John Paul II during the Solemn Opening of the 1987-1988 Marian Year, at the Basilica of St. Mary Major in Rome, have had the privilege to meet Blessed Mother Theresa of Calcutta, the Servant of God, Archbishop Fulton J. Sheen and the holy, humble and brilliant priest, the Servant of God, Fr. John Hardon, S.J.

Through my brother, a physician, I have had a personal rapport with the world-famous Tenor, Luciano Pavarotti; through a parishioner, have had the privilege of blessing the Oval Office in the White House and meeting the First Lady, Laura Bush. I have even had an opportunity to give spiritual advice to Leona Helmsley, during her time in prison, who was not really as "mean" as they said.

It has always been my goal to be a simple parish priest, as Pope Benedict had said to us, on April 19, 2005, the day of his election, "a humble worker in the vineyard of the Lord." I give the dear Lord the credit for all the blessings I have received. Often I think of the psalm, "Not to us, not to us, but to Thy Name give glory" (Ps. 115:1). As well, I wish to "Put my money where my mouth is" and to use the proceeds, if any, from this book, to benefit spreading the important message of the Mercy of the Lord. The Lord Jesus Christ tells us, "Freely you have received; freely give" (Mt. 10:8).

Several of those who have reviewed the manuscript have asked me how I could possibly remember so many names, details and dates. Even as a young boy, my Mom called me "Elly," a nickname short for elephant. She would tell me, "An elephant never forgets!" At first, I thought this was her own funny expression, which she heard in her childhood, and then I learned that the origin of this phrase seems to go back to observations that elephants follow the same paths and hand down genetic memories of directions and places even across generations. Who knew?

I have relied heavily upon my love for the Holy Word of God, as well one of the favorite books of many, *The Imitation of Christ*, written by the Flemish monk, Thomas à Kempis (1380-1471). He gives us excellent advice throughout his writings, and in particular, I think of the following, "Listen in silence to the words of the saints; and let not the parables of the ancients be displeasing to thee" (Bk. 1, ch. 5). Pope St. Clement, the fourth bishop of Rome (+100) wrote, "Follow the example of the saints, because in following them, you will become a saint."

Over the years, I have been inspired by the lives and words of so many saints, who have truly become my "Heroes in the Faith" and subsequently, the thoughts and writings of many of them are incorporated throughout these pages. It has been my hope to share with the readers the fruits of my years of spiritual reading, and pass along so many wonderful thoughts and writings to others. They have inspired me to try my best to follow the advice of St. Paul, "Run the good race to win the prize… not the perishable crown, but an imperishable one" (I Cor. 9:24-27).

I have seen, in the saints' lives, the mercy and goodness of the Lord, which has been received, recalled and shared with others. St. Bernard of Clairvaux (1090-1153) wrote, "The saints have no need of honor from us; neither does our devotion add the slightest thing to what is theirs. But I tell you, when I think of them, I feel myself inflamed by a tremendous yearning" (Disc. 2, Opera Omnia Cisterc. 5, 364 ff.).

All of the remembrances contained in this book are true, and I consider them beautiful pearls and gems that have enhanced my life. They have all been wonderfully connected, to make up a sparkling necklace, which has been strung together with one thread that is the goodness, love and mercy of God. It is my hope that the reader will learn more about the bountiful mercy of the Lord, realize His mercy in their own lives and bring that mercy to others, as we help each other persevere on the path that brings us to the kingdom of heaven.

# Part One

# REMINISCENCES

# 1

# Early Blessings

## Where are They?

In September 1970, I began my High School years at St. Benedict's Preparatory School on High Street in Newark, NJ, just down the block from St. Michael's Hospital, where I was born. The Benedictine Monks, from the Abbey located there, operated the school. Toward the conclusion of my sophomore year, they decided to suspend operations, and I then continued my education at Seton Hall Preparatory School in South Orange. It would be on that same campus I would eventually receive both the Bachelor and Master degrees in the coming years.

The title of this chapter is a theme that has come to me many times over the years. In Grammar School, our study of English was limited to nouns, verbs, adjectives and adverbs and the like. However, in High School, we studied both American and European literature. The words of the title of this chapter, "Where are they?" are taken from the Latin expression "*Ubi sunt?*" This is the shortcut for a larger verse which goes like this,

> *Ubi sunt qui ante nos*
> *In mundo fuere?*
> *Vadite ad superos*
> *Transite in inferos*
> *Hos si vis videre.*

This translates into English as,

*Where are they*
*Who were in the world before us?*
*You may cross over to heaven*
*You may travel into hell*
*If you wish to see them.*

The first person to introduce me to this theme was Mr. Richard Binkowski, my sophomore English teacher. We students referred him to as "the Bink," although, in retrospect, I could even perhaps say "affectionately" so, since he was the gentleman who most helped me to appreciate the beautiful traditions of the classics throughout the centuries: Chaucer and Keats, and the list can go on and on. This was also the time that I got introduced to the Anglo Saxon epic poem, *"Beowulf,"* and it is from that work that the words above are located.

In one sense, the expression, *"Ubi sunt"* can be seen as a reminiscing or looking back to the "Good ole' days." I do often think of those simpler times, decades ago, when there was certain camaraderie of schoolmates, whether it was in High School, or in the seminary, and wonder where they all are now. Most of my classmates from the seminary days went on to Ordination, and are now serving the Lord and His Church as priests today. The High School classmates are married, and leading lives filled with their wives, work and families. Perhaps, by now, some have grandchildren as well. I wish all of them well, and thank the Lord for the times of fellowship that we had together.

In a larger sense, those two words *"Ubi sunt"* still have crossed my mind very frequently over the years, throughout my travels. I had the opportunity to visit Istanbul, and in particular the beautiful Church of *Hagia Sofia*, which means "Holy Wisdom." It is now a museum, and still considered the epitome of Byzantine architecture. I could not help but think of the Emperor Constantine the Great, (274-337) who planned that city as Constantinople, and according to legend, began this Patriarchal Basilica. It was finished by the Emperor Justinian I, (484-565) and dedicated on December 27, 537.

The day of the solemn dedication, history tells us that both the Emperor and Patriarch Eutychius walked in the church that day side by side. I can only imagine the throng of faithful filled with great joy and I cannot help but wonder, "Where are they now?" I hope and pray the Lord had mercy upon their immortal souls, and they are with Him in the heavenly kingdom.

When I have had the opportunity to travel to other ancient sites, such as those at Ephesus and Athens, and have seen splendid cathedrals in Ravenna, Chartres and Winchester, the foundations of which are so ancient, I frequently think of those artisans who sacrificed decades of their lives in constructing these masterpieces and wonder, "Where they are now?" Even in Rome, among the ruins of the ancient Forum, and in the grottoes under the Basilica of St. Peter, one can think of the many that preceded us walking in those same pathways.

Then, of course, I cannot help but think of myself, as well as those whom I love, and wonder where we will be in another thousand years, or even another fifty years. Our lives come and go so quickly, and each of us is just one heartbeat away from eternity, so we need to do the best we can in the time allotted to us. There is a verse that comes to me, which often helps to put things in proper perspective, "Remember your last days, and you will not sin" (Sir. 7:36).

We are indeed blessed that we have a loving, merciful Heavenly Father Who is "Rich in mercy" (Eph. 2:4). He sent His only Son, Who understands the limitation of the human condition and our fight against the "world, flesh and the devil." I truly believe that the Lord is on our side, to help achieve our desire: to dwell with Him in heaven. St. Paul wrote, "If God is for us, who can be against us" (Rom. 8:31)?

When I was in Istanbul, I saw men on the street with beads in their hands. These looked like rosary beads, but were not marked off with decades. A priest friend, traveling with me, said that they were used to name the attributes of God. When we were in the Grand Bazaar, I found one of the prayer beads, among one of the 4,000 shops located there, and as I was counting the number of the beads, was told by the owner that there are 33 beads. There are 99 attributes of God in the Muslim tradition, and it is the practice to go around the beads three times, recalling the titles of God. Some of these are: "The only One, the Omniscient, the Mighty, the Glorious, the Generous, the Most Compassionate, the Tenderly Merciful and Consoling, the Most High."

However, I was told that there is no reference to God as a Father. This is apparently not part of their tradition, as it is in ours. We heard these words from the Lord Jesus who called His Father "Abba" which means Father, or even more intimate than that, perhaps more like "Daddy." When the Lord was asked how we are to pray, He instructed us, and began with the words "Our Father" (Mt. 6:9, Lk. 11:2).

We can feel the Lord's comfort and care, just as a child, who approaches their parent for their needs, help, pardon and love. Jesus tells us that His Heavenly Father will help us in our needs,

> "What father among you would hand his son a snake when he asks for a fish? Or hand him a scorpion, when he asks for an egg? If you then, who are wicked, know how to give good gifts to your children, how much more will the Father in heaven give the Holy Spirit to those who ask Him" (Lk. 11:11-13)?

As this work of my reminiscences continues, there will be many people mentioned herein, although some are relatives, most of them are fellow pilgrims along the path. Many of them I have had the privilege to serve, and even prepare to depart this earthly pilgrimage and join the many who have gone before us "Marked with the sign of faith" as we hear during the Eucharistic Prayer at Mass. Often, when thinking of them, the words "Where are they?" and I hope and pray that "They may rest from their labors, for their works accompany them" (Rev. 14:13). May that also be the case for all of us, who wish to persevere in the love of God, and be one day admitted to the company of the Lord and His saints and angels in the kingdom of heaven.

# Grandma Serafina

My grandmother, Serafina Armento Fiore, was born on July 23, 1907 in Tricarico, in southern Italy. I believe that my early love for her was based on the same admiration that many grandchildren have for their grandparents. Visiting her home was always a special treat. For example, at the holidays, there were all my aunts, uncles and cousins, and there were at least twenty, perhaps closer to thirty of us, around the Dining Room table for the all-fish traditional Christmas Eve Italian meal.

Those Christmas Eves seem like just yesterday, with the live eels swimming in the bathtub, since they would be prepared for cooking at the very last minute. Even though it is more than four decades ago now, I can still remember seeing them still wiggling in the frying pan, after they were skinned and dredged in flour! Those were happy days, filled with such wonderful memories.

As I grew older, and was in my early teens, in the year 1969, my grandmother had a heart attack, and lived with us in her recovery. When it was realized that she could not return to her home, she stayed with us almost three years. Little by little, she would tell me stories from her early life. For example, she explained to me, that in those days, the young women still went to wash the family laundry in the stream, with the bushel basket full of the laundry, carried back and forth on their heads. It was a different age.

In Italy, they had been considered a middle class family, and she was sent to a school run by a convent of religious sisters. Besides the regular subjects, they prepared their trousseau and hand embroidered, in beautiful cut work, sets of sheets, pillow cases, table cloths with matching napkins, and other items, to get ready for their marriage some day. In the end, she had twelve of every item, which filled an entire trunk that she eventually brought with her to America, as a young bride. As they did this work, she and the other young women learned to sing the parts of the Mass in Latin, and she would often sing those to me.

One day in June 1976, after lunch, I set up a tape recorder and brought up the subject of all the litanies and songs that she learned in the convent in her youth. Without her knowing it, I recorded them and am so happy that I did so. When I then showed her that I had taped her singing, within the hour, she had made a list of additional songs that she wished to be recorded, so now I have at least two hours of her voice, and I truly consider those tapes to be worth their weight in gold, and encrusted with diamonds.

She had been a very attractive young woman, as I have seen from her photos, with a round, cherubic face, and two large dimples in her cheeks that were seen frequently, as she was always happy and smiled a lot. In fact, it had been a framed photo of her, on the piano of her cousin in New Jersey in the 1920's, which attracted the attention of her future husband, Rocco Fiore. He learned that she was from the same town, and he began a courtship through correspondence.

However, her first vocation, I had learned, was to become a religious sister. Her inner goodness, beauty and piety had been noticed by the holy bishop in the hill town, the Servant of God, Bishop Raffaelle delle Nocche, who served there from 1922-1960. The cause for his beatification was opened in November 1968.

The bishop was in the process of forming a new institute of religious sisters, the Disciples of Eucharistic Jesus, known as the *"Discepole di Gesù Eucharistico"* and invited Serafina, then approaching nineteen years old, to become the first Mother Superior. She told me that she had prayed about this, and believed in her heart, that it was the plan of God for her. However, when she went to ask her father, Antonio, for his blessing, he absolutely refused. There was no way to persuade him to relent, and she had to tell this to the bishop.

However, she had remained faithful to the Lord, and each day read the Liturgy of the Hours, as the priests and religious do, at first in Latin, and later in Italian. She told me that in her early years, she had a great devotion to the Sacred Heart of Jesus. She had told the Lord in prayer, that although she could not serve Him and His church in religious life, from then on she would be considered *"Serafina di Gesù"* (Serafina of Jesus). She related to me that the Lord spoke to her heart in prayer and He told her that from now on He would be called *"Gesù di Serafina,"* (Jesus of Serafina).

Within about a year, the courtship through letters began, with her future husband, Rocco. He was working in the United States as a tailor and furrier, and they decided to get married. He returned to Italy with the wedding gown, as was the tradition, and they were wed in the Cathedral on December 1, 1928. Her cousin, Rev. Pancrazio Toscano, performed the wedding and the bishop was there as well, to give them the final Nuptial Blessing. After a honeymoon in Rome, they prepared to immigrate to the United States aboard the ship *"Augustus."*

Their four children were born in Newark, New Jersey: Paolina (Pauline), born in 1930, Assunta (Susan, my mother), born in 1931, Emilia (Emily), born in 1935 and their son Antonio (Anthony), born in 1940. Just like many immigrants, they too, made many sacrifices and prospered in their new life in America. They were a family of love and faith, who were hard-working and dedicated to attendance at Mass and reception of the Sacraments.

Unfortunately, my grandmother became a widow at a young age. In October 1952, her beloved husband, Rocco, died of a brain tumor. It was a sudden and devastating loss, he was only 48 years old and she was 45. Grandma Serafina related to me that she then grew cold toward the Lord and did not want to hear about God or religion. She felt that she had been so faithful to God throughout her life, and how could He do this to her? Her attitude persisted until the following June, when one day, she was in the kitchen, and the Lord Jesus spoke to her soul in Italian, saying, "Serafina of Jesus, why have you abandoned Me? I wait for you."

My grandmother told me that she then went into the pantry, where she kept the calendar, and realized that it was the Feast of the Sacred Heart of Jesus, which had been her favorite feast day since her youth. She began to weep, realizing that she needed to recommit herself to the Lord Jesus once again, since He alone would help her through her grief and pain. And so, she went to confession, and resumed her spiritual life, which, beside regular attendance at Holy Mass and receiving Holy Communion, included the Liturgy of the Hours and praying the Rosary daily. When I think of my dear grandmother's story, I think of the passage of Sacred Scripture in which the Lord Jesus talked about the lost sheep and said that, "There is such rejoicing among the angels in heaven for the one sheep, that has returned to the flock" (Lk. 15:10).

At 45, she was still young and very attractive, as I have seen in photographs, and there were several suitors interested in her, but she decided not to remarry. There was a position available at Seton Hall University in South Orange, NJ, in the residence of the priests, who served as the professors there. Although her official job was to clean their rooms, after a while, she was bringing home extra work to help darn their socks, and the like.

The President of the University at the time was His Excellency, Bishop John J. Dougherty, who was one of the auxiliary bishops of the Archdiocese of Newark, and he specifically asked that she attend to his suite of rooms. They became dear friends, and would often sing arias from Verdi and Puccini Operas together, since at times, the bishop was there while she was working. She had also built up a wonderful rapport with the priests, whom she considered "her sons" and would often invite groups of them to her home for a home-cooked meal. I recall those happy times, since we lived just a few homes away, that my Grandma was having the priests for dinner, and she was cooking up a storm.

In January 1969, while working in the priest residence, she had a heart attack, and was rushed to the hospital. I was too young to be allowed to visit her in the Intensive Care Department, but heard from my Mom and Dad that there must have been at least twenty priests around her bedside, at one point, all her dear "sons" from Seton Hall. My parents told me that the nurses in the Unit did not know what to make of it!

When she passed away on July 26, 1981, they all remembered her kindness to them, and eight of those priests, who she served so well, came to the Funeral Mass to concelebrate. Even the now aged Bishop Dougherty was in attendance, and both he and the priests remembered her with the affection of dear friends.

The goodness, kindness and charity that she showed to others were then shown to her in return. "The measure that you measure out to others will be measured back to you" (Mt. 7:2, Lk. 6:38) as Our Lord Himself tells us. I cannot help but think of one of my favorite movies, "The Wizard of Oz," made in 1939. In it, the character of the Tin Man had asked for a heart. Then, toward the end of the movie, the Wizard presented him with a clock that ticked, in the shape of a heart. He told the Tin Man that hearts are not to be judged by how much one loves, but by how much one has been loved by others.

Each year on the anniversary of the passing of my dear Grandma Serafina, I have found great comfort in the Holy Word of God, "The God and Father of our Lord Jesus Christ, the Father of mercies and God of all consolation Who encourages us in our every affliction" (2 Cor. 1:3-4). Her anniversary is on the Feast of Sts. Joachim and Ann, who were the parents of the Blessed Virgin Mary, and the grandparents of the Lord. The First Reading each year at Holy Mass on that day, is taken from the Book of Sirach,

> "Let us now praise our ancestors. These were men of Mercy, whose righteous deeds have not been forgotten. Their prosperity will remain with their descendants, and their inheritance to their children's children. Their posterity will continue forever, and their glory will not be blotted out. Their bodies were buried in peace, and their name lives to all generations. People will declare their wisdom, and the congregation proclaims their praise" (Sir. 44:1, 10-11, 13-15).

What I learned from the life of my grandmother is that the Lord will get us through even the most difficult of situations, if we stay close to Him. In Italian there is an expression, *"Aiutati e Dio ti aiuterà"* which means, "Help yourself and God will help you" or a more familiar English version, "God helps those who help themselves." The Lord Jesus had intervened in her life in the kitchen that day, and given her hope, along with the invitation to embrace Him once again in love. He gave her His healing and peace. But she needed to do her own part and recapture her joy, which she did little by little.

There is a 1952 movie about the life of Jane Froman, (1907-1980) who, although disabled, was always upbeat, and continued to entertain the troops during World War II. She lived up to her theme song which was, "With a Song in My Heart." Some might think that my grandmother had a difficult life, but for her, and so many others, there is always a song in the heart that loves God.

I have heard it said, "There is no such thing as a sad saint." The saints indeed had their sufferings and crosses throughout the centuries, but they did not despair of the Lord's mercy and help. Had they, they would never have been canonized. And so it is with you and me. We are invited to follow their example. St. Padre Pio (1887-1968) tells us, "It is difficult to become a saint, but not impossible, and the road to perfection is long, throughout one's lifetime." Although the Church recognizes some people as saints, most likely, the majority of those who enjoy the glory of heaven are known to God alone. That will be the status for most of us, who hope to persevere, live a committed life and die in the friendship of the Lord.

One day at lunch when I was a teenager, my grandmother told me the story of St. Rita of Cascia, (1381-1457) whose husband had been killed and whose two sons plotted to revenge his death. She prayed that the Lord intervene, so that the sons would not commit this serious sin. They both fell seriously ill and died. She was left alone, and decided to enter the convent. However, as a widow, she was rejected by all the orders, except one that allowed her to tend to the garden, but also made her life difficult. She suffered and carried her cross with true patience. One day, according to legend, the Mother Superior tested her obedience, and put a dried up broomstick in the ground and told St. Rita to water it daily. She patiently did so and on her deathbed, it blossomed into beautiful roses.

In the meantime, although we may have our crosses, ups and downs and we may require a lot of patience to persevere, we are not to go about our days gloomy. We can have fun throughout our years. I learned this from my grandmother, who enjoyed a good home-cooked meal surrounded by her family at the table.

When talking with a dear friend, Fr. Franco, from Montreal, Canada, I often say to him, "Fun is good," and he responds, "And more fun is even better.' It is not sinful to be a "*Bon Vivant*," and to enjoy life. We can travel, have a delicious meal with friends, perhaps with a good glass of wine now and then, and plenty of laughter and conviviality. I recall a poem by Hilaire Belloc, (1870-1953) that illustrates this,

> "Wherever the Catholic sun doth shine,
> There's always laughter and good red wine.
> At least I've always found it so.
> *Benedicamus Domino!*"

The Lord Jesus was present at the Wedding Feast in Cana of Galilee and, as would be normal, He joined in the happiness of the bride and groom. So we are invited to follow His example. It is important to do everything in moderation and balance. There is an expression, "In the middle is virtue" as the expression goes, which is attributed to Aristotle, and in Latin, *"Virtus in Medio stat."* It is based on a saying that was found etched in stone at Delphi, "Nothing in excess."

I call this my "Goldilocks Theory." From our childhood, most of us recall the story of a young girl, named Goldilocks, who was lost in the woods and found a house there. It belonged to the three bears: the Papa bear, the Mama bear and the Baby bear. She tried one chair and it was too hard, the next was too soft, however, the third was just right! Like her, we too need to avoid one extreme and the other, but find that which is "just right" according to our needs and limitations, but most important of all, always in accord with what is pleasing in the Lord's sight.

We need to keep our eyes focused on Jesus, and make sure that our thoughts, word and deeds give Him glory, and work toward the sanctification and salvation of our souls. As St. Paul said, "So whether you eat or drink, or whatever you do, do everything for the glory of God" (I Cor. 10:31). There is a well-known Latin expression that comes to mind, *"Ut in omnia glorificetur Deus"* The English translation of that motto is, "That in all things, God may be glorified." May we strive to give the Lord glory, honor and praise, with a song in our hearts, throughout our lives in this world and be joined with Him one day forever in the kingdom of heaven.

# Aunt Josephine

I consider myself blessed to come from a wonderful family on my Dad's side of the family. His father, Matteo, after whom I was named, was born in 1882, and his mother, my Grandma Francesca Cicenia, was born in 1892. Life in the little hill town of Sant'Andrea di Conza, in southern Italy, was difficult. After his first four children were born, my grandfather set off in 1916 for the United States of America to earn enough money as a tailor, so as to eventually send for the rest of the family to join him.

The children he left in Italy, along with his wife, were three daughters, Giovannina (Jenny), born in 1910, Giuseppina (Josephine), born in 1912, Concetta (Connie), born in 1913 and his son, Giacomo (John), born in 1915. After my grandfather became a U.S. citizen, he sent the money that he had earned for the passage, to his wife and they made the crossing from the port of Naples aboard a ship named *"Conte Biancamano."*

When the family arrived in the port of New York on December 8, 1929, my grandparents Matteo and Francesca were reunited, and my father Antonino (Anthony) was born, just about nine months later, at the end of August 1930. On the day of his birth, the three daughters went to work in the factory of a relative, and were sewing blouses for military uniforms. They recounted that day, after work, they arrived home, and their new brother had been born, and their mother was at the stove cooking dinner for them!

After my parents married on Sept. 24, 1955, they moved in with my Grandma Francesca, whose husband had passed away in January of that year. After my birth on Sept. 30, 1956, that was my first home. We then moved to another apartment, when my Mom was expecting my sister in 1959, but I would return there for weekend visits. The house was a duplex and my Aunt Josephine, her husband, Uncle Joe Di Pompeo, and their four children, my first cousins, lived next door. My grandmother and aunts, all who have now passed on, would call me *"Matteuccio"* for little Matteo, a nickname that I still hear used by my parents and other relatives from time to time.

I gratefully remember so many happy times, and in particular watching my Grandma Francesca and her daughters make those delicious homemade ricotta-filled ravioli, that were prepared for the big holidays, such as Christmas and Easter, when so many family members would be there for dinner. The taste has never been duplicated, and I have enjoyed more than a few ravioli over the years.

From those early days, I came to see that my Aunt Josephine was a wonderful person. She never spoke ill of anyone, even though, as with many families, there were ample opportunities to do so, with "This relative doing that" or "That relative doing this." If there was ever a conversation about someone, and the comments were turning a bit negative, she would simply say, "I wish them the very best," or "I wish them the best of luck." There was a particular kindness and gentleness about her, and an inner peace as well. Unfortunately, her husband died suddenly of a heart attack in May 1962, but as a young widow, she stayed close to the Lord. She was regular in attending Mass at our parish church in the neighborhood, where they had been members since their arrival in America.

When remembering, with fondness, my dear aunt, I cannot help but think of the four things that St. Dominic Savio, (1842-1857) wrote, as a promise to Jesus on the day of his First Holy Communion:

1. *Receive Jesus as often as possible*
2. *Try never to sin*
3. *Pray every day*
4. *Love everybody*

I consider these the ingredients of holiness, and they have a beautiful childlike simplicity about them. It is also St. Dominic Savio who told us that he would rather die, than offend the Lord by committing a mortal sin. His exact words were, "Death rather than sin." What a beautiful way to try to live our lives, in innocence and holiness. This is an invitation for all of us today as well. After all, Jesus told us, "Truly I say to you, whoever does not receive the kingdom of God like a child, shall not enter it" (Lk. 10:15).

Although my dear Aunt Josephine will most likely never be officially recognized as a canonized saint, she remains, for me, the model of a person of simple, humble faith in the Lord. Come what may, she was faithful. She passed away in December 1996, after suffering a stroke, and I offered her Funeral Mass. At the wake the night before, at least six or eight of her widow friends and neighbors came to speak to me individually and, with tears in their eyes, told me, "She was my best friend." This was the result of loving everybody as St. Dominic Savio suggests.

"Sometimes the best words are those that we do not say," another friend once told me." We need to be kind and merciful, and above all, withhold our tongues and any comments that can be hurtful. It is much better to be silent, than to be critical of others, as Jesus reminds us, "Why do you notice the splinter in your brother's eye, but do not perceive the wooden beam in your own eye" (Mt. 7:3)? We hear the words of St. James, when he wrote about the tongue, "With it we bless the Lord and Father, and with it we curse human beings, who are made in the likeness of God. From the same mouth come blessing and cursing. This need not be so, my brothers" (ch. 3:9-10).

The world and our individual lives would be in a better place, if we tried our very best to be merciful, charitable, and especially cautious before speaking. I once heard a story that a person's words had to pass through three gates, and answer a question that was asked by a guard at each gate, before being allowed to come forth from their mouth. The answer had to be "Yes" in order to proceed to the next gate. At the first gate, the question was, "Is it true?" The second question was "Is it necessary?" And the question at the last gate was, "Is it kind?" Let us try our very best to be kind, compassionate and merciful to others, since it will put our steps in the right path, the path that leads to salvation, the path that leads us to the unending joys in the kingdom of heaven.

# Crazy Him

The United States of America celebrated the Bicentennial year in 1976, since the Declaration of Independence was signed on July 4, 1776 in Philadelphia, PA. One month later, the International Eucharistic Congress was held in Philadelphia, which is called the "City of Brotherly Love." Choirs from throughout the United States were asked to send representatives to sing in a National Choir, to help provide music for the events of the Congress. At that point, I was a student at the College Seminary, located at Seton Hall University in South Orange, NJ, and a member of the Newark Archdiocesan Festival Chorale. It was from this group, comprised of mostly priests, religious and seminarians, that a delegation was invited to participate in the National Choir.

All of the members of the Choir arrived one week early, so that we could practice the music, under the direction of Dr. Peter La Manna, of the Archdiocese of Philadelphia. The rehearsals were held at St. Maria Goretti High School in South Philadelphia, and we stayed at the dormitory at Temple University, on the other end of the city. A shuttle bus brought us back and forth each day, as well as to the various events, once the Congress began. There were at least three to four hundred participants in the choir, representing the voice groups of Soprano, Alto, Tenor and Bass. Although we all practiced singing together, we were also subdivided into various groups, since there were to be several events scheduled at the same time.

The title of this chapter refers to a choral piece based on Psalm 150, "O Praise ye, the Lord," composed by César Franck (1822-1890). There was one section where we needed to rapidly sing the phrase, "Praise ye, Him, praise ye, Him" several times. Peter made all of us singers laugh, when he told us that it sounded like "Crazy Him, crazy Him." Over the years, when I come across Psalm 150, when praying the Liturgy of the Hours, as we priests do daily, I always smile while reading those words.

The congress was the event that also premiered the now well-known hymn, "The Gift of Finest Wheat," which was written for that occasion. It was a great highlight of my life up to that point, being a part of that choral group, which first performed that beautiful hymn in a wonderful four-part harmony, which is very seldom heard. The soaring voices of the many religious sisters provided a very ethereal sound.

It was at this Eucharistic Congress, that both Blessed Mother Theresa of Calcutta (1910-1997) and the Servant of God, Archbishop Fulton J. Sheen (1895-1979) were featured as speakers. One of the principle celebrants of Holy Mass was a not so well known Cardinal from Cracow, Poland, Karol Wojtyla, who would be elected Pope John Paul II, (1920-2005) in a little more than two years later.

Even though those were a very hot two weeks in Philadelphia, I do consider it a great privilege from the Lord to have been able to participate in this memorable event. There was a true spirit of collaboration and kinship among the members of the choir. Some of the religious sisters and priests had served the Lord and His Church for nearly half of a century, and some of us seminarians like me, nineteen at the time, were just starting out in our adventure in our service to Him.

This was one of those teachable moments in my life, when I realized that my commitment to Jesus Christ and His Church was being part of a glorious tradition. I was aspiring to stand on the "Shoulders of giants," as the expression goes. Those dedicated people, who were sitting right next to me, dressed in their choir robes, and had given so much of their talent and energy, with all their hearts, for so many decades, for the honor and glory of God. The Eucharistic Congress of 1976 is long past, and many, including John Cardinal Krol, (1910-1996) the Archbishop of Philadelphia, at that time, have gone to their rewards.

I have fond memories of Cardinal Krol, since several years later, a friend from the seminary invited his brother seminarians, including me, to attend the closing of Forty Hours Devotion in his home parish in Philadelphia. There, we were introduced to Cardinal Krol, and after the ceremony, we attended dinner along with the many priests in attendance, the majority of whom spoke Polish.

The Cardinal enjoyed this meal very much, seated at the center of a festive table and dressed in his full red cassock. Toward the conclusion, he began to sing Polish folk songs, some of which included birdcalls, and the priests joined in singing. We were all so delighted to see this great "Prince of the Church" as a Cardinal is called, greatly enjoying himself, amongst his brothers in the service of the Lord. He even had a playful attitude, just like a little child, and he was probably in his mid-seventies by then.

Over the years, I have had the great joy of participating in similar scenes of priestly fraternity, and the words of Psalm 133 usually come to mind, "Behold, how good and how pleasant it is, for brethren to dwell together in unity" (vs. 1). In fact, at those events, it is we priests ourselves, who quote that same verse of the psalm, when commenting on the good will, fraternal support and love that we experience while enjoying each other's company. We frequently use the Latin words, *"Ecce quam bonum et quam iucundum habitare fratres in unum."*

Those wonderful days remain very happy memories for me, to this very day, and the sweet sounds of the songs, "The Gift of Finest Wheat" and "O Praise ye, the Lord" are treasured remembrances and a gift to me from the Lord in the early years of my service to Him. Hopefully, those sweet sounds are a foretaste of the celestial choir that all of us aspire to hear one day in the presence of the Lord, together with the angels and saints in the kingdom of heaven.

# Msgr. Davis

The Reverend Monsignor John F. Davis was the Pastor of St. Michael Church in Cranford, NJ. Our family had moved there in 1972, after departing the Italian-American neighborhood in East Orange, a city close to Newark. Cranford was truly "Americana" in every sense of the word, with the Victorian homes on the banks of a rambling river; it is perennially just a lovely place.

Msgr. Davis had been a professor at Seton Hall University, and my Grandmother Serafina knew him well, since he served as the supervisor of the priest residence where she worked. He always called her "Mrs. Flower" because her last name, "Fiore" is the Italian word for flower.

Monsignor told me the story of that first day when he arrived to serve as the Pastor in Cranford. He entered the church through the side door, and the first thing he saw was the side altar dedicated to the Blessed Mother. He told me he knelt before the beautiful marble statue there, and said the words "*Maria Impende Juvamen*" which means, "Mary, bestow your help." It was the Episcopal motto from the coat-of-arms of Archbishop Thomas A. Boland, of the Newark Archdiocese who had sent him there. Many times, I have repeated those words, as I pass the statue of Our Lady in my own parish church, and in particular, whenever I visit St. Michael Church in Cranford, where Monsignor served as pastor.

It has been a great blessing in my life that he and I developed a wonderful rapport. He saw me attend Holy Mass on Saturdays, throughout my high school and college years, and we frequently struck up a conversation afterwards. I told him that I was a commuter to Seton Hall Preparatory School in South Orange, NJ, and subsequently was in the College Seminary program at the University there. He was very supportive during my studies there, as well as when I began the Major Seminary of the Newark Archdiocese in September 1977. After two years of studies there, I decided to take a break from theological studies, and I began to work and earn a Master's Degree.

It was an exciting time for me, and so I went to New York at the recommendation of a friend, who knew of an art studio that was looking for employees. It was the oldest firm in the U.S.A. for hand lettering, which is called "Engrossing." So, I joined the many in the workforce that commuted daily into New York and worked around the Union Square area, at 18ᵗʰ Street and Park Avenue, South.

Several evenings per week, I also went to school, and earned the Master's Degree in Counseling and Psychology from Seton Hall University in May 1981. As well, I continued with my artwork and taught a course on calligraphy in the local Adult School, and even did free-lance artwork at home on the weekend. Those were very happy and productive years for me, and I immersed myself in learning more about the craft of lettering.

Msgr. Davis also knew about my artwork and would often ask my opinion in helping to purchase or design a new vestment, or to design a cover for the Midnight Mass program. He and I got to know each other better and our friendship blossomed. In 1979, he wrote a book about his years as a priest entitled, *"This Priest is Thankful."* This was a compilation of his own remembrances about his then thirty plus years of service to the good Lord; it was so well-received, that the publisher then asked him to write another book. His first book contained many of his memoirs and reminiscences, and it has, in some way, been the inspiration to me to write my own book of priestly remembrances.

His second book was entitled *"Strike a Giant Bell,"* and it was about the life and papacy of Pope John Paul II. He gave me signed copies of both books, which I treasure to this day. Monsignor became a true friend to me and a model of what a priest should be. He was also a caring pastor to his flock, and an excellent homilist. His third and last book was entitled, *"An Audience with Jesus,"* which consisted of a series of meditations for use during visits to our Eucharistic Lord in the Most Blessed Sacrament. It was published in September 1982; however, I never had the opportunity to have him sign my copy.

One Saturday in that same month, after the noon Mass, Msgr. asked me to please see him for a few minutes in the Rectory. I thought for sure that it was regarding an art project, but he said to me, "Matty, it is time you go back to the seminary." He handed me a brochure and application to a seminary, which was geared toward second career vocations, since by now I had worked for some time, and he asked me to please pray about it. He had planted an important seed that day.

One month later, in late October, Msgr. Davis had been invited to be the homilist in Jersey City, NJ, for a Sunday Mass to commemorate the 100th Anniversary of the parish, where he had been born and raised. He was considered an "illustrious son" of the parish. After his years at Seton Hall University, and before his arrival in Cranford, he had served as the Archdiocesan Director for the Society for the Propagation of the Faith. He told me that, in that capacity, he got to know much of the work of the missions throughout the world. He mentioned that some years earlier, he had been offered the opportunity to become a missionary bishop in Africa, but chose to refuse that honor, since he was the only child of his aging parents, Frank and Amelia.

At that Mass in his home parish, at which he was the homilist, and in the presence of the Archbishop, who was the principle celebrant, Msgr. Davis collapsed in the pulpit. We later learned that he had a cerebral hemorrhage, and after several weeks in the hospital, he passed away on November 14, 1982 at the age of 62. He had been born in 1920, the same year as the Venerable Pope John Paul II, whom he greatly admired.

Although I had lost a good friend, I was grateful to the Lord for the opportunity of having gotten to know him well, over the last several years. There was a poem that he wrote, which was printed on the memorial card for his funeral. I have it in my Breviary and read it from time to time.

*Prayer for Faith*

> *Give me the faith that asks not why.*
> *I shall know God's answer by and by.*
> *Give me the faith that looks at pain*
> *and says, it will be right again.*
> *Give me the faith to clasp God's hand*
> *when things are hard to understand.*
> *Give me the faith to bow my head,*

*trustfully waiting to be led.*
*Give me the faith to face my life*
*with all its sorrow and its strife.*
*Then with the last day's setting sun*
*I'll close my eyes when life is done.*
*And my soul will go without a care,*
*knowing that God is waiting there.*

After his passing, I had not looked again at the application to the seminary that he had given me, and had almost forgotten about it. However, on Palm Sunday in the following year, our family went to the cemetery after Mass to bring the blessed palm to the graves of our deceased grandparents, as has been our custom for many years. My parents and I recalled that Msgr. Davis was buried in the same cemetery, so we also went to his grave, to offer a prayer for his soul, and left some of the palm there as well. It had been the first time we were at his grave since the day of his funeral.

As was our custom on Sundays throughout the year, and in many Italian-American homes as well, we had our main meal in the afternoon, after returning from church, and on this day, from the cemetery. After lunch I took a rest, another Sunday afternoon tradition in some homes, and in a very vivid dream, I saw Msgr. Davis, who told me to fill out the application to the seminary that he had given me. I did so immediately upon awakening, completed it within about 30 minutes, and even drove to the Post Office that same evening, so that it would go in the mail bright and early on Monday morning.

By that following Wednesday, the Director of Admissions of Holy Apostles Seminary in Cromwell, Connecticut called me and we set up an appointment to meet during the week after Easter. Of course, I needed to send the copies of my transcripts and other documents ahead of the meeting. When I got there, and the interview was complete, I was officially accepted and would begin the Third Year of Theology that coming September 1983. The Lord was good.

I believe that all this was in His providential plan, and that was the time and place, in His goodness and mercy, that He had chosen for me to return to the seminary.

In 1978, I learned a poem from Sister Carmel, O.P. of the forma-tion team for the seminarians at the College Seminary:

> *When the thing is not right, God says "no."*
> *When I am not right, God says "grow."*
> *When the time is not right, God says "slow."*
> *When everything is right, God says, "go!"*

A holy priest, whose cause for beatification has begun after his death, The Servant of God, Fr. John Hardon, S.J. (1914-2000) once told me, "The Will of God will not be thwarted." Yes, even at times, the Lord may give an answer to our prayers that sometimes we do not like, since we may want to hear "Yes" and the answer from Him is "No."

However, I believe that if we ask the Lord to help us with the bigger picture, the goal of the salvation of our souls, He will always supply for our needs. The Lord Jesus Christ will help us, with His grace, to persevere in doing what is pleasing in His eyes. He will never withhold His mercy if we seek Him with sincerity of heart. This is the Lord's will: our sanctification and our salvation. If we are faithful to him, He will give us a "safe landing," as a friend of mine once told me, but He does not promise that the ride will be without its bumps on the way. It is up to us to make the right choices, to live in His love and friendship daily in this world, so that we may be joined to him forever in the kingdom of heaven.

# All Things Beautiful

Shortly after our family moved to Cranford in fall of 1972, a brochure arrived in the mail from the local Adult School program, that offered a class in calligraphy. I thought it might be a great opportunity to learn the techniques of lettering, and so I gave it a try. I had always been artistically inclined, throughout the grammar school years, and had enjoyed studying art books. When I was around ten, I located a dip pen and jar of India ink and would try to imitate the alphabets that I saw in a Speedball lettering pamphlet, but never had any formal training.

The class was just great, and it led to an avocation of lettering and heraldic art which I have continued to enjoy over the years. I became a member of the "Society of Scribes" in New York City and went there to take classes with other calligraphers, who were our teachers, some of whom were well-known throughout the world.

When I started working and was earning a salary, I took the opportunity to travel to Washington, DC, London and other locations in Europe, to pursue my interest in the fine art of illumination, as seen in the medieval manuscripts. My admiration for the beauty and grandeur of the great cathedrals and the many world famous palaces and museums of Europe began at that time. For me, it has become a place of renewal and refreshment, a place to "recharge my batteries."

I recall the words of the Russian author, Fyodor Dostoevsky, (1821-1881) who wrote, "Beauty will save the world." I believe beauty will help to keep us sensitive, upbeat and uplifted amid life's trials and difficulties. It reminds me of the words of St. Paul "Overcome evil by good" (Rom. 12:21, also see Amos 5:14). It may be an oversimplification, but I see "Good as beautiful in the Lord's sight" and "Evil as ugly before Him." I am often reminded of the English author, John Keats, (1795-1821) who wrote, "Beauty is truth, truth beauty." He is also the author of the sonnet, "*Ode on a Grecian Urn*," which contains the memorable line, "A thing of beauty is a joy forever."

My attitude has tried to be, throughout the years, to "Accentuate the positive and eliminate the negative, latch on to the affirmative and don't mess with Mister In-Between!" My parents told me that these were the lyrics of a song written by Johnny Mercer, and that when they were younger; they would dance the jitterbug to it. They were excellent dancers in their day.

Over the years, I have come to see beauty of the Lord also in people. The beauty on the outside of a person is a reflection of the beauty and inner goodness on the inside of the person. We can just look at Blessed Mother Theresa of Calcutta as an example. Even though she might not have been considered very attractive according to the standards of the world, her interior love for the poor, the sick and abandoned truly shined forth from the inside, and was made manifest through her vibrant smile and glistening eyes. During the homily at her Beatification, on October 19, 2003, the Venerable Pope John Paul II called her "An icon of the Good Samaritan, who went everywhere to serve Christ in the poorest of the poor."

The beauty found in the Lord's creation is a positive thing, which has greatly enhanced my life. The earth and all in it gives the Lord "The glory that is due to His Name" (Ps. 33:8). In my travels, I have seen the handiwork of the Lord in the natural cathedrals that reflect His splendor in the magnificent Fjords of Norway, the impressive Grand Canyon and the scenic vistas of the Amalfi coast. I also have come to see the artistry of mankind throughout the centuries, in their spectacular monuments. Man-made beauties such as the Piazza of St. Peter's Basilica, the great Pyramid of Giza and the picturesque village of Santorini in Greece can take one's breath away, and does mine.

Actually, some of the most breathtaking moments for me have been right in my own backyard, when the sunlight makes the autumn leaves glow on a beautiful blue-skied afternoon. I recall the short poem that Sister Catherine, M.P.F., my sixth grade teacher, put on the bulletin board in the classroom and I think of it each year as I see those leaves glisten,

> *Golden leaves and*
> *Smiling blue skies;*
> *Man desires,*
> *God supplies.*

During my time working in New York, I applied for and was granted a special Reader's card for the Rare Book Room of the New York Public Library on Fifth Avenue in New York City and there I could actually hold medieval manuscripts and study them up close. One was allowed to bring a pencil, but not a pen, to sketch designs from them. It was an exciting time, but all the while, in the back of my mind, I realized that my true vocation was to serve the Lord someday as His priest, and this was somewhat of a hiatus in that process.

One day, while I was visiting Millie Van Leuven, my mentor in calligraphy, she was working on several rough drafts for a lettering project and a few of them were discarded. I literally picked one out of the garbage, one of the first drafts, with the intention of looking at her lettering to see just why it had been rejected by her. Then I realized that the quote was just wonderful. It was short, but meaningful and read:

> *The brook would lose its song*
> *if you took away the rocks.*

With her permission, I took it home, and within days it was framed and hung above my desk. It has had a prominent place in my bedroom in every rectory where I have been assigned, and has meant a lot to me over the years. It is a reminder that even though there may be difficulties that have to be surmounted, just like those rocks in the brook, they add a dimension, that otherwise, would not be there.

There would be no music or "babble" in the babbling brook, without them. Sometimes, they may be as small as pebbles and other times they may be large as boulders, but they are there for a reason, perhaps to test us, as they add twists and turns in life's journey. May that journey, with its many ups and downs, strengthen us and urge us to put greater trust in the Lord, and help to lead us to our ultimate destination, the kingdom of heaven.

# Dominican Family

My long and happy relationship with the Dominican family began in 1973, when I was in High School. By the Dominican family, I am speaking about the religious order founded by St. Dominic Guzman, (1170-1221) who laid the foundations for the Order of Preachers in 1217, during a time when the Albigensian heresy was growing stronger daily. The work of his new religious order was based in Toulouse, France, and it was there that he earnestly asked the Blessed Virgin Mary for her assistance in destroying this heresy.

According to tradition, Our Lady instructed him to preach about the Rosary to the faithful, as a safeguard against heresy and vice. From that time on, St. Dominic promulgated the Holy Rosary in his preaching. Throughout the centuries, and even in Papal encyclicals, he has been seen as its founder and originator. He died at the age of fifty-one, exhausted by the many austerities and labors in preaching the Word of God. After his death, the order that he founded is more commonly referred to as the Dominicans, in honor of its founder. Throughout the centuries, various popes have encouraged the faithful to pray the Rosary, as a means to draw closer to Christ.

On October 16, 2002, as he began the twenty-fifth year of his pontificate, the Venerable Pope John Paul II promulgated his Apostolic Letter, "*Rosarium Virginis Mariae*" (On the Most Holy Rosary). In it, the Holy Father reminded us that praying the Rosary is an opportunity for "Contemplating Christ with Mary" (no. 9). He reminded us that,

> "The Rosary, precisely because it starts with Mary's own experience, is an exquisitely contemplative prayer. Without this contemplative dimension, it would lose its meaning, as Pope Paul VI clearly pointed out: 'Without contemplation, the Rosary is a body without a soul, and its recitation runs the risk of becoming a mechanical repetition of formulas, in violation of the admonition of Christ, In praying do not heap up empty phrases as the Gentiles do; for

they think they will be heard for their many words'
(Mt. 6:7)" (no. 12).

When I was in High School, there was a publication entitled
*"Our Lady's Digest"* in the library. I enjoyed reading the articles
regarding the Blessed Mother, and since I had an appreciation for
artistic things even back then, I greatly admired the illustrations. In
each issue, there were prints of beautifully hand-cut silhouettes, with
a theme that always included the Blessed Virgin Mary, according to
the liturgical season. The magazine credited the artwork to Sr. Mary
Jean Dorcy, O.P. Eventually, I wrote to the editor to inquire about
the artist, and learned that she was retired, and living in Seattle,
Washington. Then, I wrote to her and we developed a pen-pal type
relationship. This was long before the days of e-mail and the like.

Later, I learned that she was the author of many books, and one
of them was entitled, *"St. Dominic's Family,"* which included the
stories of the lives of almost 350 famous members of the Dominican
Order, those already recognized by the Church as saints, through
canonization, as well as those in the process. My interest in the
Dominican Order progressed, and since I was already praying the
Rosary daily for some time now, I felt a certain kinship.

When Sister Mary Jean celebrated her 50th Jubilee of Profession
in 1984, I was invited to attend the Mass of Thanksgiving on that
joyful occasion, and was happy to finally meet her. She was crippled
with arthritis for the last 20 years and in a wheelchair. Sadly, the
fingers that had cut such beautiful silhouettes to honor Our Lady
and the Infant Jesus were all gnarled. She passed away in Mary's
month on May 5th in the Marian Year 1988, just a few months after
my Priesthood Ordination.

Another of my associations with the Dominican Order began for
me in 1981, when Msgr. Davis, my pastor in Cranford, asked me
to help him purchase a few sets of priest's stoles for concelebrants,
so that they would all be matching. He suggested that I go visit the
Dominican Nuns in Summit, New Jersey, about a 15-minute ride
from Cranford. It would also help the nuns in their apostolate, since
they made vestments as a means to support themselves.

I soon learned that the priests comprise the first branch of the Dominican family and these Cloistered Sisters are members of the second branch, and live in a Papal Enclosure. They took turns each hour of the day and night, to pray in the Presence of the Eucharistic Lord, which is called Perpetual Adoration of the Blessed Sacrament.

When I went there, picked out the fabric and placed the order, the sister in the vestment department was very pleasant, and wanted to know more about me. I told her that I was really on a hiatus from the seminary, and hope to serve the Lord as a priest some day in the future. I mentioned that I was currently working in New York City as an artist specializing in hand lettering. She told me that the sisters there had been doing lettering as part of their apostolate, but there were no lessons given to them since the 1940's and maybe they could use a refresher course at this point. I was happy to offer my help. After a few weeks, the Mother Prioress received permission from the Archbishop, and I now could go into the cloister area to give the sisters a few updated lessons.

My star pupil was Sister Carol Marie, O.P., who showed great promise. She was enthusiastic in learning about the new techniques and materials and we also hit it off quite well. Sister liked to laugh and joke a bit during the lessons, as to break up the school-like atmosphere. Whenever I went to another workshop, whether in New York City, Washington, DC or elsewhere, regarding lettering techniques or laying gold leaf, as part of illumination, I would rush back with freshly made photocopies "hot off the presses" to share with her, in order to help in perfecting her lettering techniques.

Sister was from Miami Beach, Florida and she had even tried out for the Olympics, in the area of diving, in her youth. She is just about fifteen years older than me, but looked then, and still looks much younger than her age. She has the swimmer physique: tall, lean and agile. The other sisters along with her in the Monastery in Summit are spiritual powerhouses in my opinion. Their every word and action seemed to be sanctified by the Lord, as they tried to conform themselves to Him in every way, by their lives of prayer and work. They truly live these words of St. Paul, "And whatever you do, in word or in deed, do everything in the name of the Lord Jesus, giving thanks to God the Father through Him" (Col. 3:17).

My relationship with the Dominican Nuns developed and certainly has been a great blessing to me. I learned all about their life, and how they support themselves, eat from the produce of their own garden and are even buried in the cemetery on the property. It was the gracious and merciful Lord at work in my life, I am sure, because those nuns, behind the scenes, were steadily praying for me to return to the seminary, and be ordained a priest. Soon, I learned about the third branch of the Order, which include the active Dominican Sisters as well as the Lay Dominicans. And so, I began to take classes on Dominican spirituality, and was professed, taking the name, Brother Rosario in honor of the Holy Rosary. This was on the feast of St. Dominic in 1983.

There were also a few surprises in store for me, regarding my connection with the wonderful cloistered Dominican Nuns. While I was in the in-between period from the seminary, and living with my parents, I received a phone call that there was a Dominican priest visiting from Rome and, if I would like to attend the morning Mass, then I could have breakfast with him. I was happy to do so, and to my surprise, the Dominican priest turned out to be Mario Luigi Cardinal Ciappi, O.P., (1909-1996) who had served as the personal theologian to the Holy Father since 1955.

We had an interesting and wonderful conversation in Italian, and at the end of it, he asked me to make sure to visit him in his apartment in the Apostolic Palace the next time I was in Rome. I happily did so a year or so later. On another occasion, there was another visitor from Rome, who the sisters asked me to assist at Holy Mass and then visit at breakfast. He was the Dominican theologian, Fr. Jordan Aumann, O.P. (1916-2007), whose book, "*Spiritual Theology*," I had read.

One of my most memorable experiences was when I was instructing Sr. Carol Marie in the art of lettering, since we had classes every few weeks, and I noticed that there was a large watch on her wrist, that kept moving every time she was writing. At that, I mentioned I had not noticed that watch previously, to which she responded that her old watch had stopped working.

She went on to explain that when a sister needed a replacement of an item such as a watch, one of the sisters is assigned to take her request. The community has a few extra watches in a shoebox, for those who may need them. Sister mentioned that recently a wealthy woman's husband had passed away, and she brought some of his things to the sisters. On further inspection, I realized that sister was wearing a man's Rolex watch. With that, I said to her, "Sister, I think that watch is worth a few thousand dollars!"

She seemed just so detached from all things financial, since behind those monastery walls, all the sisters seemed literally to be "In this world, but not of this world." As the Lord Jesus said in the Gospel, "They do not belong to the world any more than I belong to the world" (Jn. 17:16). Sister Carol Marie was very innocent in her response, when she told me, that the most important thing is that it kept the right time so she could be punctual in doing all her duties. Years later, I have been reminded of this whenever I use the Preface for Lent II which states: "You teach us to live in this passing world with our heart set on the world that will never end."

With the help of their prayers, I did return to the seminary and was ordained to serve as Christ's priest, and am ever grateful to the good Lord for the beautiful rapport that I developed with the dear Dominican Nuns over these decades. Sister Carol Marie, several years later in fact, had a life changing experience. When her dear mother was seriously ill in Florida, she received special permission to attend to her in her last months. There, she realized her desire to aid those who are dying, and serve the Lord in that capacity.

There is a branch of the Dominicans that are active sisters and she made the official change to the Dominican Sisters of Hawthorne, New York, who exclusively take care of patients with incurable cancer. This group was founded by the Servant of God, Mother Mary Alphonsa, (1851-1926) whose name was originally Rose Hawthorne, the daughter of the author Nathaniel Hawthorne. After several years serving in the house for the infirmed in Philadelphia, Sister Carol Marie became the first Mother Superior of the branch that was opened a few years ago in Kisumu, Kenya.

Over the years, I have been so edified to learn of the wonderful work of mercy in the name of the good Lord that is being done by Sister Carol Marie in Kenya. I hear from her every now and then when the Internet connection is working, on that side of the ocean. I admire how she has been called to continue to serve the Lord whole-heartedly, but now in a more active apostolate, and not inside the cloister. It has been a pleasure to help her, by sending packages with Rosaries and holy cards to be distributed in her work. She told me the story of a woman who died, while clutching in her hands the card of Jesus as portrayed in the Divine Mercy image. She said that she held it so tight that they could not remove it, and brought her to the morgue with it still in her hands.

The lives of so many dedicated religious over the years have been an inspiration to me as well as a sign of the goodness of the Lord. They follow the commandment of Jesus, "Love your neighbor as yourself" (Mt. 24:36, Lev. 19:18) and the "Golden Rule," as it is called, "Do to others as you would have them do to you" (Lk. 6:31). It is Sister Carol Marie who, some years back, had first told me, "The patient needs a project" to occupy oneself, when one is a bit down and needs to go outside oneself.

May the good work of so many dedicated people in the name of the merciful Lord, bear much fruit and may the Good Lord reward their dedicated labors. He is never outdone in generosity, so when they end their earthly pilgrimages, may they be joined with Him for all eternity in the kingdom of heaven.

# The Eternal City

Once I was accepted into the seminary and began classes in September 1983, it was necessary to locate a diocese to sponsor me. This way, at the end of theological studies, I could be ordained for service as a priest. Over the years, I had gotten to know a wonderful and brilliant Jesuit priest, the Servant of God, Fr. John Hardon, S.J. He was truly a holy man and in fact, after his death in December 2000, the documentation for his beatification was initiated. Whenever I learned that he would be giving a talk or conference in the area, I made an effort to attend. Afterwards, I usually tried to exchange a few words with him, if it was possible.

One time, in Plainfield, NJ, there was a four-week series of talks, with a closing Mass on the last evening. I volunteered to serve the Mass, and we spoke for a few minutes in the sacristy beforehand. He inquired if I had ever considered entering the seminary. I told him that I had completed the first two years of theology studies in the seminary and currently was working. Thereupon, Fr. Hardon offered his help to me in the future, should I need it.

Sometime later, I telephoned Father, who was residing at St. Ignatius Church in New York City, and we had an appointment. During it, I explained that I was to begin at Holy Apostles Seminary come September. He then suggested that I write to the bishop of a diocese in the northeast, whom he knew well, and that he would put in a good word for me. I followed his counsel, went through the interview process, and was accepted to that diocese. There was one stipulation, that after the successful completion of my seminary studies, I needed to serve a pastoral year there, from summer 1985 to 1986. I believed that was fair and logical, since they needed to get to know me better.

All looked well and after graduation, I began my service in a parish. The pastor, Fr. Mike, and I hit it off at first, and then I realized that he was missing from the parish more and more. He would leave each Monday about mid-day and return on Saturday morning for the weekend. The resident priest, who taught in a local Catholic High School, would offer the weekday morning Masses. Throughout the course of the year, I got to know the local clergy, by attending meetings to represent the pastor, whether they were regarding catechetic preparations or other matters. I also saw them at hospitals and Nursing Homes when I did the weekly visitation.

The parish was located in a coal-mining town and there were churches on practically every corner, that were built to serve the needs of the different nationalities of immigrants that came from throughout Europe, to work in the mines. Some said that the opposite corners had a bar, and some of them actually did. In the parish duties, I tried to do things "according to the book" as the expression goes. Holy Apostles Seminary, where I had attended, was a solid seminary and trained us seminarians to do things according to the mind of the Church.

However, Fr. Mike was more progressive, and there eventually arose a tension. This was brought to a greater awareness when two of the three transitional deacons, who were to be ordained to the Holy Priesthood in June 1986, had left the diocese, to join a group that was considered "too traditional." They preferred only to offer Holy Mass in Latin, which is now known as the Extraordinary Form of the Holy Mass, according to the Missal of Blessed Pope John XXIII.

Unfortunately, after this, in the eyes of that particular diocese, "to be traditional" had become a bad thing, since they had lost two men who were very near to being ordained. And so, Fr. Mike used this to my disadvantage, and in my evaluation, after one year of service in his parish, he wrote that I was too much on the traditional side, and not the type of priest the church of today needed. Regrettably, it had served as the "kiss of death."

The vocation director called me, and during a subsequent meeting, handed me a letter, which released me as a seminarian. He told me there was nothing negative in my file, but they were not interested in "my style." I was just a few weeks away from Ordination to the Diaconate, and was very disappointed. A priest friend had told me about the well-known Catholic author from Savannah, Georgia, Mary Flannery O'Connor (1925-1964). She had commented that sometimes one suffers, not for the church, but can suffer from her. It was certainly not an easy time for me, but as I thought then and still firmly do so today, with the Lord's grace, we can surmount any and all difficulties, if we put our complete trust in Him.

After the meeting with the vocation director, I went to visit a colleague in that same diocese who was recently ordained a priest in the prior June. He was shocked at the news, as were the other local clergy that I had gotten to know over the course of the year. Many came to my defense, and then contacted both the bishop and vocation director, asking for reconsideration, but it was not to happen.

There was a certain tension in the Church at that time, and was very well stated by Pope Benedict XVI in his letter to the bishops of the world that accompanied his July 7, 2007 *Motu Proprio, "Summorum Pontificum,"* (Of the Supreme Pontiffs). The Holy Father wrote of the somewhat difficult times that followed the Second Vatican Council and its implementation, "I am speaking from experience, since I too lived through that period, with all its hopes and its confusion. And I have seen how arbitrary deformations of the liturgy caused deep pain to individuals totally rooted in the faith of the Church."

I recall hearing an expression, "If you marry the spirit of the age, you become a widow in the next." The Servant of God, Pope Paul VI (1897-1978) once commented in a speech on June 30, 1972, "From somewhere or other, the smoke of Satan has entered the temple of God." On December 7, 1968, the same Pope had earlier stated in a speech to the Lombard College in Rome, "The Church is in a disturbing period of self-criticism or what could better be called self-demolition." Unfortunately, this period of confusion lingered on for some time.

Within a month of my departure from the diocese, Fr. Mike, my former pastor, had left the priesthood and got married. The priests of that area once again asked for reconsideration of my case, but it was again denied. Those good priests supported me all the more now, and they wrote letters of recommendation for me. My newly ordained priest friend then told me of a colleague of his, who knew the bishop of Ponce, Puerto Rico, and could put in a good word on my behalf. I gratefully accepted the offer, and in autumn 1986, sent a letter to Bishop Juan F. Torres, accompanied by the appropriate documentation and copies of all the letters of recommendation from the many priests who had written them.

In January 1987, I received a letter from the bishop, in which I was "tentatively accepted" as a seminarian for the Diocese of Ponce, and was asked to go to Rome for a five-month spiritual formation period. The good Lord had gotten me through a very difficult situation, and there was light at the end of the tunnel, and I was even headed to beautiful Roma! Rome has always been one of my favorite places to visit. There is an expression, "When one gets tired of Rome, one gets tired of life."

In February, I arrived in Rome and became familiar with the daily schedule of the seminary, which included meditation prior to Holy Mass and the various conferences and duties. The months flew and I truly had many wonderful experiences while living and studying in Rome, the Eternal City. These included the opportunity to attend the ceremonies of Holy Week, presided by the Venerable Pope John Paul II. Over the years, I had visited Rome several times as a tourist, but now, residing there from February to June, it was a completely different experience than just a few days there.

The seminary residence was called the "*Nepomuceno*," named after the Bohemian martyr, St. John Nepomucene (1340-1393). The Diocese of Ponce rented one of the wings there for the seminarians. As well, I got to know Marco Nunzi, who was a seminarian from the Diocese of Orvieto, a beautiful hilltop city north of Rome. We became good friends and often we would take a walk in the seminary garden together after lunch. I wanted to perfect my knowledge of the Italian language and he wanted to perfect his English language skills. He was ordained to the priesthood just a few months after me, and we remain lifelong friends.

When I arrived in Rome, the Season of Lent was about to begin, and I soon learned about the Stational Churches of Rome. This is a tradition where each day throughout Lent, there was a particular church that had been selected from the early centuries, as the location for Holy Mass for that day. I tried to attend as many as I could, since they were held at five o'clock in the afternoon, when there were no other commitments at the seminary at that hour.

On one occasion, I went to confession and told the priest that I was trying to get over a big disappointment, and then briefly outlined the circumstances. He quoted to me the words of the first Pope,

"But what credit is there if you are patient during suffering for doing wrong? But if you are patient when you suffer for doing what is good, this is a grace before God" (I Pet. 2:20).

I had done nothing wrong, but had been suffering, and so that quote really helped me to put things in perspective and got me through. I later learned that this priest was actually a bishop. He was Bishop Pavel Hnilica, S.J., (1921-2006) who was from Slovakia, and was secretly ordained a bishop in 1950 at the age of only 29, just three months after his Priesthood Ordination. He had known persecution, living under the Communist regime and was part of the underground church. In my few months in Rome, I got to know him, and had the opportunity to have lunch together at his residence.

There is an expression that "God writes straight with crooked lines." Only the Lord can do this, and bring a person from point "A" to point "B" in a circuitous, but providential fashion. I believe that His plan was about to unfold in my life. I put my trust in Him and Our Lady, that if it be God's Holy Will, I would be given the opportunity to serve Him as His priest. It was up to Him now, to put all the pieces of the puzzle together as only He could do. However, I would collaborate and do my part to the best of my ability.

As the weeks progressed, I inquired into attending a Papal Audience that was held every Wednesday, throughout the year, and was present at that of March 25, 1987, the Solemnity of the Annunciation. On that day, the Holy Father promulgated his encyclical "*Redemptoris Mater,*" (Mother of the Redeemer) and announced that there would be a special year dedicated to the Blessed Virgin Mary, called a "Marian Year," from the Vigil of Pentecost, June 6 of that Year, to conclude on the Solemnity of the Assumption of Mary, August 15, 1988. This year was seen, by many, to unofficially commemorate the bi-millennium of the birth of the Blessed Virgin Mary. It was also a time of spiritual preparation, asking the help of Mary, for the upcoming bi-millennium of the birth of the Savior in the Great Jubilee Year 2000.

I sensed that, at long last, I was in the right place at the right time, and hopefully, would be ordained, both to the Diaconate and Holy Priesthood, during the course of the Marian Year. I poured out prayers to the Blessed Mother, to receive this great grace and favor, through her powerful intercession, during this year dedicated to her. The previous and very first Marian Year had been instituted by the Venerable Pope Pius XII (1876-1958) in 1954, to commemorate the Centenary of the Definition of the Dogma of the Immaculate Conception.

Actually, on March 25th, I arrived at the Audience Hall extra early, so that when the doors were opened, it was possible to locate a seat where our Holy Father, Pope John Paul II was to pass. As he approached me, the pope took my hand, and after I venerated the Papal ring with a kiss, as is the custom, he asked from where I had come. After answering his question, I added, "Holy Father, please pray that I will be a good and holy priest." He then responded, "You will be... and pray that I will be a holy pope!"

After his death in April 2005, the procedure for his beatification and canonization began not long thereafter, and at the time that I write these words, the church has conferred upon him the title "Venerable." As for me, I hope and pray that those words of the Venerable Pope John Paul II will come to pass, that I will be "a good and holy priest." Of course, that all depends on my own collaboration with God's plan of sanctification for me. Over the years, my dear Mom and Dad always taught their three children to "Do the right thing." Many times, I can vividly recall them telling us, "If you are going to do something, then do it right, or not at all." And so, I knew from the very beginning, that if I was going to accept the Lord's call and serve Him as a priest, that I would do my very best to live a holy and committed life, and to glorify the Lord through my service in the Holy Priesthood.

The day before the opening of the Marian Year, the Rector of the Seminary announced that he had received six tickets from the Vatican Ceremony Office to attend the service and pray the Rosary with the Holy Father, at the Basilica of St. Mary Major, the next day. He asked us to please raise our hand, if we were interested. I did so, and was given the last of the tickets, and was so thrilled that I would be there for history in the making.

It was a splendid afternoon at the Basilica of St. Mary Major and one that I will never forget. The Marian Year had officially opened. Shortly after the service of prayer with the Pope, I knelt before the image of "*Salus Popoli Romani*," which means "Mary, Health of the Roman People" that is venerated in the Basilica. I never prayed so hard in my life, and said, "Blessed Mother Mary, I know that you can do it, please help me by your prayers to Jesus, to be ordained both a deacon and priest in this your Year." It came to pass as I had hoped and prayed. God's good plan was coming to fruition in my life. The Prophet Isaiah wrote, "God acts on behalf of those who wait for Him" (Is. 64:4).

When I departed from Rome, and arrived back to the United States, the seminary officials there had sent a positive report to the bishop of Ponce. Shortly thereafter, Bishop Torres' letter to me arrived on July 16, in which he asked me to arrive in Ponce by mid-October. He asked me to complete a Spiritual Retreat, in preparation for Holy Orders, prior to my arrival, since the Diaconate Ordination was scheduled for October 30.

The good plan of the Lord and the prayers and help of Mary were falling into place, and my desire to serve the Lord in the ordained ministry was soon to become a reality. This is when I was inspired to choose the verse of Sacred Scripture that would be printed on the holy card for my Ordination, "The Almighty has done great things for me, Holy is His Name" (Lk. 1:49). These were the words spoken by Mary to her cousin Elizabeth, in her song of praise for the Lord's goodness, called the "*Magnificat*." These are also the very first words of Holy Scripture that I quoted in this book, since I try to live with a sense and spirit of gratitude for all the good Lord and His mother have done, and continue to do for me.

Truly, I considered it a miracle of the Lord and Blessed Mother that had been granted to me, after a prior disappointment, and I recalled the phrase, "The stone the builders rejected has become the cornerstone. By the Lord has this been done; it is wonderful in our eyes" (Ps. 118:22-23) and "With God all things are possible" (Mt. 19:26). And so, it appeared my desire serve the Lord, as His priest, was to become a reality. We priests "Bring God to souls and bring souls to God," so that together, we can glorify Him in this world and in the kingdom of heaven.

# 2

# The Villalba Years

## Fr. Villanueva

On Friday, October 16, 1987, I arrived in the diocese of Ponce, Puerto Rico with the hope of serving there someday as a priest. Bishop Torres met with me the next day, and during our very cordial meeting, informed me that I had a Moral Theology exam the following Monday at the Catholic University. This was to be an oral exam, wherein I would be asked questions, and had to answer them verbally. Everything was contingent on the fact that I needed to pass that exam, to be ordained a deacon on the coming October 30 and to the Holy Priesthood on January 11, 1988. He told me that his original intention was to ordain me a priest on May 13, the Feast of Our Lady of Fatima. However, there was an urgent need in the parish where I was to be assigned, and he had dispensed me from the period of time usually between the Diaconate and Priesthood ordinations.

When I was in Rome from February to June of that year, I was given about twenty-five Moral theology points to review all in preparation for the exam. I prayed to St. Joseph of Cupertino, (1603-1663) who was a Franciscan priest. He was a bit clumsy and not construed as intelligent, and he too knew his limitations. However, he loved the Lord and the Blessed Mother Mary, and asked her assistance to persevere to become a priest.

The day of his final exam arrived, that would decide whether or not he would be advanced to Holy Orders, and his bishop, opening the Sacred Scriptures, pointed to a passage referring to Mary and asked the seminarian to explain it. He spoke of Mary so beautifully that the bishop began to weep, and allowed his Ordination to proceed. After his canonization and the accounts of his life were related, St. Joseph has been considered the patron of those preparing for an exam. So I poured forth my prayers to the Lord, and asked the guidance and help of St. Joseph of Cupertino.

The day of the test arrived for me, and the professor, Fr. Diaz, was very kind and cordial, but toward the end of our time together, he asked a bit of a tricky question. It involved the fictional case of a priest, who was in very serious sin. The only priest to whom he could confess, prior to offering Mass, would apparently know about the sinful matter involved. This would mean breaking the seal of confession. I responded that the priest who was in mortal sin should make a perfect act of contrition to Almighty God, as best as possible, in order to offer the Mass worthily. Then, at his earliest possible opportunity, he should go to confession to another priest, who had no knowledge of the situation. I stated that "under no circumstances," was it allowable for a priest break the Seal of Confession. Then Fr. Diaz broke into a big smile and said, "Let the Ordination proceed!"

It was a great blessing to me from the Lord, through the intercession of good St. Joseph of Cupertino. The entire path of studies and training that I had trodden leading up to Ordination was coming to fruition, since I would be ordained to the Diaconate in 11 days. I called my parents, sister and brother and they were thrilled and got plans ready to be with me in Ponce for the Ordination.

A wonderful and holy priest, Msgr. Emilio Valdes befriended me, upon my arrival to reside at the seminary. He had served as the Rector of the Major Seminary in Havana, Cuba, but had left there at the time of political unrest. He offered his assistance in reviewing for the exam, and was a great help. He also offered to drive me to see the Church of Our Lady of Mount Carmel, in which I would serve as both deacon and priest.

The day following the Moral Theology exam, he brought me to the small town of Villalba, where the parish is located, which was nestled in the hills of the central mountain range, called *"La Cordillera Central"* which runs from east to west across the island. It impressed me as just picture-perfect beautiful, especially a day or two after a rainfall, when the vegetation is at its greenest. The large white adobe-style church and the plaza were the centerpiece of the town and the green mountains were in the background.

I had my early experiences in the service to Our Lord and His Church there, where I performed my first Baptisms and Weddings as a Deacon. After my Ordination to the Holy Priesthood, on one of the most happy and memorable days of my life, I continued my service at the parish in Villalba. It was there that I both heard my first confessions and offered my First Mass.

The parishioners in Villalba were very devout, thanks to the hard work of Fr. Fausto Ramos, who had been pastor there for almost three decades. He was from Spain, and had fought in the Spanish Civil War, before entering the seminary. He was very well-loved and thanks to his strong teaching of the Catholic faith, Villalba was known as one of the places that remained faithful, while in other towns, some Pentecostal churches had sprung up.

I came to see firsthand the dedicated love for the Lord of the devout parishioners there. My first Holy Week as a priest was spent there, and each of us priests spent between 6-8 hours daily in the confessional. Each year on Good Friday, there was a procession after the 3:00 pm Celebration of the Lord's Passion. During it, a statue of the Lord Jesus Christ, depicted in repose after His death, and in a glass casket, was carried through the winding streets, as if to bring Him to the sepulcher to be laid to rest. Following it, was a statue of the Lord's mother, Mary, which was dressed in mourning clothing, including an embroidered long black dress. It was completed with a black lace veil and a white lace embroidered handkerchief in her hands, representing Our Lady of Sorrows.

This was a tradition that had been taken from the south of Spain, in particular, the Andalusia region, where many Puerto Ricans can trace their heritage. In that little town of Villalba, there were roughly about 7,000 to 8,000 people who followed in procession. In the

Season of Lent, the pastor had decided to postpone all Baptisms until Easter Sunday, since it was a way of emphasizing the connection between the Lord's Triumphant Resurrection and the Sacrament of Baptism. Then on Easter Sunday, I had the privilege to baptize 65 babies in one ceremony after the last Mass. It was just wonderful.

Each weekend, I was scheduled to offer six Masses in six different small chapels in the surrounding *"Campos,"* or sections that comprise the town. There were two Masses on Saturday evening, at 5:00 and 7:00 p.m. and then I began with two Masses on Sunday morning at 9:00 and 11:00 a.m. There were another two Masses on Sunday evening at 5:00 and 7:00 pm. They were all preceded by confessions. For some of the remote chapels in the mountains, I had to be picked up and driven there in a jeep, because there were many hairpin turns and no guardrails and I was not familiar with driving in those hills. By the end of the weekend, one was tired but fulfilled.

In addition to the pastor, Fr. José, and myself, there was a third priest who served the needs of the flock at the Our Lady of Mount Carmel Church in Villalba. He was Fr. Francisco Javier Villanueva, from northern Spain. He was ordained in 1946, and came to Puerto Rico when Blessed Pope John XXIII (1881-1963) had asked priests from Spain to please volunteer and serve in the other Spanish speaking parts of the world.

After I got to know him, for the first month or two, he told me many wonderful stories from his early life. He was born and raised in the Basque region of Spain, near San Sebastián, and taught me a few of the unique words from that part of his region. We would sit at the kitchen table after lunch, which was the main meal each day, and on one occasion, when the pastor was on his day off, and it was just the two of us, we had a great extended visit.

He told me that shortly after his Ordination to the Holy Priesthood in Spain, he was asked to fill in for one month, as the chaplain at a Catholic Hospital in Madrid, before beginning his first assignment in a parish as a newly ordained priest. The day that he began his service, the director of the hospital informed him that there was a very important patient there, and he was to bring Holy Communion to her every day. This was the Servant of God, Sister Lucia dos Santos, (1907-2005) the Carmelite sister, who was one of the three children that were visionaries of the Blessed Mother at Fatima, Portugal in 1917. Fr. Villanueva was given strict orders not to speak with her, either before or after giving her Holy Communion.

However, somehow during the course of that month, they had a brief conversation one day, which he told me, had changed his life. Sr. Lucia had told him about the look of great sorrow on the face of Mary, when she related to the three children that "Many souls go to hell." Our Lady said that it is a horrible place, and then she showed the children a vision of hell. Fr. Villanueva told me that throughout his many years, he never saw such sorrow on the face of anyone, as he had seen on the face of Sr. Lucia as she related this to him.

At that point, I could see a look of great sorrow on his own face, as he told all this to me. He said that we are to take our salvation very seriously. We need to be people with a deep prayer life, so that we do not get involved with evil things, which will lead to losing our soul forever. We are to do our very best not to go astray, especially priests, who are more under attack from the evil one. His conversation and his good example reminded me then, as it does now, of the sage advice given by Our Lord to live a holy life and choose the right path. Jesus tells us,

> "Enter through the narrow gate; for the gate is wide
> and the road broad that leads to destruction and those
> who enter through it are many. How narrow the gate
> and constricted the road that leads to life. And those
> who find it are few" (Mt. 7:13-14).

Fr. Villanueva lived these words, and put them into practice and truly tried to be a holy priest. He was the celebrant of the first parish Mass every morning at 6:30 a.m., and would unlock the church at 5:30 a.m. and sit in the confessional awaiting any possible penitents. He kept his own confessional door open, so that he could be in prayer for that hour in the presence of the Blessed Sacrament. He lived very simply and ate sparingly, and I believe that all his earthly possessions filled one suitcase. When he went back to Spain each year, for a visit with his family in the Basque area, he was never sure if he would be returning to Puerto Rico.

I believe that Our Lord in His great love and mercy for me, as well as the Blessed Mother, to whom I had consecrated my priesthood, had put me in the right place and time to live in the same Rectory as this holy and dedicated man of God. The way that his own encounter with Sr. Lucia had a great influence on his life as a priest, I believe that it did the same for me. As a newly ordained priest, it helped me set my own spiritual priorities, and over the years has helped me focus on the reality of sin and that it is truly a battle to be holy. In Spanish, it is called "*En la lucha*," which means "Amid the fight."

We are all united in the Mystical Body of Christ. St. Paul wrote about the many varying members that make up the "Body of Christ" (Rom. 12:5). The Communion of Saints emphasizes this connection of all the members united under Jesus Christ, the Head. It consists of three sections: the "Church Triumphant" in heaven, the "Church Suffering" in purgatory and the "Church Militant" still on earth. The word "militant" means that we are here still, amid the battle, for the salvation of our soul and we are to, "Work out your salvation with fear and trembling; for it is God who is at work in you, both to will and to work for His good pleasure" (Phil. 2:2b-13).

There is a very well known hymn "For All the Saints," that most of us hear, unfortunately, only once each year, on All Saints Day. It has a second verse that I have found very inspirational. A part of that verse goes like this, "We feebly struggle, they in glory shine." The saints are in the part of the Mystical Body of Christ called the "Church Triumphant." They are those members in the Communion of Saints that have triumphed in the battle of good versus evil in their lives, and chosen the path of light over darkness. We look to the example of the saints of all ages, many known to Almighty God alone. When they were on earth, they also feebly struggled, but they cooperated with the grace and plan of the Lord and now gloriously shine with Him in the kingdom of heaven.

# Doña Luz

Those first few months in Villalba were happy ones for me, and the Lord provided a loving family that was very kind and welcoming. This was the family of Doña Luz Maria Cintrón. The word "Doña" is a title of respect shown to an elderly woman; the male equivalent would be "Don," like the saint, Don Bosco. Her little house was probably one of the original wooden structures from the establishment of the town in 1917. In fact, the coat-of-arms of Villalba has a background, or field, in the green color, with a white church in the center, surrounded by five small white homes, which depict the first houses in the small town. Doña Luz's home was located directly behind the church, and probably was one of those found on the shield.

As an Ordination gift, one of the families gave me a puppy, who my pastor gave the name, "Maurie." Every night after the evening 7:30 Mass, I would take a walk, along with the dog, and pass her and her family sitting on their balcony. At first, we exchanged a few words and eventually, I was invited to join them and sit down to visit. They became like a second family to me, since I was far from home. When it was Christmas Eve or Mother's Day, and I was a bit homesick for my family in New Jersey, I was included in their family gatherings. On Sunday evenings, after all the weekend Masses were finished, I took the opportunity to unwind with Doña Luz and her son Roberto, who came in for the weekend from San Juan, along with some neighbors. We had cheese, crackers and refreshments and a few good laughs and that very special ingredient, love.

During one visit, Doña Luz spoke very candidly with me and told me that she had not always been the best role model. She explained that when she was young, she had studied with a doctor and learned how to give injections. She had served practically as the town nurse, in the absence of a physician, and that she became well-known in that little town. She was a very beautiful young lady and the gentlemen were smitten by her good looks. She also told me that over the years, she had six children with several different men.

One day, an elderly parishioner, Doña Gertrudis, came to the Sacristy after Mass and asked to speak with me. We went to the rectory to talk and there, she told me to be very careful, and to discontinue going to the home of Doña Luz. She said that she was an "Indecent person" and I should not associate with such people since I was a priest, and it would damage my good name in the town. I was somewhat shaken up by this, since I had really become fond of my new Villalba surrogate family.

Of course, I immediately thought of my patron, St. Matthew, who was a tax collector. He was considered a public sinner and a traitor, among his contemporaries, the Jewish people, since he worked for the Romans, their oppressors. The Lord Jesus had called Matthew to follow Him and he left his post collecting taxes in Capernaum, and even invited the Lord to his home to eat. I was in good company, I thought, because Jesus too, was criticized for associating with sinners. But this, after all, was Villalba, a small town, and everyone liked to talk, and in particular see what the new priest was up to. I thought to myself, "Better safe than sorry," and that maybe I should distance myself from Doña Luz and her family. With that, I asked the Lord for His guidance to do the right thing.

Not long after that, I took ill with the flu and was in bed with a fever for several days. The word of my illness apparently spread throughout the town, and the people at daily Mass all heard about it, including Doña Gertrudis. However it was only Doña Luz, then aged 78, who arrived at the Rectory and climbed the steep stairs to my bedroom and brought me homemade soup and a native tea, called *Té de Naranjo*. It was made from the leaves from the bitter orange plant, and steeped with a little sugar. She had been taught this natural remedy; a tradition of the indigenous people from many years earlier, and it really did help.

The Lord had given me a great sign. The mercy and kindness of Doña Luz had come through. Yes, she had made her mistakes sure enough, in her youthful days and had realized that, and had repented of it, but she was a better person now. In the merciful eyes of the loving Lord, it does not matter where you start, but where you finish. She knew that I was far from my Mom and Dad and was sick in bed, and made the effort to bring me comfort, in particular during a time of illness. Just like the story that Our Lord told us about the King, who had called the blessed into the Kingdom. He said, "When

I was hungry, you gave me to eat, when I was thirsty, you gave me to drink, when I was ill you visited me" (Mt. 25:35-36). It is on this same Gospel passage that the Corporal Works of Mercy are based.

Before I was given a new assignment and left the beautiful town of Villalba, I have another memorable image of Doña Luz, which stays in my mind. She worked with a program called "*Hogares Crea*," which means "Creating Homes," which helped young people, who came from broken homes. They were now in a rehabilitation facility, after being involved with a serious problem, whether drug related or the law. They would come to our little town of Villalba on occasion, to be of help cleaning up the plaza and Doña Luz reached out to them. Sometimes forty or fifty young men and women would arrive, and eventually each of them would stop at the home of Doña Luz for a visit and a bite to eat.

On one occasion, she had made one large pot of *Arroz con Habicuelas*, which were Rice with Beans, that she had prepared early in the day. The young people, who at about eighteen to twenty one years old are always hungry, would then eat from that one pot of rice and beans all day. At the end of one particular day, she was tired from being the hostess to so many and rested on the porch as usual. Doña Luz, with tears in her eyes, told me it was a truly a miracle from the Lord, how all those people had eaten from that one pot of food all day long, just like the multiplication of the loaves and fishes that never gave out, and to this day I truly believe that was the case.

Years later, when I became pastor at Holy Rosary Church, I often thought of Doña Luz. There was a very kind woman who so thoughtfully looked out for my welfare, Theresa Bucci, who was in her late 70's when I arrived in 2002. When she came to Sunday Mass, if she saw that I was ill with a cold, cough or even a fever, she would go home, and within hours, call to say that she was coming over to drop off a pot of homemade chicken soup, complete with vegetables and noodles. It is wonderful and caring people such as these, who bring joy to a priest's heart, to see that the love which he has in his heart for others, is, every now and then, returned by the kindness of his flock.

Unfortunately, I lost a dear friend when Theresa had a serious stroke in early April 2008, and passed away about ten days later.

When she was still in and out of consciousness, I held her hand and told her in Italian, "*Gesù ti aiuta*" which was actually our southern Italian dialect version of "*Gesù ti aiutera*'" in proper Italian, to which she faintly whispered back, "I know." In one of her favorite aspirations, she would often say in Italian, "*O Gesù mio, misericordia,*" which means: "My dear Jesus, be merciful to me." I have incorporated this in my own life and so, when I am stopped at red light while driving, would repeat those same words, or at times, "Lord Jesus Christ, have mercy on me, a sinner," and as well, "Jesus, I trust in You." In this way, I have found that one can live in the presence of the Merciful Savior throughout one's day.

Let us be grateful to the good Lord for those wonderful people, such as Doña Luz, Theresa and so many others, who have shown love and compassion to us. For me, they are signs of the Lord's mercy, goodness and love. May those who have gone before us in faith be rewarded for their acts of charity, and may we be reunited one day with them in the kingdom of heaven.

# Birthday Cakes

My birthday is on the last day of September, and in 1988 it was the first one that I was to spend in Puerto Rico. Over the years, I had spent birthdays away from my parents while in the seminary, and was not expecting to be "down in the dumps" when the day arrived. My folks, sister, brother and some relatives and friends had sent greeting cards that arrived a few days earlier, which were displayed on my desk. When the housekeeper, Ana arrived to bring the laundry, she noticed the cards, and asked when my birthday was. When I told her the thirtieth of the month, in just a few days, she asked what I was doing to celebrate. Of course, I had no plans whatsoever, as I was far from home, and tried to make light of it.

Maybe down deep, one still does feel a bit homesick from time to time, especially when one's birthday rolls around. However, I had made a commitment to the Lord and His Holy Church to serve Him as a priest, and this is where He wanted me. I knew that it would involve sacrifice, and at sometimes there were more sacrifices expected than at other times, but we are not to shrink from accepting it. At my Priesthood Ordination, during the ceremony, the bishop reads an Instruction from the Rite of Ordination, which is addressed directly to the person about to be ordained. The bishop says, "Model your life on the mystery of the Lord's Cross."

Over the years, I have looked at the commitment of the priest and in fact, all Christians, as the commitment of fidelity we hear in the marriage vows: "I promise to be true to you in the good times and the bad, in sickness and in health." We all have our ups and downs, but we need to be faithful to the Lord and trust in Him, and He will get us through every circumstance. Of course, the trouble comes in when we do not abandon ourselves to His plan. It is by sin, saying "No" to God, and "Yes" to our own ways, that we can confound the good plan of the Lord from unfolding.

The day of my birthday arrived, and I was greatly surprised. It looked like Ana had spread the word around the town, that the new priest's birthday was here and that he was far from home. The door at the rectory was busy practically all day, with well-wishers who brought me cards, flowers and about five different birthday cakes!

By the end of the day, truly I had tears welling up in my eyes, to realize the way that the Lord came through for me. The words of the Lord came to life on that very day for me, and many times thereafter. St. Peter told the Lord Jesus, "We have left everything to follow You." Jesus said,

> "Truly I say to you, there is no one who has left house or brothers or sisters or mother or father or children for My sake and for the Gospel's sake, but that he will receive a hundred times as much now in the present age, houses and brothers and sisters and mothers and children along with persecutions; and in the age to come, eternal life" (Mk. 10:28-30).

Throughout the years, this quote from Sacred Scripture has been replayed in my mind many times. In the various assignments where I have served in parish ministry, there have been so many wonderful folks who have opened their hearts and homes to me. They knew that my parents live in New Jersey, and so invited me to spend special holidays at their homes. I jokingly refer to them as my "surrogate sisters and brothers," and have had the blessing to baptize their children, and now see them in their High School years. In fact, with one lovely family that I have gotten to know well over the years, we refer to our gatherings as meetings of the "Corks and Forks Club," since there is usually a good glass of wine that accompanies our meal.

At times, I have been invited to arrive early and help prepare the meals with them. For this we have coined the fond term, "Culinary Therapy." There have been a lot of laughs and just old-fashioned good clean fun which has enhanced my life, and which I have seen as the providence of the Lord for one of His unworthy priests. As priests, we are to follow the advice of St. Paul, "Rejoice with those who rejoice and weep with those who weep" (Rom. 12:15). And so, I have not just been there for fun and food, but when there is illness or the passing of a loved one in their family, I am there too. My folks always taught me not to be just a "fair weather friend."

It is a good thing to be "emotionally involved," in the best sense of the expression, and not detached from one's flock, but to love, nurture and care for them. We hear in the Holy Word of God that Our Lord Jesus wept at the death of His dear friend Lazarus. The Dominican priest, Père Lacordaire, O.P. (1802-1861) wrote that priests are "to be a member of each family, yet belonging to none." This is contained in his inspirational poem found below:

### Thou art a Priest Forever

*To live in the midst of the world with no desire*
*for its pleasures; to be a member of every family,*
*yet belonging to none; to share all sufferings; to*
*penetrate all secrets, to heal all wounds; to daily*
*go from men to God to offer Him their homage*
*and petitions; to return from God to men to bring*
*them His pardon and hope; to have a heart of fire for*
*charity and a heart of bronze for chastity;*
*to bless and to be blest forever. O God, what a life,*
*and it is yours, O Priest of Jesus Christ!*

Although there have been sacrifices, as I look back, I can say that the blessings have far outweighed them. Over the years, I have spoken to my brother priests, who were to celebrate their Fiftieth or even Sixtieth Anniversary of Ordination, and have frequently asked them if they would do it all again. They always answer with a strong voice, and without an instant of hesitation, "Absolutely!" This is the goal for all of us, not just priests and religious: to be faithful to the Lord, even with the sacrifices that may entail, in order to achieve our goal. That is to draw closer to Him in love and friendship in this world and to live in the house of the Lord forever in the kingdom of heaven.

# The Wedding

Early on a Tuesday morning in April 1989, my pastor in Villalba, Fr. José ask me to please perform a wedding that afternoon. He was scheduled to witness the vows of the couple that day, but another commitment had arisen and he needed to be elsewhere. He explained to me that the couple was expecting a child and they wanted to be wed before the baby was born. He told me that it should be just a simple ceremony, without a Nuptial Mass and there would be no music. The hour arrived and there were about ten people in the church. Besides the bride and groom, were both his and her parents, the best man, maid of honor and a few friends.

However, I decided to make this event special and memorable for the couple, as I am definitely not a "no-frills" type of person. With that, I put on my cassock, my finest lace-trimmed surplice and my most beautiful white stole complete with gold embroidery, which was purchased in Italy. The bride was in a simple white dress, without a veil, and she was very pregnant indeed. There was to be no procession and they were all sitting in the front pews waiting for me. I introduced myself and offered them my congratulations, and then I asked if all those who were planning to attend had arrived and whether we were ready to begin. There was a feeling of tension, and even hostility, since the bride and groom's parents probably were very unhappy about the entire situation.

There was a very strange and uncomfortable feeling inside of me, as well; since I had performed already many weddings in that church, particularly around Christmas Eve, when many couples like to combine the happy event of their marriage, along with the family gathering for the Savior's birthday. However, this event did not that have joy-filled atmosphere that usually precedes a wedding; it was far from it. So I took a deep breath, collected my thoughts and glanced over at the statue of the patroness of the parish, Our Lady of Mount Carmel. I asked Mary and her Son, the good Lord for their help, as I had done so many times throughout my life.

I invited the bride and groom to come to the foot of the altar and the two witnesses to their left and right, all facing me, as is normally done during a Wedding. Just as I was about to make the Sign of the Cross to begin the ceremony, I told them that we have to wait a minute because something was missing. With that, I went over to the statue of the Blessed Mother, where there were beautiful white daisies that were put there for the Sunday Mass just a few days before. I plucked about four or five branches out of the vase, in the sight of all present, and smiled from ear to ear as I handed it to the bride and said to her, "This is what was missing: you need a bridal bouquet on this special day, these are from Mother Mary for you."

A smile came upon everyone's face. Thanks be to God, the tension was broken. The short ceremony went well, and at the end, there were still many smiles amid the newly married couple and their parents, now the new in-laws. Someone brought out a camera and the makeshift bridal bouquet came in very handy when it was strategically placed to camouflage the new bride's apparent condition. Within a week, I learned that a baby boy was born to the couple.

Throughout the years, now decades, I have thought about this couple and the wedding that could have been truly the worst wedding of my priesthood, but in fact has became one of the most memorable. It was all by the grace of God, not my doing. The saints tell us that it is the Lord Who acts; we are just His instruments. We are almost like spectators of those great and wonderful works that He does through us. And so, we give due glory "To Him Who is able to accomplish far more than all we ask or imagine, by the power at work within us" (Eph. 3:20). The Lord and Our Blessed Mother had inspired me to diffuse a tense situation with a simple smile, a little kindness and a few flowers.

It may be childlike of me, which is not really always a bad thing, but I cannot help but think of a line in a song from the movie, "Mary Poppins," that was "Just a spoonful of sugar helps the medicine go down." A little sweetness, tenderness and mercy never hurt anyone, and even can turn an unpleasant situation into a good and positive one.

We always have a choice. We can do things with anger and pain or do them with kindness and compassion; it is our call and our own way of demonstrating to others that we are trying to live a Christlike life. If you, the reader, think that I am "goofy," since, as a fifty-plus year old priest, I am quoting Mary Poppins, sorry, but this is the way I am, and have been instilled with this positive attitude in my upbringing, so we can all blame it on my folks! I am sure that there are a lot of worse case scenarios than this, believe you me.

St. Francesca Cabrini, (1850-1917) who was the first national-ized American citizen to be canonized said, "We cannot all do con-spicuous things for God, but let us do well, all that He asks us." A more recent future saint, Blessed Mother Theresa of Calcutta has told us, "We cannot all do great things, but we can do small things with great love." St. Paul tells us, "If I give all I possess to the poor and give my body to flames, but do not have love, I gain nothing" (I Cor. 13:3). This is the wisdom of the saints. Let us try our best to follow their counsel, so we can be joined one day with them in the presence of the Lord in the kingdom of heaven.

# The Doves

Over the years, I have often told people that our lives are a series of ups and downs, hills and valleys or, as they say in Spanish, *"arribas y abajos"*. The Lord is with us to help us get through the joys and sorrows, the good times and bad. This is similar to the wedding vows, wherein the couple promises fidelity to each other, come what may, throughout their lives together.

A few years back, I was visiting Rome and saw a large sign outside the Church of St. Eustachio, which is located between the Piazza Navona and the Pantheon. It announced an upcoming Parish Mission, and the theme of it was, in Italian: *"Chediamo al Signore la grazia di affrontare, con serenita` e coraggio, la vita di ogni giorno"* which means, "We ask the Lord the grace to accept, with serenity and courage, the challenges of daily life." All that I had with me, in my pocket, was a scrap of paper and a pencil, and so I wrote down those words.

It had given me an insight that it is only with by grace and help of the Lord that we can courageously and peacefully accept that which He sends our way. It is not easy, but helps us to grow in the school of holiness. Many of the candidates that the Church considers for canonization are judged, not only on the virtuous life they led, but on "Heroic Virtue," the way in which they courageously confronted the many difficulties that they were sent.

In my own early life as a priest, I can indeed say that I have seen so many dramatic, as well as touching moments, the ups and downs, as it were, ranging from the belly-laughable to the near tragic. When my first Lent as a priest was approaching, the parish received a phone call to please bring Blessed Ashes to a group of soldiers at Fort Allen National Guard Base in Ponce, which was about twenty minutes away.

When I arrived to impose the ashes on that very hot afternoon, I found that all of the soldiers, a total of about fifty, had green camouflage paint on their faces. Needless to say, as I put the ashes on their foreheads, I needed to maintain a straight face and not burst out laughing. It took me a few days to get the green tint off my thumb as I recall! This was one of my most laughable moments that

I have experienced, and the following account is one of the most near tragic.

The doves, in the title of this chapter, refer to the Spanish words, "*Las Alondras,*" which was a neighborhood about a ten-minute drive from the center of the town of Villalba. It was considered the best development in that vicinity, with lovely sprawling one family homes and some space for a front and back garden. I got to know several families there. One day in late August 1988, a woman who I will call Rosa, came to the Rectory. It was a sunny Thursday morning and she asked to speak with me. She was in her mid-thirties, just a bit older than me at that time.

We went into a private office and there she burst into tears, telling me that she needed my advice. She told me that her husband, who I will call Juan, was on the verge of committing suicide. She recounted that he had been very "down in the dumps" for several weeks, and had been preparing her, by telling her things like, "All will be alright for you and the children, the house and car are all paid. When I am not here, you will all be fine." She knew that he was not planning to just move to another place.

I suggested that the three of us meet as soon as possible, but she said, "No, he cannot know that I came here to speak with you!" So I suggested a plan, whereby I would go to their home and pretend to be lost, and ask them for directions to another home. I hoped and prayed that the Lord would understand if I played a bit of "make believe" to reach out to help Juan from a tragic death.

We agreed on that plan, and that she would be outside her home about 8:45 that evening, when I would pull up with my car, looking for directions. We did exactly that, later that same evening, and she invited me into their home. She acted surprised, and told her husband that the young priest, the "*Padrecito*" was lost, needed directions and that she had invited me to bless their home, since I was there. Juan looked very sullen and before long, the three of us sat down for a little visit.

During our chat, I learned that they had both been born and raised in Villalba and had also been married there. After that, I began to comment how good the Lord had been to them. They had been so blessed with a wonderful life together, their two children, ages

8 and 10, their health, a beautiful home and good employment. At first, Juan was not buying any of this, so I took another approach, mentioning that for all of us, life has its ups and downs. No one can escape the sorrows and disappointments that come along with the joys and triumphs.

The conversation continued, and I mentioned that we are not alone throughout our lives, since we have the help and grace of the Lord, Who helps to get us through it all. The Lord provides us with blessings, and as well, He sustains us in times of difficulty. None of us knows what tomorrow will bring but "*Con la ayuda de Dios y la Virgencita, todo se puede*" which means, "With the help of God and the 'little' Virgin Mary, you can do anything." This is a variation on one of my very favorite quotes from one of St. Paul's letters, "I can do all things in Him, Who strengthens me" (Phil. 4:13). I still repeat this to myself many times in the course of the day.

Soon, it seemed that there was a small breakthrough with Juan. I had given it "my all" to help him see the blessings of the Lord in his life. He was listening intently, and eventually there was a slight mist in his eyes, and I could see that he was going in the right direction. By then, I had been there almost thirty minutes, and did not want to overstay my visit. Since I was there to bless their home as well, we called over their son and daughter and the five of us formed a circle. In the prayer, I thanked the Lord for the many blessings that He had bestowed on their marriage and family, and together, we asked the Lord to help them in their daily crosses.

In conclusion, I asked the Lord God to send His holy angels to protect their home, and dispel the enemy, who, with his lies, brings doubt and discouragement, but rather, to send them confidence and hope in the Lord. By the end of the blessing, Juan, Rosa and I had tears in our eyes and together with the children, had a "group hug" as they call it nowadays. As I went back to the car and waved goodbye to them, I said to the Lord quietly in my heart, "If I never do another good thing in my life, please remember this visit on my behalf come the day of my judgment."

During my visit, I had encouraged Juan and Rosa to stay close to the Lord through daily prayer, regular attendance at Holy Mass, Holy Communion and in particular, to avail themselves of the Sacrament of Confession when needed. Subsequently, I did see the family regularly at Mass and after a few weeks, Rosa stopped by Rectory office to tell me that her husband was doing much better. I told her that it had all been through the grace of God, since it was the Lord who put us together in the right circumstances. I recall the wonderful words of St. Thérèse of Lisieux, (1873-1897) called the "Little Flower" who wrote, *"Tout est grâce, vraiment, tout est grâce"* which means, "All is grace, truly, all is grace."

Years later, when I saw the movie, "Schindler's List" there was a line in the movie that was from the Jewish Talmud, "Whoever saves one life saves all mankind." I then recalled my visit with Rosa and Juan and thanked the Lord for that blessed opportunity to be His instrument of healing and peace, amid a difficult period of crisis for them both. This story is a reminder that the Lord never abandons us, if we put our trust in Him. He will get us through, even when things seem desperate, and as if no solution is in sight. There is always hope. That is what brought Rosa to the rectory that day. The Letter to the Hebrews reminds us,

> "Do not love money, but be content with what you have for God has said, 'I will never desert you, nor will I forsake you' that we may say with confidence: 'the Lord is my helper, I will not be afraid; what can man do to me" (Heb. 13:5-6)?

We ask the Lord to help us in all of our needs, and in particular, to help us keep our eyes focused on the most important of all goals, to live daily in His love and friendship and to be with Him forever in the kingdom of heaven.

# 3

# The Danbury Years

## Father Joe

After several years of service in the Diocese of Ponce, Puerto Rico, I felt it was time to return to the New York area, to be closer to my parents in northern New Jersey. When I arrived in Puerto Rico in 1987, both my brother and sister were still living at home. However, in 1989, my brother was accepted to Medical school and went to Omaha, Nebraska, and in January 1990, my sister had married and moved to Milan, Italy. And as I was living in Puerto Rico, none of the three children were in close proximity to my parents. So I thought that one of us should be nearby our folks, especially in case of an emergency.

A priest friend suggested that I write to Bishop Edward M. Egan, of the Diocese of Bridgeport, Connecticut. It was located not far from my folks in New Jersey, and this priest was a friend of his and offered to put in a good word for me. With the permission of the bishop of Ponce, I began service in the Bridgeport Diocese on July 31, 1991. After just six months at St. Charles Borromeo Church in Bridgeport, I arrived in St. Joseph Church, Danbury on February 14, 1992. It was a beautiful Romanesque church, with a lot of activity, a Grammar school, and five priests in the rectory. Besides the pastor and two associate pastors, one of whom was now me, there were also two retired priests in residence.

I enjoyed the Danbury years very much, and there are very happy memories from my service there. It was a city filled with many faithful people and I enjoyed the Novena Prayer Group on Tuesday evenings, as well as the fidelity of those going to Confession. This was a place where there were still two priests in the confessionals every Saturday morning from 11:00 am until Noon, then again from 3:00 - 4:00 p.m.

It was always a blessed opportunity to bring the loving mercy of the good Lord to others, in what has been called the Sacred Tribunal of Penance. I prefer to think of the priest as the "Physician of souls" where he has the opportunity to look into the depths of the soul of the penitent, help them to see the error of their ways, then tell them those most consoling words that Our Lord spoke to the woman caught in adultery, "Go, and from now on, do not sin anymore" (Jn. 8:11).

Somehow, I often think of the seminary days, when we were asked to help in a local parish, and get a taste of parish life. I was asked, as a seminarian, to hear the practice confessions of the children who were preparing for their first Penance. When one little boy came in, I reminded him that he did not have to tell me his real sins, since I was not really a priest, and that this was just practice. His name was Brucie and he had a little lisp, which was awfully cute when one is seven years old. He told me that he had fought with his sister, disobeyed his parents and pulled the tail on the dog. I said, "Well, did you pull the dog's tail by accident or was it on purpose?" and he answered back, without missing a beat, "No, it was on purpose!" Well, I had to stop myself from bursting out in laughter, and thought to myself, "How can I ever hear confessions as a priest someday?"

But, I truly believe that the good Lord gives us, His priests, the wisdom and grace that we need to help meet the people in the confessional where they are at. We must be kind, patient and merciful. Of course, we see St. Peter carrying two keys when he is depicted. One is gold and the other is silver. The gold key loosens on earth, and thus it is loosened in heaven. We forgive them their sins, they are forgotten on earth and in heaven, and they move on. The silver key binds them. We need to admonish and correct them, and tell the truth in love. I once heard it said, "Truth without love is harsh, love without truth is mush, to tell the truth in love is compassion."

Father Joe was one of the retired priests living in the rectory. At the time, he was in his early 50's, but had an operation several years prior for a tumor in his brain, and sadly, was not the same person he used to be. He had served as the Catholic chaplain of the State University, located in Danbury, and I learned that after many years of service there, both the students and faculty alike loved him. However, they began to see a change in him since he began acting strange. Some thought that he had unfortunately developed a drinking problem, since he was slurring his speech. One day, he passed out and when they brought him to the hospital, they discovered a tumor in the area of his pituitary gland and removed it. He had not been the same since then.

I think of Fr. Joe and his many hours in the confessional, and remember those days as if they were yesterday. In May 1994, he was to celebrate his 25th Anniversary of Ordination to the Priesthood, also known as his "Silver Jubilee," and by then, his health was really failing, and did not have the stamina to offer a Mass of Thanksgiving. My heart really went out to him and I thought I would try to make this beautiful and momentous event in his life a little special. I was brought up this way, to "go the extra mile" as they say.

So, the night before the date of his actual anniversary, I decorated the door of his room with a big glistening silver number "25" that I had cut out from cardboard, and covered with aluminum foil. I affixed silver streamers going all around the frame of the door, from top to bottom, and was still on the ladder putting the last streamer in place, when he came up the stairs to his room and saw what I was doing and he broke into tears. He was so grateful that I wanted to make, his otherwise unremembered day, a somewhat memorable one for him.

I believe that this is what our lives should be. I once heard the expression: "Do random acts of kindness" and really believe that the "Planned acts of kindness" go a long way too. I also remember hearing that "Jesus has no hands in this world, only yours." We need to continue His work, and to bring His comfort, consolation, mercy and healing to others and our dear Lord will see and be pleased. Our generosity to others will come back to us in good measure and overflowing. He cannot be out done in generosity, as I have heard it said. The Lord Jesus gives us wonderful words of wisdom to help us live a caring, compassionate and mercy-filled life,

> "Stop judging and you will not be judged. Stop condemning and you will not be condemned. Forgive and you will be forgiven. Give and gifts will be given to you; a good measure, packed together, shaken down, and overflowing, will be poured into your lap. For the measure with which you measure will in return be measured out to you." (Lk. 6:38, Mt. 7:2, Mk. 4:24).

These reminders help us to be generous and ever-ready in doing acts of kindness for others. Our Lord will be pleased with our efforts. It is He Who "Watches over the way of the just" (Ps. 1:6) Not that we are looking for recompense, but this is His promise. The only reward we ever need is eternal life. We need to keep in focus our goal, to live a holy life and after a holy death, be with the Lord for all eternity in the kingdom of heaven.

# Children

Over the years, I have enjoyed seeing children growing up. I love to see them take their first steps, and be there to witness that excitement and pure joy on their faces. They are so adorable at about eighteen months old. It is great to see them spread their wings and grow into their own personalities. After they accomplish something important in their development they say something like, "I am not a baby anymore, I am a big boy/girl, now!" It is good to support them, show that they are loved, and to tell them that God loves them, that they are to be friends with God and thank Him for all His blessings.

In February 1995, Peter must have been approaching his fourth birthday. By then, I had been assigned to the parish in Danbury for three years, and I knew him since when he was about six months old. Both of his parents served as Lectors, and would come to the sacristy before Mass to review the Readings. And so, I had known Peter and felt comfortable enough to joke a bit with him.

I remembered the story of the girl called Little Red Riding Hood when I was a little boy. There was the part when the wolf was impersonating the grandmother, and the girl notes the big ears and nose. I said to Peter in a joking manner, as Little Red Riding Hood said to the wolf who was in disguise, "My, Peter, what big ears you have… My, Peter, what a big nose you have…" etc, and he gave me a blank stare. I then said, "Don't you know this? It is just like the Little Red Riding Hood story, when she talks to the wolf, right?" To which he responded, "I don't have that video!" At that moment, I knew then that the days of telling Grimm's fairy tales from my childhood had taken a back seat to the age of computer-animated cartoons and video technology.

Not long ago, I was reading a magazine, and saw a one-box comic of a father tucking in his daughter at bedtime. She was depicted as young, only about five years old, and was clutching a teddy bear, that she had in bed with her. The caption over the father's head read, "Would you like Daddy to 'text' you a bed time story?" Things certainly have changed.

It was in my service as a priest in the parish in Danbury that I became an uncle. My sister, Suzanne, traveled to Milan, Italy in

1985 and there met a fine fellow, Giuseppe Pasini. After a courtship, they were married on January 13, 1990 and moved to Milan, to begin their family. I was happy to be able to perform their Wedding Ceremony in the same church where our parents were married in 1955. Their three children are Francesca, born 1991, Stephen, born 1992 and Victoria, born 1997. I was greatly honored to baptize all three and gave them their First Holy Communion.

For my parents' Fortieth Anniversary in 1995, we all took a family vacation to celebrate. It was a cruise from New York to Bermuda. One afternoon, we were near the pool on the deck of the ship, and some of us were in the pool enjoying the refreshing water. My niece Francesca, then not yet four years old, stood by the edge of the pool and said, "I am afraid to go in, because I might drown." I told her, "But you know that I am your uncle and I love you, and I will make sure that you won't drown."

That was all it took, and she jumped right into to my arms and enjoyed herself, splashing up a storm! That was a lesson to me to this day of childlike trust. She knew that she would be in good hands. Children are completely dependent on their parents for everything: to keep them fed, clean and dry and put a roof over their heads. They are totally in the care of their parents.

In the Gospel, Jesus talks to his chosen apostles to set them on the right track, at a time when they all seemed to be looking for positions of importance, we hear the Lord gently tell them,

> "At that time, the disciples approached Jesus and said, 'Who is the greatest in the kingdom of heaven?' He called a child over, placed it in their midst, and said, 'Amen, I say to you, unless you turn and become like children, you will not enter the kingdom of heaven. Whoever humbles himself like this child is the greatest in the kingdom of heaven'" (Mt. 18:1-4).

We need to keep that simple childlike faith and trust in Christ, and put our hand in His hand, that He might lead us and guide us in the paths of righteousness. His mercy and kindness will be upon us, if we place all of our trust and hope in Him. We hear, "Our soul waits for the Lord who is our help and our shield. For in Him our hearts rejoice and in His Holy Name we trust" (Ps. 33:20-21).

How wonderful if we could keep that simple, trusting faith just like those children who prepare for their First Holy Communion. The catechism question that so many of us remember from those days, "Why did God make you?" The answer was then and now, "God made me to know Him, love Him and serve Him in this life, and to be happy with Him forever in Heaven." May this childlike answer help all of us, in guiding the decisions in our lives and remind us of our goal which is to get to the kingdom of heaven.

# Light of Christ

The parish at St. Joseph in Danbury had a well-attended Catholic Grammar School. We priests assigned to the rectory took turns in offering Holy Masses on the First Fridays of each month and the Holy Days. On the Solemnity of All Saints in the year 1994, there was a Mass at which the school children attended. The celebrant was Fr. Larry Carew, who was also assigned to the parish, and he asked the children a question during the homily, "Who is a saint?" A little third grader looked at the stained glass window and pointing to it, said, "A saint is someone the light shines through." Fr. Larry later told me that he was practically speechless after that comment. How true a statement, the Light of the Lord certainly shines through the life of a saint. The little child said it much better, and in more simple terms, than all of us priests in that parish, put together, could have said.

Some years ago, I learned of a poem that was read over the radio, by King George VI (1895-1952) of England, on December 25, 1939. It was a time when the citizens of the British Empire faced another World War. Amid the gloom, the king brought back a tradition that was begun by his father, which was an annual Christmas message to all inhabitants of the Empire. The speech would go on to be famous. King George VI, not usually a compelling speaker, reassured his people by quoting a poem that was written in 1908 by Minnie Louise Haskins,

> *"I said to the man who stood at the Gate of the Year,*
> *'Give me a light that I may tread safely into the*
> *unknown.' And he replied, 'Go out into the darkness,*
> *and put your hand into the Hand of God. That shall*
> *be better than light, and safer than a known way.'"*

The Venerable Cardinal John Henry Newman (1801-1890) expressed this same idea in a more poetic way in a few lines from a much longer prayer written by him,

*"Flood my soul with Your spirit and life.*
*Penetrate and possess my whole being so utterly,*
*that my life may only be a radiance of Yours.*
*Shine through me, and be so in me*
*that every soul I come in contact with*
*may feel Your presence in my soul.*
*Let them look up and see no longer me,*
*but only Jesus!"*

It was also Cardinal Newman who wrote the Hymn, "Lead, Kindly Light," in 1833. The last verse, for me, has always been the most moving, when he wrote, "Lead, Savior, lead me home in child-like faith, home to my God, to rest forever after earthly strife, in the calm light of everlasting life."

As Christians, we are to radiate the light of the Lord, and shine that light forth to others. I recall a quote from the well-known physician, Dr. Elisabeth Kübler-Ross, (1926-2004) who was a Swiss-born psychiatrist and the author of the groundbreaking book, *"On Death and Dying."* She likened people to stained glass windows, and said that when the sun is bright, they sparkle when you view them from the inside. However, it is only when it is dark outside, that the light from within reveals their true beauty.

In happy times, it is easy to sparkle and be bright. However, it is in those dark times or difficulties, when the interior light needs to come through, in order to show forth the beauty of the windows from within the church building. All of us need to keep that light of Christ burning from within, by cultivating the childlike spirit and keep your faith simple by "Departing from evil and do good" (Ps. 3: 27).

If we live in the Lord's friendship, then the Fruits of the Holy Spirit will be evident in our lives. They can serve as that burning Light of Christ and can shine through, so that our good works can give witness to the power and goodness of the Lord. Jesus tells us,

> "You are the light of the world. A city set on a moun-
> tain cannot be hidden. Nor do they light a lamp and
> then put it under a bushel basket; it is set on a lamp

stand, where it gives light to all in the house. Just so, your light must shine before others, that they may see your good deeds and glorify your heavenly Father" (Mt. 5:14-16).

The choice is always ours. A friend once told me a Chinese proverb, that made me laugh right out loud, but he applied to our spiritual lives, "He who walks in the middle of the road, gets hit by rickshaw both ways." Two paths are set before us, and let us choose to walk as children of the light, and not of darkness. We hear two diverse paths contrasted by St. Paul, who delineates the Fruits of the Holy Spirit,

> "I say, then: live by the Spirit and you will certainly not gratify the desire of the flesh. Now the works of the flesh are obvious: immorality, impurity, licentiousness, idolatry, sorcery, hatreds, rivalry, jealousy, outbursts of fury, and acts of selfishness, dissensions, factions, and occasions of envy, drinking bouts, orgies, and the like. I warn you, as I warned you before, that those who do such things will not inherit the kingdom of God. In contrast, the fruit of the Spirit is love, joy, peace, patience, kindness, generosity, faithfulness, gentleness, self-control" (Gal. 5:16, 19, 21-23).

Let us try our very best to walk as children of the light of Christ and reject the darkness. This way, after a faith-filled and faithful life on this earth, we can be illuminated by the perpetual light of the Lord, which awaits us in the kingdom of heaven.

# Leona

Throughout our lives, I believe that one of the most important things for us is not to go into the "carpentry business." We are not to construct our own crosses, or to add more wood to the one that we already have. Unfortunately, as weak human beings, we can so easily get involved with the wrong things. In other words, one would not walk in the good and righteous paths, but the wrong and dangerous ones. It is so very easy to just let things slide, but takes a concerted effort to do the right thing.

When I was assigned to the parish of St. Joseph Church in Danbury, I would offer Holy Mass on Sunday afternoons at the Danbury Federal Correctional Institution. Sometimes, the inmates would ask me why God did this to them. I would try to be as diplomatic as possible, but also gently remind them that they must have done something "Not quite right" at some time to be where they were.

One of the more famous inmates was none other than Leona Helmsley, (1920-2007) whom I met one Sunday before Holy Mass. It was on her birthday July 4, and the year was 1993. Leona saw me there, and asked for a minute of my time. She told me that her husband Harry had been very good to Cardinals Spellman, Cooke and O'Connor. With that, I told her that I was just a simple parish priest, and not in a powerful position as all of those important people. However, I gave her a piece of advice, "Carry your cross every day with God's help." I also told her to make sure she complied with the rules, try not to make any trouble, and then things will go better for her and she might get back home even sooner.

I realized that Leona was not a Christian, but there was no better advice that I could give to her. Apparently, she was consoled by my few words, and her eyes began to get misty. Then I gave her a special blessing, since she mentioned it was her birthday, and also gave her a little embrace to encourage her. She gave me a hug and kiss on my cheek as well.

Later that night, I called a priest friend, who was then assigned to a parish in Pennsylvania, and told him of my unexpected encounter with Leona and how I received a nice hug and kiss from her. He responded, "Too bad she didn't give you a diamond brooch!" It seemed that I could not stop laughing that evening, and I think of his comic response every now and then when I need a good laugh from the past.

It is with a spirit of cheerfulness that we are to carry the cross. Of course, this is easier said than done. Jesus tells us not to draw attention to ourselves when we are amid sacrifices or suffering. We hear in the Gospel of St. Matthew, "When you fast, do not look gloomy like the hypocrites. They neglect their appearance, so that they may appear to others to be fasting. Amen, I say to you, they have received their reward" (ch. 6:16).

When I was visiting the beautiful island of Bermuda, I went into one of the clothing shops. There was a section in it, where they sold the uniforms for grade school children. Since it is an island that takes its traditions from England, their mother country, each school has its own coat-of-arms, which are stitched on the jackets and shirts. One of the mottos of the school crests was for the Whitney School and it struck me, it was embroidered in Latin, "*Magnanimiter Crucem Sustine*" which means, "Carry your Cross Magnanimously."

The word magnanimous comes from two Latin words, "*Magna*" meaning great and "*Anima*" meaning spirit, and literally it means "With a great spirit." The word has many connotations, such as courageously, unselfishly, noble in mind and heart, and to be generous in forgiving without resentment or revenge. With all my heart, I truly believe that the Lord will help us in carrying our crosses by His mercy and grace. We need to be confident in asking His assistance, and to involve Him every step of our path to glorify Him, as we try our best to:

> *Carry your Cross*
> *Like Christ*
> *With Christ and*
> *For Christ.*

Perhaps Blessed Mother Theresa of Calcutta said it best, "The more we embrace the cross, the more we become like Jesus." The more we become like Jesus, the more we grow in His love and friendship, and so steady our feet on that path that leads to our friendship with Him forever in the kingdom of heaven.

# Farewells

Over the years, I have heard it said, "For some people death comes like a thief, and for others it comes as a friend." When I was assigned to the parish in Danbury, part of my duties was to cover the responsibilities of the hospital chaplain on his day off. With that, I would carry a pager from 8:00 a.m. each Wednesday until 8:00 a.m. on Thursday. This was for emergencies, in most cases. On Wednesday, May 4, 1994 about eight o'clock in the evening, the pager went off. Right away, I called the hospital and was told to get there as soon as possible.

There, I found a 35-year-old man, who was unresponsive in the Emergency department. The doctors and nurses had a very solemn and grim look on their faces, when I entered the room. It looked serious, so I gave him the "Farewell package" to get him into heaven: Absolution from his sins, the Sacrament of the Anointing of the Sick and the Apostolic Blessing with the Plenary Indulgence. As I was about to leave the room, the doctors and nurses all said, "Please stay, we need as many prayers as we can get." This was the first time I had heard this from them, as they usually want me out of there promptly, so they can have the extra space for equipment.

Soon, I learned from his wife, Sue, that her husband, Kevin, had been exercising and she heard a thump in the room, since he had collapsed. Unfortunately, I later learned that Kevin had an aneurysm in his brain that had burst. The surgeons there at Danbury Hospital performed emergency surgery to correct the problem and at first, it looked like there was slight improvement. Although I was no longer on duty as the fill-in hospital chaplain, once Thursday morning at 8:00 a.m. arrived, I returned over the course of the next few days to see how that young man was improving.

Shortly, I met Kevin's mother, Mona, his brother, Mark and his sister, Ann, and I learned that Kevin and Sue had two young daughters. Soon, there was an entire support system of prayer and caring composed of many family and friends, who were sitting outside the Intensive Care Unit, just waiting for the opportunity to go see Kevin, if even for just a few minutes.

Regrettably, by the following Monday, May 9, his condition had taken a bad turn, and Kevin was declared clinically brain dead. For sure, it was devastating news to them, but I was amazed at the strong faith of all involved. They commended him to God, and each went into say their last farewells. I learned that the nurses were very kind and sensitive and had allowed, even suggested, that Kevin's wife, Sue, lay on the bed with him, those last hours, to hug him and kiss him goodbye. These words from *The Imitation of Christ* come to mind, "Blessed is the man that has the hour of his death continually before his eyes, and daily puts himself in order for death... for the Son of Man will come at an hour when He is not looked for" (Bk. 1, ch. 23).

The family had decided to help others, by donating some of Kevin's organs to those awaiting transplants. It truly was a learning experience for me, to see the grace and mercy of the Lord working in them and sustaining them, in a time of such difficulty. Death had indeed come as a thief, to take away a handsome and talented young man, in the best years of his life. We hear in the Book of the Prophet Isaiah, "For My thoughts are not your thoughts, nor are your ways My ways, says the Lord" (ch. 55:8).

The family, as well as the doctors and nurses, would have liked to see a different outcome, but it was not the Lord's plan. After Kevin's funeral, I have kept in touch with the family, still to this day. I have the opportunity to visit with Kevin's dear mother, Mona, a few times a year. When her son, Mark, visits from Los Angeles, California, she usually lets me know, so I can make sure to get there, for an enjoyable visit and a cup of tea.

Mona, and her now deceased husband, Desmond, were born and wed in Ireland, not far from Dublin. She was very attractive in her youth, and still remains so now, in her later years. She was a stage actress not far from Dublin and I always have enjoyed hearing her stories of the old days. I learned that Mona is a woman of great faith, and that she put her sorrows at the foot of the cross, and united her own pain to that of the Blessed Virgin Mary, who also was there with her dying Son.

The Lord, by His merciful healing, has gotten Mona and the entire family through the years that have passed since the sad days of Kevin's illness and death. I considered it a privilege to have been part of those days, and gotten to know this wonderful family during their time of loss. Hopefully, I was able to bring the Lord's healing, comfort and mercy to them when they most needed it. To this day, I believe that I got out of this experience infinitely more than I put into it, and truly thank the Lord for putting me in the right place at the right time, to be His unworthy instrument, and to bring some of His healing to them at a time of great pain.

On October 2, 1993, I performed the wedding of Sean and Jennifer. They were a beautiful and sweet young couple, and I enjoyed getting to know them, during the time that we were preparing the pre-wedding documents. Eventually, I even had the honor of baptizing all three of their sons over the years. They invited me to their wedding reception, to offer the blessing and to then stay for the dinner, to enjoy the evening with their relatives and friends. I was seated at the table with the groom's grandparents, Ray and Alba, who were just about ten years older than my parents at that time.

Sean's grandmother, Alba was tall and elegant, and yet so much down to earth, she had a straight posture and looked much younger than 71, her age then. We had a fun time that evening, around the table, and I learned that their family originated from the Province of Avellino in Italy, as did my father's side of my family. I got to know the entire family, brothers, sisters and all the cousins and it reminded me of my own family.

They told me that Alba's father had named two of his daughters after two daughters of the King of Italy, Victor Emmanuel III of the House of Savoy, (1869-1947). "Molly" was named for Princess Mafalda, (1902-1944) and "Yolly" was named for Princess Yolanda, (1901-1986). I thought, "Wow, these are my kind of people!" As well, they told me that Alba had been named for the first white light of dawn, which was at the very time of the day that she had been born.

By the end of the evening, they told me that we have to "get together." Over the years, I had heard this more than a few times and regrettably, it seldom materialized, but this time it was different. They soon called me and I was treated like one of the family. Just like my own family, they enjoyed their main meal on Sunday around one o'clock in the afternoon, and it was a big event. It included pasta, meatballs, homemade red wine, all followed by espresso coffee and pastries. It was just like old days, I thought. There was enjoyment, laughter and that most important ingredient of all, love, around the table. Alba knew that my favorite Sunday meal was ricotta cheese-filled ravioli, and she would make dozens of them, and any that were leftover, were always sent back with me to enjoy during the week ahead.

As a priest, I had missed all this, but long ago, while serving in Puerto Rico, I realized that it was all part of the sacrifice involved in serving the Lord as a priest. However, it was just great to have this fun time together every once in a while. I saw these meals and visits with Alba, Ray and the family as a great blessing from the Lord, that I could received such nurturing and love from a wonderful family.

I would visit from time to time and then, when I got transferred to the parish in Stamford, some distance away, it became more difficult, but we would still be in contact. The years took their toll on both of them, and I learned that Ray was admitted to a Nursing Home for dementia. I would still go visit Alba on a Sunday afternoon every month or so, and now we would have our Sunday afternoon meal at a local restaurant and then go visit her husband.

After our visit to Ray, I always offered to drive her to the supermarket for a few groceries, and since it was close to the cemetery, we would usually stop there to say a prayer at the grave of her son, Ray, Jr., who had died many years earlier. He was the father of Sean, the groom of the wedding. Alba's dear husband, Ray passed away on September 3, 2004, at the age of 85, and thereafter Alba began to steadily decline.

Now, each time that I visited her, Alba looked frailer and frailer. She was using a portable oxygen tank, and when we would go to visit the cemetery to say a prayer, she just rolled down the window, rather than get out of the car. She would often ask me, "Oh Father, why am I still here?" Death came as a good friend to her, when she passed away in her sleep in her home on April 19, 2006 at the age of 84. Although I was sad that I had lost a lovely and dear friend, and I would miss our visits, I was very happy for her. Her favorite song was from the era of World War II entitled, "I'll be Seeing You" and the family arranged to play a tape of that song at her wake. She was reunited with her husband and son and was now in the peace of Christ.

At first, when I learned of Alba's passing, I was scheduled to leave on the very morning of her Funeral for a spiritual pilgrimage with several priests to the Basilica of Our Lady of Guadalupe in Mexico City. Among us, I was the only one who spoke Spanish, and this trip had been arranged several months in advance. When the news of Alba's passing came, I was visiting my parents on my day off in New Jersey, and told her family that I needed about an hour to get back to them, whether or not I could be there for her funeral, due to the travel plans. I went into the kitchen to tell my Mom about Alba's passing, and saw that she was cooking ravioli for dinner. That was it! I thought, "How could I forget all of Alba's kindnesses and her delicious ravioli over the years, and not be there for her Mass of Christian Burial?"

When I explained the situation, my priest friends fully understood and I was able to take another flight and joined them much later that same night of the funeral. Alba and Ray had been kind and loving to me and I could not be just a "fair-weather friend." If I enjoyed the good times with them and their family, how important it was to be there during their time of need. She and her husband had been instruments of the goodness of the Lord to me and many others throughout their lives, and I pray that the good Lord reward them for their faith-filled lives and grant them happiness with Him forever in the kingdom of heaven.

## Sister Death

As a child, I thought of death much differently. The old-fashioned Italian wakes were truly like a scene out of a dramatic Opera come to life. They lasted three afternoons and three nights, and everyone was dressed in black from head to toe. There were the old-school Italian women, who, at times, actually screamed and wailed while they cried. When I went on a Retreat for Priests to the Holy Land in January 1993, for my Fifth Anniversary of Ordination, I heard this same wailing sound from the minaret for the Islamic prayer. I then realized that the Saracens had invaded some parts of southern Italy, where my family originated, and perhaps this is why the southern Italians incorporated the Middle Eastern tradition of wailing.

Over the years, I began to look at death in a new way. I came to learn that the feast day of the saints is on the date of their death, called the "*Die Natalis*," the day they are "Born into Eternal Life." Several years ago, I heard the expression that "The day of our death is the most beautiful day of our lives," and have used that quote at funerals. I have tried to remind the mourners that, although it is a sad and difficult time for them, it is not so for the deceased. Although, at times, some people may leave this world, even in sometimes a sudden or tragic way, it is still the day that they have achieved the goal for which we came into this world, which is to leave this world, and see the Lord face to face, if they have been faithful.

St. Francis of Assisi (1181-1226) in his beautiful poem, The Canticle of All Creatures, wrote,

> *Praised be You, my Lord through Sister Death,*
> *from whom no one living can escape.*
> *Woe to those who die in mortal sin!*
> *Blessed are they she finds doing Your Will.*
> *No second death can do them harm.*

Over the years, and in my various travels, I went to the Etruscan city of Tarquinia, in central Italy. Their civilization flourished several centuries before Rome was even founded. Each stone sarcophagus in the museum there had the image of the dead person, carved as if reclining on a couch, with their arm propped on a pillow to hold up their head. I thought, "All that they needed was the remote control for the television." When I saw those ancient tombs, I questioned the tour guide why the deceased were depicted and positioned as they were.

The guide explained that for the Etruscans, death was like a banquet, and this was the position which was taken by the guests at a banquet at that time, when they "Reclined at table" and would be enjoying themselves. I recalled the words of St. Paul regarding the wonderful banquet that awaits us in heaven, "No eye has seen, no ear has heard, and no mind has imagined the things that God has prepared for those who love Him" (I Cor. 2:9).

We need to remember that we must be prepared to enter the banquet. The Lord Jesus told us the Parable of the Wedding Feast, which the king held for his son. However, some of the guests were not properly dressed with a wedding garment. That wedding garment is symbolic of our soul, which we are to keep free from sin at all times, since "No one knows the day or the hour" (Mt. 24:36, Mk. 13:32). We also hear the words of the king, when he addressed one of the guests and said, "My friend how is it that you came in here without a wedding garment? But he was reduced to silence" (Mt. 22:12).

The Universal Church saw the passing of our beloved Vicar of Christ, Pope John Paul II on April 2, 2005. I recall the moving words that evening at 9:37 p.m. Rome time, spoken by a member of the Papal Household when he announced to the world that "Our Holy Father, John Paul has returned to the house of the Father." This is a beautiful sentiment that has helped the mourners realize the Heavenly Father's house is the destination for all of us.

Over the years, I have had the occasion to go to more than the average amount of wakes, and offer words of consolation to the family. It is my preference to go at the very beginning, actually even before the visitation by the public begins, since just the immediate family is there to mourn for their beloved deceased relative. This is a time of most pain for them and I want to be there with them and for them, when they most need me. As Christ's representative, it is the best time to give them a few words of comfort in their time of sorrow, and help to dry their tears. I have seen some touching moments as the family expresses their emotions at that time.

There was one woman who knelt by the casket of her deceased sister and told her, "I will see you in heaven." On another occasion, an elderly family member approached the deceased and said, "I won't be far behind, see you real soon!" This reminds me of the last letter written by St. Thomas More, (1477-1535) to his daughter Meg, as he was in prison awaiting execution, "Pray for me, and I shall pray for you and all our friends, that we may merrily meet in heaven."

Death is a certainty for each one of us. We need to live in expectation of it and always have our "spiritual baggage prepared" for our departure. We never know the day or hour, as the Lord Jesus reminded us when He told the parable of the man who stored up his barn with provisions for years to come and said, "Fool, this night your life will be required of you" (Lk. 12:20). St. Paul tells us, "To live is Christ; to die is gain" (Phil. 1:21).

There is a story of the well-known French Dominican priest, who was considered a renowned preacher, Père Henri Lacordaire. He became well-known for his beautiful sermons and they were collected in a series of books. When he was dying, he became fearful, so one of the priests near his bedside tried to encourage him, saying to him, "Just think of all the sermons you preached." The dying priest responded, "If God does not bring them up, neither will I." We need to try our best to make the Lord happy by the way we have lived our lives, since He will one day have to judge us.

Over the years, I have had the opportunity to work with many Funeral Directors in the various parishes in which I have served. This has been an education for me, since I got to know more about the "nuts and bolts" regarding the reality of death. This began when I was stationed in Danbury, and an elderly priest who resided there in retirement, Fr. Walter, had passed away. The pastor asked if I would go to help the funeral director to put the vestments, which the priest wears during Holy Mass, on him, since they were getting his body ready for the viewing.

We priests pray the beautiful Vesting Prayers, as we put on each vestment, as a reminder of their symbolism. It is a tradition that a priest usually dresses a deceased priest in the vestments, while praying the prayers. The morticians are not familiar with these prayers or the vestments, as are we priests. So, I had to go "behind the scenes" as the expression goes. It was a learning experience that helped me to understand better those words from the first Book of Sacred Scripture, which I have repeated numerous times on Ash Wednesday, over the years, "Remember man that thou art dust, and unto dust thou shall return" (Gen. 3:19).

Throughout the years, I have built up a good rapport with the funeral directors, and in fact have even heard a few good confessions as they were driving me to the cemetery for the Rite of Committal Service. They have invited me to their birthday and anniversary parties, as well as Christmas staff parties, and we have had a few good laughs along with our food and drink. I told one of them that, in spite of the circumstances of the death of someone, I always enjoy coming to their Funeral Home, as I feel that I am among good friends. I told him, "You put the word 'fun' in funeral!" It reminded me of the Etruscans who saw death, not as something to be feared or dreaded, but rather the opportunity to join in that sumptuous banquet, the great feast that awaits those who have been faithful.

I hope to keep that in mind, and not be in dread of the hour of my own passing from this world, but see it as "The most beautiful day of my life," when my earthly pilgrimage will be complete. St. Jean Vianney once said, "To die well, we must live well." Sacred Scripture tells us, "Be faithful unto death and I will give you a crown of life" (Rev. 2:10). May a holy life lead us to have a holy death, and admit us to the great eternal banquet, to be enjoyed for all eternity in the kingdom of heaven.

# 4

# The Stamford Years

## Luchie

The name "Luchie" is actually a nickname that my brother Anthony, who was born in 1964, used for one of his more renowned patients. He had graduated Medical School in 1993 and was then accepted in an Orthopedic specialization. In the summer of 1998, he was working at Lenox Hill Hospital in New York City, where he was accepted for a sub-specialty fellowship in total joint replacement. There, he had the opportunity to work with a world famous surgeon, who sometimes performed up to six joint replacements daily.

One of the patients that summer was the world famous Opera star, Luciano Pavarotti (1935-2007). He had his left hip and right knee replaced. My brother, Anthony, assisted during the surgery and subsequently helped "doing the rounds," to follow up with the postoperative patients. The head surgeon asked him to see how Luciano was progressing, and my brother struck up a rapport with him, and they even conversed in Italian.

Toward the end of his hospital stay, Mr. Pavarotti, now referred to as Luchie by my brother, asked the chief surgeon that Anthony help in his rehabilitation. And so, my brother accompanied him back to Italy for the two-month long follow up care at his summer home in Pesaro, on the Adriatic Sea. Our family was very happy for my brother to have this opportunity and in particular, my sister and her family who live in Milan, Italy, were hoping that they would be able to see their brother and uncle. And so, when Anthony asked for a few days free to take the train to Milan to see the family, Luchie told my brother that they were welcome to come to Pesaro for the weekend, as his guests. They did just that and had an enjoyable time there. As they were leaving there after a few days, it happened that the shoelace of my six year old nephew, Stephen, was untied, and so Luchie bent over to tie it for him. My sister, Suzanne has that moment recorded in a photo.

My brother had even called me, to ask if I wanted to come for a few days to Pesaro as Mr. Pavarotti's guest. However, it is not easy to just go to Italy at the last moment for a few days, and beside that, I was uncomfortable with the situation. It had been public knowledge that Luchie had left his wife and three grown daughters, after many years of marriage, and gotten involved with his personal assistant, Nicoletta. I just did not feel it was the right thing to do, being there under the same roof, as if I was condoning the situation.

In November of that year, Mr. Pavarotti was to perform at a special Gala Event at the Metropolitan Opera House in New York City. This was in honor of the Thirtieth Anniversary of his debut there. During his two-month stay with Mr. Pavarotti, my brother had spoken about my parents and myself to Luchie, who now wanted to meet us, since he had already met Suzanne and her husband and children. We were invited to attend this performance and meet the great singer afterward in his dressing room. There were many well-known people in attendance. A few rows of seats in front of us were Mayor Rudolph Giuliani and Joe Torre, manager at that time, of the New York Yankees Baseball Team. To be sure, it was an enjoyable and memorable evening.

After the concert, we were escorted backstage and practically "bumped into" the famous tenor, Placido Domingo, as well as the vibrantly beautiful soprano, Cecilia Bartoli, who also were waiting near the dressing room to congratulate Luciano on his superb performance. We eventually were escorted in to have a brief, but very cordial visit and a photograph taken with our now dear Luchie. At the end of the visit, he spoke to me in Italian and said, "*Padre, prega per me,*" which means, "Father, pray for me." I gave him the Lord's blessing and a kiss on his forehead, and promised that I would certainly do so.

The years passed and we learned that, within one year, both of Luchie's parents had died and that Nicoletta, now his wife, had given birth to twins, but although the little girl was healthy, the little boy had died. We learned that it was a very sad and difficult time for Luchie, since he still kept in touch with my brother, and so I prayed for him even more. We then learned that he was diagnosed with pancreatic cancer and the prognosis did not look good. I remembered the words of our Lord Jesus, "What good does it profit a man to gain the whole world and lose his own soul" (Mk. 8:36)?

I thought that poor Luchie had given much joy to so many people throughout the world, through his God-given talent of singing, and now he will be leaving this world, having made some big mistakes. Had he put his spiritual priorities in place? If his bags were packed to leave this world, in what state was his soul, when he had to make an account of his life on earth before the Lord? I asked the Lord to have mercy upon him and grant him salvation. I believe that there was a great outpouring of love and prayers for him around the globe, as many realized that he would soon be departing this world.

When I learned that Luciano Pavarotti passed away on September 6, 2007, I called my brother to give him my condolences, since he had lost a good friend. Shortly thereafter, I learned that the wake and funeral would be in the Cathedral of Modena, Italy, where he was born and raised, and that the bishop there was to offer the Funeral Mass. At first, I thought that was unusual, until I soon learned that in his last few days, Luchie had asked to see a priest, and had been reconciled to the church, through the last sacraments, shortly before his death. I was so happy to hear that, and when speaking to other priests and friends, they too were relieved that he had repented of his errors and died in the Lord's friendship. It has been said, "Every saint has a past, and every sinner has a future." This is attributed to Oscar Wilde, (1854-1900) an Irish poet. A friend once told me, "The Church is not a museum for saints; it is a clinic for sinners."

The merciful Lord came through for him! A man who brought joy to so many people, through his God-given talent, would not be deprived the opportunity to hear the angels chant God's glorious praises in the kingdom of heaven. I remember reading in the Diary of St. Faustina, (1905-1938) this quote revealed to her by the Lord, "The greater the sinner, the greater the right he has to My mercy" (Diary #723). There is an old song, some may call "sappy" but I like it actually, it is entitled, "He'll always say I forgive."

May many people come to realize that the Lord God is like the loving father in the Parable of the Prodigal Son. He looks down the road to await the return of his son, after he squandered all his possessions. The Gospel according to St. Luke recounts the entire story but the most moving part for me is the actual moment of reunion between the father and his son,

> "But while he was still a long way off, his father saw him and was filled with compassion for him; he ran to his son, threw his arms around him and kissed him. The son said to him, 'Father, I have sinned against heaven and against you. I am no longer worthy to be called your son.' But the father said to his servants, 'Quick! Bring the best robe and put it on him. Put a ring on his finger and sandals on his feet. Bring the fattened calf and kill it. Let's have a feast and celebrate. For this son of mine was dead and is alive again; he was lost and is found' " (Lk. 15:11-32).

When I visited the Hermitage Museum in St. Petersburg, Russia, in August 2001, I had the opportunity to see the famous painting of the Prodigal Son by Rembrandt van Rijn (1606-1669). The tour guide pointed out that the right hand was painted more thin and delicate, while the left hand was larger and more muscular. The rationale was that the larger hand represents the father; however, the more delicate hand represents the love for the child that is unique to a mother. The Lord God tells us, "Can a mother forget her infant, be without tenderness for the child of her womb? Even should she forget, I will never forget you" (Is. 49:15).

May the loving and heartfelt reunion of the Prodigal Son and his father, be a reminder for us, that the Lord's invitation to return to Him is always there for us, since His mercy never runs short. He waits for us with open arms, and wants us to share in His life, love and friendship in this world, and one day, forever in the kingdom of heaven.

# Frankie

Actually, Frankie is the name of a car, not a person. I began my service at St. Mary Church in Stamford, CT on May 13, 1999. Just a few weeks later, we learned that a newly-ordained priest was to be assigned to the parish. His name was Father Ed, and he was born and raised in Colombia. I was happy to help with the preparation for his room and went to the department store, along with the housekeeper, to purchase brand new bedding and curtains, so that the new priest would have a fresh start in his new home. We put several pictures on the walls, and even had an empty frame waiting, so that he could put his ordination photo in it. It was just the perfect size, too. It was a time of happy anticipation that our team of two priests would soon grow to three. We also had a retired priest who was living in residence; he was a venerable and elderly Monsignor, and we all got along very well.

Fr. Ed arrived and he spoke to the pastor, Fr. Richard, and me that first night at dinner. He was very sincere and told us that he needed our help. He said that he was new at being a priest, and did not know what to do in his new role. He was a very pleasant young man, only in his mid-twenties, and was short in stature. In fact, he recounted that when he was in the High School Band in Colombia, he played the tuba, which was practically as big as him. The people would look at him playing the instrument and say, "*Mira al niño con la tuba*" which means, "Look at the child with the tuba."

The pastor and I called him our child, our "*Niño*" in Spanish, and he would call both of us "*Poppie*" which means Daddy or Father. And so our dear niño, Eddie had practically nothing, besides a heart full of good will, and was starting out without a car or even without a credit card. Not that these things are very important in one's life, but after all, the diocesan priest does need to go to visit the sick at the hospital, as well as the homebound, and they cannot depend on getting a ride with someone, especially if there was an emergency.

After a few months, Eddie and I had a chat about his desire to purchase a car. I offered to co-sign the loan and guarantee payment if, for some reason, he could not do so. That never occurred, since he was always faithful in his monthly car payments. He was so happy about this and we went together to various places and looked at several good used cars. I advised him not to buy "a piece of junk on wheels," that would just consume money in repairs. He purchased a car on October 4, which is the feast of St. Francis of Assisi, and when Fr. Ed and I blessed it with Holy Water that same afternoon, it was unofficially christened "Frankie" in honor of St. Francis.

Over the years, I had gotten to know a deacon from a local Stamford parish, Ramón Isidro, a wonderful elderly gentleman from Havana, Cuba. He actually had been a student, at one time, of Msgr. Emilio Valdes whom I knew in Ponce, Puerto Rico. Deacon Ramón was supportive of the new priest, and he was very happy to learn that he finally got a car, and that I was instrumental in arranging the loan. He saw me a few days later and told me very moving words: "The Lord will not forget your kindness to that young man. He will reward you greatly, you wait and see. His generosity and mercy will accompany you for this good deed you did."

Of course, I never helped Fr. Ed with the hope of getting anything in return, however, in retrospect; I see that Deacon Ramón's words came true. My years of service at St. Mary Parish in Stamford were the happiest of my life. From May 1999 until my departure in September 2002, we priests were of one mind and one heart in service of the Lord and His holy people. "We loved each other with the affection of brothers," as Sacred Scripture tells us (Rom. 12:10).

The granite Gothic-style church building was truly a masterpiece set at the top of a rolling hill, and at one time was called the most beautiful church in New England. It was also a vibrant and active parish, with many Weddings, Baptisms and even Funerals. There was an active Senior Group, Bible Study, Novena Prayer Group and the list can go on and on. The good Lord had truly blessed us. We had wonderful conversation and enjoyable food at our evening meal together provided by our cook Anna, who was born and raised in Rome, Italy. She even sang Italian songs in the kitchen as she cooked, reminding me of my grandmother and family. "Better than this, one cannot get," I thought, when I was a priest in Stamford.

The year of the Great Jubilee Year 2000 was approaching, and a lovely couple in the Bridgeport diocese was organizing a pilgrimage to Rome and Assisi. They invited me to serve as the spiritual director on the trip, and to offer daily Mass in the various Basilicas for the group. I was greatly honored to serve as the group chaplain, and even received a discount on my trip. There was a single supplement for the room that I had to pay, and thought it could be put toward helping Fr. Ed to come join me on this Holy Year Pilgrimage, so this young priest could have the experience of visiting the Eternal City.

We asked the pastor's opinion, if both his assistant priests could be gone from the parish at the same time, for eight days, and we received his blessing. Fr. Ed was absolutely thrilled, and Rome was beyond what he ever expected. Years later, he still spoke of the trip, and suggested that we plan a pilgrimage there together. This we did in April 2008, and had over fifty participants who greatly enjoyed our Pilgrimage to the Shrines of Italy.

We hear from St. Peter, in the Sacred Scriptures, "Finally, all of you, be of one mind, having compassion for one another, love as brothers, be tenderhearted, be courteous and forgiving" (I Pet. 3:8). These same sentiments are reiterated by St. Paul, as we hear, "Be kind to one another, compassionate, forgiving one another, as God has forgiven you in Christ" (Eph. 4:32). We are invited by the Lord to be people of forgiveness, healing, and compassion and to be merciful to others, just as the Lord has been merciful to each of us. This is how we can grow in grace, as we strive to be holy, and achieve our desire to live in God's love and friendship on earth and in the kingdom of heaven.

# F.R.O.G. Sunday

This is probably the strangest title for one of the chapters in this book of reflections. In October 2000, I was at the desk in my office at St. Mary Church in Stamford, when the mail arrived, and in it was a catalogue from a church goods store. I rarely flip through them, but for some reason, I did so this time, and I'm glad that I did. There was an item that immediately caught my attention. It was a little plastic green frog with big white bulging eyes, just about two by two inches in size. It had the letters F.R.O.G. written on its back. The explanation read that this meant: "Fully Rely On God." I loved it and called the company right away, and had 150 of them sent to me.

I had been very "frog-favorable" for many years. In the mid 1970's I heard a story about two frogs that were out hopping around one day, and it was getting very hot, so they went into a barn. There, they saw a big vat of cream, and both jumped in it to cool off, but the vat itself was deep, and there was nothing from which to leap in order to exit. Try as they did, it was not looking good for them. One of the frogs got exhausted and gave up, yes, he "croaked." But the other frog kept trying with all his might, and eventually churned some of that cream into a large pat of butter, from which he sprang off, exiting the vat to his freedom. The moral of the story is to persevere, churn away and do not give up, just like that second frog and all will work out.

There was a children's Mass every Sunday at 9:00 a.m. and my plan was to give out the frogs then, to the children and anyone who wished. The cute little critters arrived within a week, and I picked a Sunday in the month of November, just before Advent began, and the color of the vestments that the priest wore were still green, and I "unofficially" designated it as F.R.O.G. Sunday. At the Mass, I told the boys and girls, both young and old, that we will be beginning a New Church Year in a few weeks, with the start of the Season of Advent. No one knew what the new church or civil year ahead would bring, but we should totally place our trust in God to get us through it.

Then I showed them the tiny plastic frog, and explained the writing on its back, and told them it was a reminder to fully rely on

God. We are to "Put all our cares on Him" as we hear in the Sacred Scriptures (I Pet. 5:7). The Lord Jesus will take care of us, and help us through all the ups and downs. We hear His words in the Gospel, "I have told you this so that you might have peace in Me. In the world you will have trouble, but take courage, I have conquered the world" (Jn. 16:33).

The news of Frog Sunday at St. Mary Church that Sunday in late November got around. The phone started ringing on Monday morning. Everyone wanted a frog! Of course, I needed to order additional dozens of them right away, then handed out another batch the next weekend, but did save just a few to give to the infirmed in the convalescent homes and the home-bound. Each time I gave a frog, along came the explanation, that although they may be a real cute little green thing to look at, there is a deeper significance to them: that we rely on the Lord God, and we put our trust firmly in Him. As St. Paul wrote, "We know that all things work for good for those who love God, who are called according to His purpose" (Rom. 8:28). We hear a few lines later: "If God is for us, who can be against us" (vs. 31)?

About two years later, when I was transferred to my first pastorate in September 2002 to Bridgeport, I received an anonymous gift shortly before I departed. It was a plant in a green ceramic planter that had a green frog as part of its design. When I opened the card, it was unsigned, but just had four words written: "Fully Rely On God." I kept one of the little plastic frogs and it sits on my desk as pastor, and look at it every day, as it is right by the telephone. I hope the others who still have a frog do the same.

For me, my little green plastic friend helps to serve as a pleasant reminder that we are to trust in the Lord God, and place our confidence in Him. May we do nothing to destroy His good plan for us, but let Him work though us, His unworthy instruments, that we may cooperate with his plan of holiness each day by "fully relying on God" in this earth and be with Him someday in the glory of the kingdom of heaven.

5

# The Bridgeport Years

## The Banana

O n July 31, 2002, I received a phone call from Bishop William Lori, of the Diocese of Bridgeport, CT, in which I serve, inviting me to become the pastor of Our Lady of the Most Holy Rosary Church in Bridgeport. I was grateful to him, and promised to do all things "For the greater glory of God" in Latin, "*Ad Maiorem Dei Gloriam.*" It was the feast day of St. Ignatius Loyola, (1491-1556) the founder of the Society of Jesus, also known as the Jesuits, and that is the official motto of that order.

A few weeks later, on September 8, I was installed as the twelfth pastor there. In its golden days, Holy Rosary had been a flourishing parish, founded to serve the needs of the Italian immigrants and subsequently their children and grandchildren. It was founded in 1903, although the baptismal records date from 1895, since it had been a small mission chapel attended to by the Scalabrini Fathers from New Haven, CT, before being designated a parish.

Over the decades, the City of Bridgeport unfortunately saw a steady and sad decline. There were many factories that flourished in the era of the 1930's and 1940's when Bridgeport was the third most industrial city in the world, but they eventually all closed. At one time, it had been called the "Arsenal of Democracy," since it was the world headquarters for Remington Arms, which made the guns for the United States Military, including those used in both World Wars. With the loss of jobs, came the exodus from the city and new problems of poverty arrived. Unfortunately, the parochial school had closed two decades before my arrival, and over the years, many of the second and third generation children of Italian immigrants had moved to the suburbs.

The motto of Holy Rosary Parish was: "We do not have quantity, but quality!" The weddings and baptisms had been very infrequent, so as the pastor, my ministry had been based on serving the needs of the elderly, infirmed and dying. A dear priest from New Jersey, Fr. Anthony, who was a colleague from the seminary, told me that my mission is like that of St. Joseph of Arimathea, who helped with the burial of Jesus, "To help the beautiful old people prepare to meet the Lord." Yes, this is the true goal of theirs, and each one of our lives, to live in the presence of the Lord in the joy of heaven for all eternity.

Even though the inner city neighborhood in which the parish lies has its challenges, with God's help one makes the best of the situation, if they make up their mind to do so. It is said, "Resiliency is when, in tough situations, while some people snap, others snap back." My favorite quotes from Sacred Scripture came to mind frequently in my pastorate at Holy Rosary Church. They are, "I can do all things in Christ, Who gives me strength" (Phil. 4:13) and the words of Our Lord Jesus Christ which are complimentary, "Without Me, you can do nothing" (Jn. 15:5).

Over the years, I tried to outreach to the members of the Hispanic community, who mostly reside in the former Italian-American neighborhood, and scheduled an additional Sunday Mass in Spanish. However, most of the people were already participating in the other area parishes, which offered Mass in the Spanish language. Our Spanish Mass attendance was low and after one year, it was discontinued when the attendance was down to only two people.

My knowledge of the Spanish language from my years of priestly service in Puerto Rico had come in useful, and I enjoyed socializing with the local people, in particular those that came to the parish Food Pantry each week. Besides the weekly distribution of food to the needy in the neighborhood, we also distributed toys and gifts as Christmas approached. In addition, during those few days that preceded Thanksgiving, we distributed over three hundred food baskets, which included a frozen turkey in each of them. I think of the quote from the Book of Psalms, "Happy are they who consider the poor and needy. The Lord will deliver them in time of trouble" (Ps. 41:1).

When I need a few groceries, rather than drive to the big supermarket a few miles away, I usually went to the local little market run by a Spanish speaking family, called a "*Bodega*." One day in early April 2006, I went to that local market for just a quart of milk. When I was at the checkout line, there was an elderly gentleman in front of me, who was purchasing a quart of milk and three bananas. He spoke in Spanish to the cashier, and apparently did not have enough money, so he tore off one of the bananas from the small bunch. After the cashier weighed the two bananas, he then had enough money for the purchase to be completed.

Since I was the next person in line, I saw the lone banana sitting there by the cash register, so I decided to purchase it, to give it to the elderly gentleman, since his plan was to purchase all three of them. I did so, and caught up with him outside the store and handed the banana to him, saying, "*Disfruta esta banana tambien*" which means, "Enjoy this banana too." He smiled widely at me and thanked me, "*Gracias, Padrecito*." This means "Thank you, little Father." As he continued on his way, I silently said a few words to the Lord, asking Him to please grant me His help and mercy when I most needed it.

Several weeks later, the last week of May, it was time for my summer vacation. I was to serve as a priest chaplain aboard a Cruise ship for nine days from Civitavecchia, the port of Rome, Italy, to various ports in the Mediterranean Sea, including the Greek Islands. It was going to be a great adventure, and I had really been looking forward to it for some time.

An adventure it was indeed, from the first few hours after I landed at the Rome airport! After landing, I took the train to the Rome station and when getting off the train, I had my carry on luggage over my shoulder and was holding a piece of luggage. Unfortunately, my foot slipped off the little step getting off the train and missed the platform and it went right down into the gap between the train and platform. The other leg went straight out and I sank into the hole, with the luggage falling on top of me. It was a real mess, I felt banged up, from head to toe, and was certain that I had broken a bone or two, and thought for sure that I'd never get to see Greece now.

The people on the platform, who were nearby, at first all screeched when they saw what happened, but were very kind and solicitous and immediately came to my aid. They lifted me up from the gap, as well as the luggage that was on top of me, and then helped me to stand up. They also called for the First Aid department of the train station, to bring a wheel chair. Besides being a bit shaken up, I was pretty scratched up, and my forehead, elbows and knees had been scraped and were bloody, it was a pretty ugly-looking scene. By then, the wheelchair had arrived, but before sitting down, I thought that it might be best to put pressure on my left leg that was the most aching and full of blood at that point.

Then, I somehow recalled that my Mom had told me years ago: "If you can stand up on your leg, it is not broken." I thought, hopefully that comment by her had not been just a wives' tale, but really true. So I began to walk, and in fact, almost hop around, to see if my leg could take the pressure. Soon, I realized it was completely fine, not broken at all, thank God. Then I immediately recalled the banana! I had given it to that elderly man a just few weeks prior, and had asked the Lord to remember that very small act of kindness and prayed that He please give me mercy and help when I needed it. That little banana came through, I thought to myself!

The kind folks from First Aid had bandaged me up, and I had one day to visit beautiful Rome, before embarking on the cruise ship. The next day, when I got aboard the ship, I went to the office of the Cruise Director to introduce myself, and inquire as to my duties aboard as the chaplain. He told me how happy he was to have a chaplain this sailing, since the last two priest chaplains had both broken their legs, and were unable to even embark. One of them had to be flown back to the United States, and the other priest ended up having surgery, and was still recovering for two weeks in a hospital in Rome. After hearing that, I rolled up my Bermuda shorts slightly, to let him see that my leg was bandaged, and explained to him that I was almost the third priest cruise chaplain with a broken leg, due to my fall at the train station.

Over the years, I have recounted this story, and have asked the listeners to "Give a mercy banana away" by doing acts of mercy, compassion, caring and kindness to others, especially those in need, and to please do it with their hearts, and to ask the Lord to have mercy upon us in our needs. The Lord Jesus tells us in the Beatitudes, "Blessed are the merciful, for they shall receive mercy" (Mt. 5:7).

Perhaps, I was somewhat selfish on the day that I offered the banana to that elderly gentleman, and asked the Lord for mercy for myself. In my preaching, I have suggested to the listeners that we are to "Put mercy in the spiritual bank." By acts of kindness, we can fill up the mercy account and ask the good Lord to distribute it, giving it away when needed, as He sees fit, perhaps to one of the most discouraged persons, most in need of His healing, mercy and love.

I cannot help but think of the story of the conversion of the people of Nineveh by the preaching of the prophet Jonah. By our acts of penance and sacrifice, we can offer them so that the Lord have mercy upon us and upon others, as He did upon the people of Nineveh. Through Jonah's preaching, the people of Nineveh believed in God, and proclaimed a fast and put on sackcloth. Even the king of Nineveh laid aside his robe, covered himself with sackcloth, and sat in the ashes and proclaimed a fast,

> "By decree of the king and his nobles: 'Neither man nor beast, neither cattle nor sheep shall taste anything; they shall not eat, nor shall they drink water. Man and beast shall be covered with sackcloth and call loudly to God; every man shall turn from his evil way and from the violence he has in hand. Who knows, God may relent and forgive, and withhold His blazing wrath, so that we shall not perish.' When God saw by their actions how they turned from their evil way, He repented of the evil that He had threat-

ened to do to them; He did not carry it out" (Jon. 3:7-10).

One also recalls the account in the Book of Exodus when the Lord God was displeased with His chosen people, since they had not been faithful, but rather made an idol out of gold. After the Lord had been so good to them, by bringing them out of a life of slavery in Egypt, this is how they repaid the Lord God of Israel. And so, the anger of the Lord flared up, but Moses beseeched the Lord to "Turn from Thy fierce wrath" (Ex. 32:12) and the Lord did so. And so, our beseeching the Lord, by our prayer, sacrifices and acts of compassion, all done with a sincere heart, can obtain His mercy upon us.

There was a prayer that the Blessed Virgin Mary taught to the three children in Fatima, Portugal in July 1917, which comes to my mind. Our Lady asked that this prayer be recited after each decade of the Rosary, "O my Jesus, forgive us our sins, save us from the fires of hell, and lead all souls to heaven, especially those in most need of Thy Mercy." We ask that the Lord choose who are to be the recipients of His mercy, since He is aware of those that may be most in need, the dying, the discouraged, and especially those who have no one to pray for them.

One of the prayers of the Chaplet of Divine Mercy as revealed to St. Maria Faustina by the Lord Jesus is as follows: "For the sake of His Sorrowful Passion, have mercy upon us and on the whole world" (Diary #475). The Venerable Pope John Paul II, known as the great Mercy Pope, during one of his last visits to his native land, Poland, added a variation to that prayer, "For the sake of His Sorrowful Passion and Glorious Resurrection, have mercy upon us and on the whole world."

It is never too difficult to be kind and considerate. We can never run out of mercy, in the same way that the Lord never runs out of mercy for us. As William Shakespeare (1564-1616) wrote in *The Merchant of Venice*, "The quality of mercy is not strained, but drops as gentle rain from heaven upon the place beneath. It is twice blest: it blesses him that gives and him that takes" (Act IV, Scene 1).

This idea of the perpetual replenishment of the bounteous mercy of the Lord also comes to us from the Book of Lamentations in

Sacred Scriptures, "I will call this to mind, as my reason to have hope: the favors of the Lord are not exhausted, His mercies are not spent. They are renewed each morning, so great is His faithfulness" (Lam. 3:21-23).

At the meetings I attended in preparing for the Mercy Congress, one of the speakers commented that, "Mercy is the true face of God, it is the true face of the Church, and it is the true face of man." By our living mercy, may we receive it, and be admitted one day, by the Merciful Father, into joys of the kingdom of heaven.

# Charter School

The parish of Holy Rosary Church had a Parochial School that was constructed and dedicated in 1960. With the departure of many parishioners to the suburbs, the enrollment decreased and the decision was made to close the school in the 1980's. It is a well-maintained facility and we had rented it to a Charter School as a source of income for the parish. The school was geared to helping Inner City children have a more specialized education, than perhaps they would have received in the Public School. The focus is on academic excellence and motivating the students to do their best. There are posters in the hallways that depict a mountaintop, and the goal is to reach college.

Every so often, I needed to go from the Rectory to the school in case a piece of their mail got delivered to us or vice-versa. On one occasion, I was impressed by a certain expression that I heard for the very first time. The students were lined up to leave the gymnasium and the teacher said to them, as if a battle cry: "Keep your eyes..." and the students responded, "On the prize."

Of course, I realized that they were talking about academic achievement, perhaps that good grade on their next spelling test, or graduating and getting accepted into High School, then College. However, the expression made an impression upon me, as regards to our eternal salvation and of course, the prize, in my mind, was to achieve our eternal destiny, which is to get to heaven. If we miss that, we have missed it all. St Peter encouraged the believers in his day to persevere in "Obtaining as the outcome of your faith the salvation of your souls" (I Pet. 1:9).

Later that same afternoon, a Christmas card arrived from my dear friend, Sr. Carmel, O.P. and she wrote in it, the very same message she has written to me, since she was on the formation team in College Seminary in 1974: "Matty, let us keep our eyes fixed on Jesus." Later that very night, I called a dear priest friend, Father Anthony, to say hello and our conversation ended up talking about perseverance in doing the Holy Will of God, and the duties entrusted to us priests in our particular circumstances. He told me, "Keep your eyes on the prize." That was the third time I had read or heard that expression in the same day. We are reminded of this in the Holy Word of God. We hear in the Psalms: "Yes, like the eyes of a servant on the hand of his master, like the eyes of a maid on the hand of her mistress, so our eyes are on the Lord our God, till we are shown favor" (Ps. 123:2). In the Letter to the Hebrews we hear about keeping our eyes fixed on Jesus:

> "Therefore, since we are surrounded by so great a cloud of witnesses, let us rid ourselves of every burden and sin that clings to us and persevere in running the race that lies before us, while keeping our eyes fixed on Jesus, the leader and perfecter of faith. For the sake of the joy that lay before Him, He endured the cross, despising its shame, and has taken His seat at the right of the throne of God" (Heb. 12:1-2).

It is not easy to arrive at the prize, as there are many ups and downs, discouragements and distractions along the way. However, we need to keep the prize in our hearts and minds daily, and endure even hardships, if we need to do so, in order to achieve it. St. Paul reminds his readers of the value of offering up one's sufferings as part of achieving the prize,

> "For this momentary light affliction is producing for us an eternal weight of glory beyond all comparison, as we look not to what is seen, but to what is unseen; for what is seen is transitory, but what is unseen is eternal (2 Cor. 4:17-18).

In our lives, we reap that which we sow. Our good works and efforts produce good results, and are appreciated in most circumstances by others. What we do for the love of the Lord with all our hearts is seen by Him, and sometimes by Him alone. At times, others may even misjudge even our very best intentions, as we have seen in the lives of many saints throughout the centuries.

There is a legend of a woman by the name of Euphrasia, who lived in Constantinople at the time that the *Hagia Sofia*, the great church dedicated to Holy Wisdom, was being built. It is said that praise for the building of that beautiful basilica was given to her, and not the emperors, because she was a poor widow, who drew from her mattress "A wisp of straw and gave it to the oxen" that brought the marble from the ships. God needs each one of us to give our own straw, to aid in constructing our own temples, that are built, not with marble, but with grace that we receive in the sacraments.

When He told us, "If you love Me, keep My commandments" (Jn. 14:15), the Lord Jesus invited each of us to do the best we can, for love of Him. He invites each of us to love Him as He has loved us. We hear in the Holy Word of God, "We love, because He first loved us" (I Jn. 4:19). The Lord will give us the grace we need, if we draw near and make Him the very center of our lives. We need to keep our eyes fixed on Him and strive to please Him, since He is the ultimate prize, Who alone can give us eternal life. We ask the Lord's mercy upon us. He offers us the opportunity of living in His beautiful friendship. We suffer, and at times, regrettably, it may be of our own making, since our poor choices have brought us down dangerous paths. Other times, the Lord can send us afflictions as a "Wake-up call" as it were, to remind us, "If we repent, He will relent." He does this to spur us on to greater holiness.

These have been called Deuteronomic sanctions throughout the ages of our salvation history, as we learned in Scripture class in the seminary. When the ancient chosen people of Israel turned their face from the Lord, they usually "got clobbered" by their enemies, and big time too! This is how it is explained in the Holy Word of God:

> "Here, then, I have today set before you life and prosperity, death and doom. If you obey the commandments of the Lord, your God, which I enjoin on you today, loving Him, and walking in His ways, and keeping His commandments, statutes and decrees, you will live and grow numerous, and the Lord, your God, will bless you in the land you are entering to occupy. If, however, you turn away your hearts and

will not listen, but are led astray and adore and serve
other gods, I tell you now that you will certainly
perish; you will not have a long life on the land, which
you are crossing the Jordan to enter and occupy. I
call heaven and earth today to witness against you:
I have set before you life and death, the blessing
and the curse. Choose life, then, that you and your
descendants may live, by loving the Lord, your God,
heeding His voice, and holding fast to Him. For that
will mean life for you, a long life for you to live on
the land which the Lord swore He would give to your
fathers Abraham, Isaac and Jacob" (Deut. 30:15-20).

So it was then, in the time of our forefathers, so even it is now
for us, for God is pleading with us to choose life. We do this when
we keep the commandments and follow the teachings of our loving
mother, the Church. If we turn to the Lord in our moments of needs
and temptations, He will give us the help we need, to keep our eyes
fixed on the prize. St. Paul tells us, "Where sin abounds, grace far
surpasses it" (Rom. 5:20). We are reminded as well, "But God, Who
is rich in mercy, because of the great love He had for us, even when
we were dead in our transgressions, brought us to life with Christ"
(Eph. 2:4-5).

The merciful Lord invites each one of us to walk in His light. The
star of Bethlehem that appeared at the darkness of midnight when
the world lay in sin and error still brightly shines for us today. It has
been written on Christmas cards throughout the years, "Wise men
still seek Him." We are invited to accept guidance by the Light of
the Lord, which is manifested through His holy spouse, the Church,
as it continues to teach and proclaim the message of the Lord.

The church is called *"Lumen Gentium"* meaning the "Light to
all Peoples" and lovingly helps each of us in our progress toward
our salvation, and encourages us to keep our eyes on the prize. The
church is our loving mother and teacher. Although the world sets
other standards, our standard is the Son of God. Pope Benedict XVI
reminded us of this on April 18, 2005, the day before his election,
when he warned that "We are moving toward a dictatorship of rela-

tivism, which does not recognize anything as certain, that has as its standard one's own desires."

We are to put away the darkness and confusion that the world offers, since it is only by living in the Light of the Lord that we can best see the prize ahead. Let us work hard to achieve the goal, and avoid distractions, so that we can keep our eyes focused on it. That prize is the crown of glory that awaits us in the kingdom of heaven.

# Orvieto

When I lived at the seminary in Rome in 1987, prior to my arrival in the Diocese of Ponce, Puerto Rico, I got to know a fellow seminarian, Marco Nunzi, and we have become good friends. My friendship with him has led to my happy affiliation with his diocese, that of Orvieto in central Italy, about one hour north of Rome. It is also famous for its crisp white wine that is well-known worldwide.

My visits there have become a great blessing for me, truly a gift from the gracious and merciful Lord God, to enhance my life. This picturesque hill town has a stunning Gothic Cathedral, which was built in the 14th century and is called the "Golden Lily' among Italian cathedrals. Its construction began during the pontificate of Pope Urban IV, (1195-1264) to commemorate and provide a suitable home for the Corporal of Bolsena, where a miracle occurred in 1263, during his pontificate.

The story of the miracle is a very moving one. There was a priest from Bohemia, named Peter of Prague, who had doubts about the validity of transubstantiation, when, although the bread and wine retain their outward appearance, they are changed to the Sacred Body and Blood of the Lord Jesus, with the words of consecration during Holy Mass. And so, he went on pilgrimage to the tomb of his patron, St. Peter in Rome, to ask for an increase in his faith. On his return back to his home, he offered Holy Mass at the Basilica of Saint Cristina, in the nearby town of Bolsena. When, at the appropriate time during the Mass, he broke the consecrated host, blood began to flow, staining the corporal, or square piece of linen on the altar.

The Lord had heard his prayer and increased his faith. The priest then rushed into the sacristy, with the bleeding host that he had placed inside the corporal, which he had folded. The drops of blood left stains on both the corporal and on the marble floor. The participants at Holy Mass saw the blood that was dripping, and followed the priest into the sacristy, to see if he was ill. There, he explained the entire matter to them. The word got to the local bishop, John, right away who sent delegates to Orvieto, just a few miles away, to explain all this to the pope, who was there, at his summer residence.

And so, Pope Urban IV personally went to investigate, and met Bishop John at the bridge over the Charo River. He then returned, accompanied by the cardinals and the faithful, and carried the blood-stained corporal in procession to Orvieto, and showed it to the faithful from the front of the then Cathedral of St. Prisca. This was considered the first *Corpus Christi* procession. The blood-stained cloth is now enshrined in the Chapel of the Corporal inside of the cathedral. One year later, the same pope instituted the feast day of the Solemnity of the Body and Blood of Christ, to be celebrated in perpetuity, throughout the church. All of this has been illustrated in the beautiful frescos in the Chapel of the Corporal of the Cathedral.

A very interesting part of this story is that in 1246, there was a religious sister in Liège, Belgium, St. Juliana of Mont Cornillon, (1193-1258) who had a vision of the Lord Jesus Christ, Who showed her a luminous moon with a black spot on it. When she inquired of the Lord what this meant, He told her that the moon represented the Church's Liturgical year, but that the black spot on it signified that there was something missing. The Lord Jesus told her,

> "I desire to set up a special Feast for My Church Militant, because this Feast is most necessary. It is a Feast of the Most High and Most Holy Sacrament of the Altar. At the present time, the celebration of this Mystery is only observed on Holy Thursday. But on that day, it is mostly My sufferings and death that are thought about. Therefore, I desire that another day be set apart, in which the Most Holy Sacrament of the Altar shall be celebrated by all of Christendom! The first reason why I am asking for this special Feast Day is so that the faith in this Sacrament would be confirmed by this Feast, when bad people would attack this mystery in the future. The second reason is so that the faithful would be strengthened on their way to virtue by a very great love and adoration of the Blessed Sacrament, and the third reason is so that because of this Feast and the loving attention given

to it, reparation would be made for the insults and lack of respect shown to the Blessed Sacrament."

St. Juliana went to the Mother Superior and explained all this to her, then together they went to the Archdeacon of the diocese. He then explained the matter to the bishop of Liège, who established the Feast of the Body and Blood of Christ only for that diocese. It was this very Archdeacon, who later became Pope Urban IV. His name as Jacques Pantaleon, and was elected to the papacy in 1261. Perhaps this helps to explain the pope's readiness to establish the feast day of the Solemnity of the Body and Blood of Christ, and extend it to the Universal Church with the papal Bull, *"Transiturus,"* which he promulgated on August 11, 1264.

Pope Urban IV had invited several important theologians of the time to prepare the Office, which included the official liturgical prayers and texts for the liturgical celebration. The theologians included St. Thomas Aquinas, (1225-1274) who, at that time, was residing in Orvieto, and held the chairmanship of the Theology department at the Monastery of St. Dominic. Also assigned to the task was St. Bonaventure, (1221-1274) a member of the Franciscan Order, who was from the picturesque hill town of Bagnoregio, which was just a few miles away.

When the day arrived for them to present their texts to the Holy Father and the members of the papal court, in residence at Orvieto, St. Thomas was asked to come forward first and he proceeded to read what he had composed. Among them were the hymns that are so well-known to all of us today, *"O Salutaris Hostia,"* "O Saving Host," as well as *"Tantum Ergo Sacramentum,"* which has been translated as "Down in Adoration falling." There was also the beautiful hymn *"Pange Lingua Gloriosi,"* which has been translated as "Sing, my tongue, the Savior's glory" and the Sequence for the Mass, entitled *"Lauda Sion Salvatorum,"* which means, "Jerusalem, Praise your Savior."

When St. Bonaventure heard the moving texts of St. Thomas, he was filled with emotion, and impressed with their beauty. He then took his own manuscript of that which he had written for the Feast, and ripped the pages up right in front of the Pope and all of those present, explaining that they were as nothing, compared to those presented by St. Thomas.

According to a long standing tradition, shortly thereafter, St. Thomas was praying in the Church of St. Dominic in Orvieto, and the wood carved image of the Crucified Savior spoke to him saying, *"Bene scripsisti de Me, Thomma"* which means, "You have written well of me, Thomas." The Lord then asked St. Thomas what he would want in return, to which St. Thomas so humbly responded, "Only Thyself, Lord." Not long after his encounter with the Crucified Lord, St. Thomas would write, "The end of my labors has come. All that I have written appears to me as so much straw, after the things that have been revealed to me."

That very crucifix is still in the same chapel in Orvieto, and when I have gone there to pray before it, it has brought to mind the important fact that we are not to look for any earthly honors or glories, but that which is always the most important of all: the intimate friendship with the loving and merciful Savior, and to please Him in all things. He will help get us through the pilgrimage of life and by His grace, help us to arrive at the only honor we seek, to be with Him forever.

During my time as a seminarian and after my ordination, I would go to visit Fr. Marco in Orvieto. At first, I went there as a tourist on vacation. Eventually, I began to help with the Masses in the parishes, convents, nursing homes and even the Cathedral. Over the years, my one week stay there for my summer vacation, became extended to two or even more. Fr. Marco and I would spend some time, between religious duties, visiting the shrines of the various saints of the region of Umbria.

Together, we saw the Basilicas of St. Clare and St. Francis in Assisi, as well as the town of Greccio, where St. Francis displayed the first Nativity scene. We also visited the Shrines of St. Rita in Cascia, the hill town of Norcia which is the birthplace of Sts. Benedict and Scholastica, as well as the Churches dedicated to St. Christina in Bolsena and St. Bonaventure in Bagnoregio.

When the bishop of Orvieto, Bishop Decio Grandoni, was planning to retire in November 2003, he was aware of my years of service in his diocese over in the summers, and he decided to nominate me as an Honorary Canon of the Basilica Cathedral of Orvieto. Bishop William Lori, of the diocese of Bridgeport, graciously gave his permission and the official document is dated September 8, 2003. As an honorary Canon, I have the duty to offer Holy Mass, once each month, for the other Canons, both living and deceased, and I am remembered in their Masses as well. There is also special canonical vesture that we are entitled to wear, but I felt embarrassed to even order it, and postponed doing so. The Lord Jesus told us, "He who humbles himself shall be exalted, and he who exalts himself shall be humbled" (Lk. 14:11, Mt. 23:12).

However, about two years later, a priest friend in New Jersey told me that he was going to have a service of Solemn Vespers, which included a procession. He mentioned to me that there would be other Canons in attendance, wearing their canonical vesture, and asked that I could do the same, so I did eventually have the Canon's garb made, but have worn it very infrequently.

My affiliation with the beautiful town of Orvieto and the diocese there continues to this day, and I truly thank the Lord for this great blessing that He has bestowed upon me. The picturesque place, with its glorious cathedral and, winding medieval streets is like my "Home away from home" and for me, truly a "Bit of heaven on earth" as the expression goes, a foretaste of the great joy that awaits us all in the true home in the kingdom of heaven.

# The Supreme Law

Unfortunately, this is a sad story. On Saturday, September 1, 2007, I was planning to visit with a dear priest friend in Stamford. We were going to have a relaxing dinner together, after we both had offered our evening anticipated Masses. However, he had called earlier that day and told me that he was not feeling well, asking if we could reschedule. And so, it seemed like an opportunity to have a quiet meal and evening by myself and do a little reading after my bowl of soup. In retrospect, I can see that it was all orchestrated by the providential plan of the merciful Lord Jesus. No sooner had I finished the soup in the kitchen of the Rectory, and the phone rang.

It was one of our musicians who asked me to please rush to the hospital, since her nephew Michael had overdosed. I went to my car and got there as soon as possible. Regrettably, things looked very serious for Michael, who had just turned eighteen a few weeks prior. He had stopped breathing and the medical team was trying to save his life.

Although they would not let me in the treatment room in the Emergency department, I stood right outside the closed doors, and decided to commend him to the Lord, and therefore I gave him Absolution from his sins and the Apostolic Blessing with Plenary Indulgence. Throughout my seminary days, I never heard that it was impossible to do this, and that a closed door would be an impediment to the mercy of the Lord to a dying person. Rather, what came to my mind, at that very moment, was the exact opposite; it was the Latin maxim, "*Lex Suprema Salus Animarum*," which means, "The supreme law is the salvation of souls." The Lord's merciful help to a dying person to aid that soul, in the most extreme of conditions would not be impeded by a mere piece of wood, just a few inches thick.

Several minutes later, the door opened and a nurse with a sad look on her face shook her head, and told Michael's family and myself that he had not survived. We waited for the remaining members of his family to arrive and they too then learned the sad news of his death. While we were waiting for them, the family explained to me that Michael was unfortunately a drug addict in a rehabilitation program, and was taking methadone. Since it was Labor Day weekend, they administered the dose to him that Saturday morning, and then gave him two dosages to take home, one was for Sunday and the other was to be taken for the Labor Day holiday on Monday. Unfortunately, he had taken the both those doses all on Saturday, and it led to his death.

I could not help but think to myself that, although he had a troubled life, the good Lord was merciful at the very end and had sent a priest, even me, to be there at the right place and right time, in order to give him the entry ticket to heaven. The thought came to me then, as it had many times before, that when someone is dying, it is so important that those surrounding him or her be sure to call a priest, to help that person in their last few minutes on this earth, and bring them the last Sacraments.

At that important time, we priests are more important than the President of the United States, all the Governors and Mayors put together, and even the doctors and nurses. Only we can do that which they cannot, since we can bring the mercy and forgiveness of the Lord to that person, and prepare their soul to leave this world. We are Christ's ambassadors and are there to help admit their soul to the presence of the Lord, even if they get there at the last moment of their lives and "By the skin of their teeth" as the expression goes. Our Lord Himself did exactly that with the Good Thief, who hung on the cross next to his, when He said to him, "This day you will be with Me in paradise" (Lk. 23:43). It has been said that the thief had been a thief to the end, and had even stolen his way into heaven!

Subsequently, I made myself available to the family and offered the Mass of Christian Burial, and tried to use this occasion as an opportunity to be of comfort to them in their time of affliction and sorrow. For them, a hurricane, tornado and blizzard, all combined into one, had hit with the death of Michael. When there is a sudden or tragic death such as his, I selected the Gospel passage of the Lord Jesus Christ calming the seas during a storm.

> "Meanwhile the boat, already a few miles offshore, was being tossed about by the waves, for the wind was against it. During the fourth watch of the night,

He came toward them, walking on the sea. When the disciples saw Him walking on the sea, they were terrified. 'It is a ghost,' they said, and they cried out in fear. At once Jesus spoke to them, 'Take courage, it is I; do not be afraid' " (Mt. 14:24-27).

An unexpected storm arose and the apostles were shaken and thought that they were going to drown. Jesus calms their fears and tells them to be confident, He is there with them, even amid the storm, and all will be well. Amid a tragedy, we too feel that we are sinking, but we need to have faith, trust and courage in the goodness and mercy of the Lord, Who will help us even in the most tragic of circumstances.

What the Lord tells them, "Do not be afraid," He says this again and again through His public ministry. We hear the story of what I call a "miracle within a miracle." As Jesus was going to the home of Jairus, one of the synagogue officials to heal his daughter,

"A woman who had been suffering with hemorrhages for twelve years and she had heard about Jesus and came up behind Him in the crowd and touched His cloak. She said to herself, 'If I but touch His clothes, I shall be cured.' Immediately her flow of blood dried up. She felt in her body that she was healed of her affliction. Jesus, aware at once that power had gone out from Him, turned around in the crowd and asked, 'Who has touched My clothes?' When the woman came forward, Jesus told her, 'Daughter, your faith has saved you. Go in peace and be cured of your affliction.' While He was still speaking, people from the synagogue official's house arrived and said, 'Your daughter has died; why trouble the Teacher any longer?' Disregarding the message that was reported, Jesus said to the synagogue official, 'Do not be afraid; just have faith' " (Mk. 5:22-36).

It is our faith and abiding trust in the mercy and goodness of the Lord that gets us through the most difficult of circumstances. I recall reading an excerpt of the 1974 autobiography of Rose Fitzgerald Kennedy, (1890-1995) which was entitled, *"Times to Remember."* She related that she had been asked many times how she had dealt with so many tragedies, such as the deaths of three sons, Joseph Jr., John and Robert.

She responded that she had come to the conclusion that the most important element in human life was faith. She often heard from people who were overwhelmed with tragedies and felt desolation, and she wrote to them, to give a few words of consolation. She told them, that one must turn to God in faith, knowing that His loving kindness is never far from us. His providence never allows us to be tested beyond our strength. We need to truly believe in His presence and goodness, and that we are never alone or forsaken.

Our soloist Linda's grandson's name is Brandon. He was eight years old at that time, and a great buddy with Michael. They lived in the same house, with Michael's family on the second floor and Brandon and his family on the first. Michael had been like a big brother to Brandon, and would take the time to play with him, and they rode their bicycles together, and so Brandon was truly saddened by the death of Michael. Two weeks after Michael's death, Linda told me that Brandon had a dream and saw Michael. In it, Michael told Brandon to tell everyone that "I am happy and am with Jesus." This is our desire too, that when our earthly lives are over, we can be happy with Jesus forever in the kingdom of heaven.

# Miracle Babies

Jamie is my first cousin; she was born in April 1976, and is twenty years my junior. She is the youngest daughter of my Uncle Anthony, my mother's brother. I was always very fond of her, because she was grandchild number ten for my Grandma Serafina. It was a great joy for her to see her tenth grandchild, which she always hoped would arrive some day.

Jamie was engaged in 2003, and her husband-to-be, Dan, who was a Presbyterian, asked me to give him instructions in the Catholic faith. So we met every few weeks throughout the year prior to the marriage, and in the April before their July 17, 2004 wedding, he made his Profession of Faith as a Catholic. On their wedding day, I preached about the 3 "H's." I told them that many people would be wishing them healthy and happy years ahead in their marriage, but that my greeting card would have a third wish, for a "Healthy, happy and holy married life together." I reminded them not to forget about the third "H," the most important of all. And so, over the years since the wedding day, when we would send e-mails to each other, we would sign off, "Yours in the 3 H's, or just H H H."

Within a year, Jamie and Dan were expecting their first child, but unfortunately, before her first trimester was complete, Jamie had a miscarriage. She was very shaken up and needed not just physical, but emotional healing, from the trauma of the loss of the baby. After a few minor surgeries to correct some issues, Jamie and Dan hoped to try again. They were unsuccessful and discouraged, and so in a visit to their home, I mentioned a special saint who was the patron of women hoping to conceive.

He is St. Gerard Maiella, (1726-1755) an Italian Redemptorist brother, who died of tuberculosis in Caposele, in southern Italy, at the age of 29, but achieved great sanctity in spite of his short life. His "Last Will" consisted of a small note on the door of his monastic cell saying, "Here the Will of God is done, as God wills, and as long as God wills." There is a story that Brother Gerardo was visiting a family and dropped his handkerchief on the floor of their home. When a young daughter in the family went to return it to him, after he departed, he told her to keep it, that she would need it someday.

Years later, that same woman was having difficulty during childbirth, and she asked that the handkerchief of the holy Brother be brought to her. Immediately, the problems ended and the baby was safely delivered. That handkerchief was then handed down in that family to every woman who was about to give birth, and after several decades, only a few shreds of the cloth remain. The fame of the story spread, along with devotion to the holy brother, who was eventually canonized by Pope St. Pius X, (1835-1914) in 1904. Thereafter, St. Gerard has been considered the patron of expecting mothers.

Over the years, I have been very happy to promote this devotion to St. Gerard. I was very familiar with devotion to St. Gerard, since the National Shrine dedicated to him is located at St. Lucy's Church in Newark, New Jersey, not far from where I was born and raised. To be honest, I cannot begin to count the many couples that I have mentioned to me that they had been married for several years, and been unable to conceive. After offering to give them a blessing, all of them agreed right way, and I used the relic of St. Gerard to bless them, and ask his assistance. We prayed together to the Lord God, that through the prayers and intercession of good St. Gerard, He would grant that couple the gift of parenthood. St. Gerard has a hundred percent success rate, and has been called a true miracle worker!

When I was helping as chaplain in Danbury Hospital, one of the nurses told me she was having difficulty conceiving. With that, I gave her a blessing with the relic of St. Gerard, and within a few months, she told me that she was pregnant. She then told another nurse, and I did the same for her, giving her the prayer card, and just a few weeks later, she told me that she was expecting twins. The news got around the floor, and every time one of the nurses saw me, they would jokingly say, "Stay away from me!"

And so, I offered the same prayer and blessing for Dan and Jamie and put an entire packet together for them with some of the prayer cards, as well as the Novena booklet. I even loaned them my only relic of St. Gerard, with the promise that they would return it to me on the day of the Baptism of their child. Over the years, I had loaned out the relic about six prior times, and in every case, had the relic of St. Gerard returned to me on the day of the Baptism. That holy and innocent saint, St. Gerard, is very powerful indeed.

This was a true test of faith for Jamie and Dan. It was an opportunity for them to grow closer to the Lord and have trust in His merciful love and providential care. The third "H," for "holy," which followed the other two, "happy and healthy," now became the first "H" in the listing for them. In fact, this "H" for holy, now became a heading of its own, with two other words under its category: faith and trust. In my "pep talks" to them during this time, I kept telling them to "Be strong in Faith," (I Pet. 5:9) an expression that has very much helped me over the years. Somehow, I prefer it in Latin, "*Fortes in Fide*," since, to me, the words even sound stronger.

Over the course of almost two years, which involved additional minor surgery for Jamie, they surely got discouraged at times. However, my advice to them was to consistently stay close to Our Lord, attend Holy Mass regularly, receive Holy Communion and if needed, to seek the opportunity for the Sacrament of Reconciliation. Most of all, I told them to pray to the Lord daily, through the intercession of St. Gerard. They learned to trust in the goodness and mercy of God, and the help of St. Gerard. Jamie told me that she prayed and rubbed the relic of St. Gerard "on her tummy" every night before bed when she prayed. They also had the image of Jesus as the Divine Mercy nearby, with the words below it, "Jesus, I trust in You."

Jamie and Dan invited me to dinner at their home in the Spring of 2008. When she greeted me at the door, I noticed that her tummy looked bigger than normal, and learned the good news that she was expecting. The pregnancy was not without its ups and downs, since there was a minor capillary that ruptured, and she was worried that this pregnancy would end in another miscarriage. Thanks be to God, all went well. The Lord had used even this experience to help this young, wonderful couple to grow closer to Him. They grew in His love and friendship at an even higher and new level, by trusting in Him as they never had before.

A few weeks later, Jamie and Dan then told me the surprising news that they were expecting twins! I told them how the Lord saw their commitment to Him, and that He even made up for the baby they had lost through miscarriage. On December 18th, the two beautiful baby girls, Abigail Newman and Elizabeth Kaylen were born.

Shortly thereafter, I called to congratulate the new parents, and to thank the Lord and good St. Gerard with them.

Later that day, I sent an e-mail to them to ask if they would consider adding a second middle name of "Gerarda" for each of their daughters in gratitude to St. Gerard and they answered back an enthusiastic "Absolutely!" It was a very happy day when the relic of St. Gerard was returned to me, at the Baptism of the twins. Hopefully, there will be many more miracle babies in future years, thanks to a firm, trusting faith and persistence, in asking the good Lord's great kindness and mercy, along with the powerful intercession of St. Gerard Maiella. The Lord told us, "Ask and you shall receive, seek and you shall find, knock and the door will be opened to you" (Mt. 7:7, Lk. 11:9).

Another well-loved saint, St. Padre Pio tells us, "Put all your trust in the Most Gentle Jesus. Pray, and I might add, devoutly pester the divine Heart." May St. Gerard, a powerful saint, help us to love Jesus as he did, with a child-like simplicity and desire to do the Holy Will of God in all things. May he help us to aspire to be with him and all the saints to give glory and praise to the Lord one day in the kingdom of heaven.

# Spa Ministry

On January 11, 2008, I celebrated my Twentieth Anniversary of Ordination to the Priesthood. Those years had flown, I thought. Most of us priests like to get away after the extra preparations for the Seasons of Advent and Christmas. I have heard it said jokingly that some priests go to Florida "To check how the palm is growing for Palm Sunday." My friend, Fr. Marco from Italy, asked me to arrange a break for both of us. He too, was going to celebrate his Twentieth Anniversary of Ordination on November 13, that same year.

On Sunday, January 13, we embarked on a cruise ship, where I was to serve as the chaplain. It departed from New York harbor, and we were headed to the Caribbean for a little sun and fun. Once aboard, I noticed that there was a very special event involving various artists, whose paintings were to be auctioned. Little did I realize that the actual artists were aboard the ship, as part of promoting their original art work. There was the work of one painter, in particular, that I had admired for many years, and actually had several prints of his paintings framed and hanging in the rectory. One of his favorite subjects is Europe and he paints such spectacular vistas of Portofino, Amalfi and other places throughout the Mediterranean. And so, I was very happy to hear that he was onboard, would be giving a demonstration of his painting techniques, and hopefully I might have the opportunity to meet him.

After attending the demonstration, I was so delighted to chat with him afterward, and his wife Judy was so kind to take a photo of the two of us near one of his original paintings. A day or two later, there was a "sea day" aboard the ship, which means we were not docked in one of the ports such as St. Thomas in the U.S. Virgin Islands or Barbados, but sailing all day from one island to the next. That gave me the opportunity to the exercise in the Gym and after some time on the treadmill, went to the Spa area into the Jacuzzi and Sauna to relax. It was a co-ed facility, and when I went into the Sauna, recognized the only person there beside me. It was Judy, the wife of the artist.

In talking with her, I mentioned how much I enjoyed her husband's remarks and a sample of his painting techniques. She recalled that I was the priest chaplain aboard, since on the day of the demonstration, I offered to give her husband a blessing. When he agreed, I offered a prayer to thank the Lord for the talent that He had bestowed upon the artist. It was good to get to know her, and soon I learned that she was a Catholic, but she regretted that she had not been faithful in attending Mass as she should.

She told me that her husband, that very talented man, was an atheist and did not want to discuss anything religious with her. After a few minutes, I got the impression that "All that glitters is not gold" as Shakespeare wrote in *The Merchant of Venice*. I soon learned that Judy was in a difficult situation and marriage, as she told me that she had been "seduced by wealth and fame" and now realized that she had made a colossal mistake for these past years since their marriage in 1995.

My advice to her was to stay close to the Lord Jesus Christ, and that this is the time that she needs Him the most in her life, in order to get her through the ups and downs. "If the Lord brings you to it, He will bring you through it," I told her, and that the merciful Lord would give her the grace to embrace the cross and carry it, difficult though it may be. The cross is the opportunity to be ever closer united to the Lord. I recall a hymn from the Feast of Christ the King,

> *The head that once*
> *was crowned with thorns*
> *is crowned with glory now.*
> *The royal diadem adorns*
> *the mighty Victor's brow.*

We all have crosses. Some have larger thorns on our crowns than others, but if we are faithful in uniting our sufferings with those of our Lord Jesus Christ, we will share in His glorification as well. The Lord's suffering was turned into His triumph. After the Ascension, He heard the words from His Heavenly Father: "Well done, good and faithful servant" (Mt. 25:23). These are the most important words that all of us want to hear one day when our earthly pilgrimage is over.

Nearing the end of our spiritual conference in of all places, the Sauna, I encouraged Judy to please return to the sacraments, in particular the Sacrament of Reconciliation, and most of all, to be faithful in attending Sunday Mass and receiving Holy Communion. The sacraments, especially Holy Communion, are the best means of healing that the Lord has given us to help us live in His grace and friendship. He has not abandoned us orphans, but left us the means to grow in holiness and overcome many obstacles. I told her to trust in the Lord and explained the short prayer, "Jesus, I trust in You." That prayer is an act of Act of Confidence, reminding us that God has a plan, and we are to submit ourselves to His Will in our lives. I told her that it has certainly been a source of inspiration for me, in my own spiritual life. I wanted to share that with her, to get her through a difficult time.

Of course, the evil one uses one of his most valuable tools to hit us when we are down, that is discouragement. Sometimes we just want to give up, and do not want to fight the battle any longer. However, with the help of the Lord, and with trust in His power in our lives, we can overcome the powers that seek to destroy us. Sacred Scripture tells us, "Yet amid all these things, we are more than conquerors through Him, Who has loved us" (Rom. 8:37).

Judy remembered from her upbringing the words to "Offer it up." We have kept in touch after that vacation had ended, through e-mail and by telephone. Sometimes, I believe that a priest helps to serve as a "Spiritual coach" in another person's life. By means of sound spiritual advice, we can help the people of God, though far or near, to live a more committed and Christ-centered life. This was not the first time that I served as a spiritual director at the Spa.

A few years prior, my friend, Fr. Marco and I had again taken a winter break, when I served as a cruise ship chaplain from Santiago, Chile, under Cape Horn, arriving in Buenos Aires, Argentina. One day, after some time on the treadmill, I went to sit in the outdoor Jacuzzi on the deck, surrounded by the beautiful scenery of the mountains of Patagonia, and a fellow in his mid-thirties joined me shortly thereafter.

He soon recognized me as the priest aboard, since he attended Holy Mass on Sunday a few days prior. His name was Manuel, and he had an executive position at a bank in Mexico City. He had taken the vacation for healing, since his mother had recently passed away. He was integral in her care during her illness, and he was having a difficult time dealing with her passing. Here were the two of us, in bathing suits, sitting in the Jacuzzi, and he began to tear up, as they say, when relating the story of his mother's illness and passing.

One of the most consoling phrases that I have used in helping people in a time of loss is to tell them "Love does not come to an end with death." Your love for them continues, and their love for you does as well. There is still a spiritual connection through the Communion of Saints. I am sorry if this sounds just like an advertisement for the telephone company, but I believe that "We are all connected." St. Paul wrote, "Love is patient, love is kind... love never ends" (I Cor. 13:4,8).

Our faith tells us this, in the doctrine of the Mystical Body of Christ. Our prayers can help those in purgatory to get into heaven, and when they arrive there, they can pray to the Lord to help us as well. The Lord uses us, His priests, when and where He needs us, in order to be His instruments of mercy and healing, and to bring consolation to the brokenhearted.

As with Judy a few years later, I encouraged Manuel to draw closer to the Lord and that He would help to heal the pain. I reminded him that his separation from his beloved mother was not to be permanent. If we are faithful to the Lord and live and die in His love and friendship, we will all be reunited in the place of refreshment and eternal light, where there is no sorrow, illness and pain, but just the eternal joy of the kingdom of heaven.

# In Time of Rain

When dealing with the death of a loved one, I often quote the Gospel passage, "Mary treasured all these things, pondering them in her heart" (Lk. 2:19). I believe that the memories of the happy and good times can get us through the difficult times. In times of gloom and rain, we can still think about sunny days that made us happy. I encourage all of those who are participating at a Mass of Christian Burial to remember all the happy Thanksgivings, Weddings, Birthdays and other memorable and joyous family occasions.

In this way, the sad days of the illness and passing of a family member or friend are not first and foremost in one's mind, when thinking about the deceased. The more that a person loves another person, the more difficult it is to say good-bye. Queen Elizabeth II (b. 1926) of England, on the occasion of a remembrance service, just days after the September 11th terrorist attacks said, "Grief is the price we pay for love."

At times, when I realize that my grandparents and many of my elderly aunts and uncles are gone from this world, I find great consolation when I think of the happy times of the past. There were many special occasions when I was growing up, around the years 1962-1975, from around when I was from six to nineteen. There were many happy events such as the High School or College graduations of my cousins, or there might be relatives who would be visiting from Italy. We would give them a warm welcome with a big meal, and introduce him or her to all their relatives here, on this side of the Atlantic Ocean.

Usually, we would gather in the finished basement of my Aunt Jennie or Aunt Connie, my Dad's sisters. It would be a "cast of thousands" as they say, well, not quite. There were usually new additions to the family, with my older cousins having their infants and toddlers, who were always the center of attention. Eventually, when the meal was over, a few of the elderly uncles and cousins would bring out the mandolin and guitar and they would sing Italian songs, to the enjoyment of everyone. Some of them would even dance, and there would be good homemade red wine flowing as well. These, for me, are still fond and much treasured memories, and I truly thank the Lord for having been part of those wonderful family events.

I recall a poem that illustrated this point of recalling past mercies and blessings from the Lord, even while going through present difficulties; it is by the Scottish author, Robert Louis Stevenson, (1850-1894):

### In Time of Rain

*We thank Thee, Lord, for the glory of the late days and the excellent face of Thy sun. We thank Thee for good news received. We thank Thee for the pleasures we have enjoyed and for those we have been able to confer.*

*And now, when the clouds gather and the rain impends over the forest and our house, permit us not to be cast down; let us not lose the savor of past mercies and past pleasures; but, like the voice of a bird singing in the rain, let grateful memory survive in the hour of darkness.*

*If there be in front of us any painful duty, strengthen us with the grace of courage; if any act of mercy, teach us tenderness and patience.*

I have figured out that our interior lives could be compared to an onion. There are those outer layers, which lead to the inner core. On the outside are the peripheral things, such as getting the oil in the car changed, paying our taxes and the realities that we all have to abide by in our polite society. Yes, some of these can lead to stress. Then, as we approach the center, we locate those rings of the onion that represent the more sensitive matters, such as family relationships, as well as those people and things about which we care. At the very core of the onion is where we are to cultivate joy, hope and peace. We need to be cautious and allow nothing to invade it.

There is a quote I heard attributed to Helen Keller, (1880-1968) who suggested that the more we keep our faces in the sunshine; the less we will see the shadows. Our Lord Jesus tells us, "You are the light of the world… your light must shine before others, that they see your good deeds and glorify your Heavenly Father" (Mt. 5:14, 16). We are to be children of the Light of Christ, not the darkness, as we hear from the beloved disciple, St. John, "Now this is the message that we have heard from Him and proclaim to you: God is light, and in Him there is no darkness at all" (I Jn. 1:5).

We can find that peace, which is in the inner core of that symbolic onion, only in Jesus Christ, and put our unreserved and full trust in Him. We can nourish that inner core, through a life of prayer, and not let the outer layers penetrate and invade that inner peace. Even in great difficulties, with serious illnesses, or a very bad scenario, I can find consolation in the words of Psalm 116, vs. 10, "I trusted, even though I was sorely afflicted." We know that the Lord will not abandon us in our needs, if we cry out to him as Psalm 130 tells us, "Out of the depths I call to You, Lord; Lord, hear my cry! May Your ears be attentive to my cry for mercy. If You, O Lord, mark our sins, Lord, then who can stand" (vs. 1-3)?

The good Lord will hear us, lift us up and He will get us through. It may not be easy, there may be suffering, and it may even result in our death in this world, but this world is not the destination, it is just the earthly pilgrimage on the way to the true destination. We need to keep our eyes fixed on the goal above all goals, union with Him in this world, and union with Him in that place where there is no rain or sorrow, but only perpetual light and joy in the kingdom of heaven.

# Prunes and Plums

When I arrived at Holy Rosary Church, in September 2002, I was introduced to our two parish Trustees, one of them was Mary Lou, who was a single woman, had a career in banking, and was now retired. She was in her mid 60's at the time, was a sweet and endearing person and I very much enjoyed her humor and childlike laugh. When the parish completed its Centennial Year celebration on the first Sunday of October 2003, there was an Anniversary Mass with the bishop as the principle celebrant. This was followed by a banquet, and many of the priests who had served there, as well as the current parishioners, and those from yesteryear, were all in attendance.

Toward the close of the celebration, there was a large Anniversary Cake to serve the more than 200 guests, and I invited the two lay Trustees of the parish to please join me in cutting the cake, it was a true "Photo opportunity" if ever there was one! Then I whispered to Mary Lou, "Let's have a little fun, and feed each other a piece of the cake, just like a bride and groom do, since neither of us will ever have the chance." She giggled and with a big smile said, "Oh yes, let's!" With that, we both enjoyed that unique moment of feeding each other the delicious centennial anniversary cake!

Unfortunately, just a few months later, she was diagnosed with pancreatic cancer, and her prospects to survive were very slim. Her cousin, Anita, lives in Washington, DC, and I had heard so many good things about her. She had been born and raised in our parish, and after graduating from college in Washington, worked at the State Department. She was just around my sister's age, born in the same year. Anita would come up to Bridgeport every few weeks, but as Mary Lou's condition worsened, her trips to visit her cousin became more and more frequent. I got to know her, her husband and two beautiful children, although it was through the sad circumstances of illness. She was very thoughtful and brought her cousin great comfort in her last weeks. I would bring Holy Communion to Mary Lou several times per week, and got to chat with Anita whenever she was there visiting.

When our dear and sweet Mary Lou was nearing the last hours of her life, on August 12, 2004, she asked to have all of her cousins around her bed to say goodbye. I was there, as well, that evening, and gave her Absolution from her sins, the Sacrament of the Anointing of the Sick, Holy Communion and the Apostolic Blessing in the presence of all the relatives. After that, we held hands and prayed for the mercy of the Lord upon Mary Lou, and that the Blessed Mother Mary would protect her under her mantle. We also invoked good St. Joseph, the patron saint of a holy death, to assist her at that hour.

Mary Lou's last words to those at her bedside were "I love you all." She passed away later that evening, after all of us had left. Only Anita was there with her, and I told her to telephone me, no matter the hour. She called me to tell me of her cousin's passing in the wee hours of the morning for what, as I called it, the "de-briefing." Our dear Mary Lou had a beautiful life and a beautiful death.

Shortly after the Mary Lou's funeral, Anita and her husband invited me to spend a few days in Washington with their family. She wanted to show me the formal rooms of the State Department, where Ambassadors take their oath of office, and hopefully, she could even arrange a private tour of the West Wing of the White House. These tours are usually given by appointment only, and are scheduled in the evening, after the President goes to the residence on the second floor of the White House. We looked over the calendar, and the best date for all was November 3. We thought that was perfect, since the presidential election was the day before and, win or lose, it would be a quiet time.

However, the election was not decided on November 2nd, but on the 3rd. It was while I was on the train, on my way to Washington, that Senator Kerry made his concession speech. When Anita greeted me at the station, I soon learned that President Bush had been re-elected, and that we were scheduled for a tour of the West Wing of the White House in about one hour.

We visited the Press Briefing Room, the Cabinet Room and then went to the Oval Office. We were not allowed to go in it, but the door was open and there was a velvet rope that cordoned it off. It was very inspiring and so, a bit meekly, I asked if I could offer a prayer to invoke God's blessing upon the President and his family and give a blessing to the Oval Office. It was after all, a historic day, with the re-election of President George W. Bush to his second term. There was no objection, so I proceeded to do so, and it was a memorable and beautiful moment for me, truly a gift from the Lord. Later that night when I returned to Anita's home, I wrote it down and it is below:

*Blessing of the Oval Office*

*Almighty God, Merciful Father,*
*We ask You to bless this Office.*
*Send Your holy angels to abide here and guard it*
*against the attacks of the enemy.*

*On this day of his re-election,*
*We ask You to pour forth*
*Your abundant blessings upon*
*our President, George W. Bush.*
*Fill him with Your gifts of Wisdom,*
*Strength, Prudence and Perseverance.*

*Guide and direct his actions*
*and decisions that they be*
*in accord with Your Holy Will.*
*Grant him and his family good health,*
*happiness and Your Divine Assistance always.*

*Bless all those who work here*
*in the White House and grant them*
*the grace they need to serve well*
*the people of our great Nation.*

*We ask this through the powerful Name of*
*Jesus Christ, Our Lord. Amen.*

Over the years, I have kept in touch with Anita, and have had the opportunity to return to the White House to see it decorated for Christmas. She eventually became the Chief-of-Staff to the First Lady, and I was introduced to Mrs. Bush and had a short conversation with her and had a photograph taken together with her and Anita. When the President arrived in Bridgeport for a conference, Anita was very kind in obtaining a ticket to attend the event and I was in the second row, very close to the podium from which he spoke.

An interesting story is that in autumn of 1988, when President Ronald Reagan was finishing his second term, several of my priest friends wrote to him to congratulate him on the completion of his two terms, and to wish him their blessings. I was serving as a priest in Puerto Rico at the time. They were invited to meet with him at the White House, and were each given a set of cuff links, with the presidential seal on the front and his signature engraved on the reverse. The cuff links were impressive, and I had admired them.

When I visited the White House to see the Christmas decorations in December 2006, Anita invited me to join her for lunch at the White House employee Dining Room, called the "White House Mess." Toward the end of the visit, she invited me to her office, which was located next to the First Lady's Office. There, she gave me a pair of the cufflinks, which were given out by President Bush. I consider it another little favor from the Lord, Who had seen it was something I had admired several years prior.

I once heard the expression that in life, "Some days the Lord sends us plums, and some days we get prunes." In our lives, there are those good and joyful times, and then those difficult ones, that sometimes seem to follow right after them. The visits to the White House have been joyful and memorable experiences for me. I have seen them as a small sign of the Lord's kindness and mercy toward me, and they have served as a reminder to be grateful for all the blessings, both large and small, that have come my way.

This reminds me of the Nuptial Blessing that is given to the bride and groom on the day of their marriage, "Lord, may they both praise You when they are happy, and turn to You in their sorrows. May they be glad that You help them in their work, and know that You are with them in their need."

May the difficult days be opportunities to grow in our trust in the Lord to help get us through them. May the joyful days that we have the pleasure to experience here on earth, make us truly grateful to the Good Lord, and may they be foretastes of the eternal joys that await us, where there will be no prunes, just luscious plums, at the eternal banquet in the kingdom of heaven.

# 6

# The Mercy Congress

## The World Apostolic Congress on Mercy

In May 2007, my bishop, Bishop William Lori of the Bridgeport Diocese, invited me to be the President for the U.S.A. committee for the World Apostolic Congress on Mercy, which was to be held in Rome, on April 2-6, 2008. The idea to hold a Congress on Mercy developed following a 2005 Retreat for Priests in Lagiewnicki, near Cracow, Poland. In early spring 2007, the United States Conference of Catholic Bishops received a letter from Christoph Cardinal Schönborn, who was serving as the President of the upcoming congress, who asked each bishop's conference to participate in it.

At that time, Bishop Lori was the chairman of the Doctrine Committee of the U.S. Bishop's conference, and he was entrusted with this task, and he then asked me to head the committee. When, sometime later, I asked him why he had chosen me, my bishop responded, "I thought that you would do a good job." I hope and pray that I can live up to those words.

The scope of the Mercy Congress was not limited solely to the Divine Mercy devotion. On September 24, 2007, I joined in a meeting with the representatives from other National Committees, that were preparing for the upcoming Mercy Congress. We met at the Lateran Palace in Rome with Cardinal Schönborn, who told us "The Congress is not to be a festival of St. Faustina." His Eminence stressed that first, we need a more profound understanding of the theology of the Lord's mercy, this is to be followed by a deeper and more profound spirituality of mercy, and lastly, we can find the devotional aspect of mercy.

St. Maria Faustina Kowalska was a religious sister, who lived in Poland and the Lord Jesus Christ chose her as His personal secretary, to bring to the world a greater understanding of His great Love and Mercy. She was canonized in the Jubilee Year 2000, on the Sunday after Easter, also known as Mercy Sunday, by Venerable Pope John Paul II. This has somewhat of a similarity to the revelations to St. Margaret Mary Alacoque, (1647-1690) who lived in France, which led to the promulgation of devotion to the Most Sacred Heart of Jesus, and subsequently the establishment of a celebration on the liturgical calendar. Regarding devotion to the Sacred Heart of Jesus, Pope Leo XIII (1810-1903) wrote, "The Heart of Jesus is the symbol and express image of the infinite love of Jesus Christ, which moves us to love in return" (*Annum Sacrum: Acta Leonis*, Vol. 19, 76).

St. Thomas Aquinas tells us "Apparitions do not give us new doctrines but new graces." I see the Divine Mercy image, which Jesus wished to be displayed, as an "updated version" of the Sacred Heart image. At the time of St. Margaret Mary, the visible heart of the Lord Jesus was represented, complete with its veins, and the place where it was pierced by the lance, the drops of blood, crown of thorns and flames of fire. That was the image that the Lord desired to be manifested at that time, in the mid-seventeenth century, for diffusion throughout the world.

Now, more than three centuries later, there is a different sensitivity to that of the Baroque age. We see a more simple and symbolic image of the heart of the Lord. The red and white rays of light represent the Love and Mercy of the Lord, reaching to all of mankind. What we see in the Divine Mercy image are the interior dispositions of the Sacred Heart of Our Lord, which are not visible. They are the attributes of His great Love and Mercy, which emanate from deep within His Heart, which are manifested through the red and white rays.

These colors represent, as well, the Blood and Water that flowed from the Lord's side, when it was pierced by the soldier's lance after His death on the cross. The Lord Jesus dictated a special prayer to St. Faustina for the conversion of sinners, "O Blood and Water, which gushed forth from the Heart of Jesus as a fount of Mercy, I trust in You" (Diary #187).

In my opinion, the Mercy Congress has two integral people standing at a large door: St. Faustina and the Venerable Pope John Paul II. Both of them are pointing their fingers to the Lord Jesus Christ, and drawing our attention to His Great Mercy. They invite us to enter this great portal, and have a deeper understanding of the Mercy of the Lord. This was the great desire of the Venerable Pope John Paul II, that there be a more profound and loving relationship with the Merciful Lord, and the Mercy Congress is an attempt to continue the work that he began.

It is notable that Pope John Paul II had prepared the Angelus Message for Sunday April 3, 2005, which was to be the day after his death. The message has been called his "Testament" and was published in the *Osservatore Romano* on April 4, 2005. Pope Benedict XVI repeated those memorable words on March 26, 2007, during his pastoral visit to the Parish of the Merciful Father in Rome,

> "To humanity, that sometimes seems lost and dominated by the power of evil, of egoism and fear, the Risen Lord offers as gift His love that pardons, reconciles and opens the mind to hope. It is love that converts hearts and gives peace. How much the world has to understand and welcome the Divine Mercy."

To paraphrase the great St. Augustine of Hippo (354-430) in his Confessions (Book X, 27) we can come to see mercy as "Ever ancient, ever new." We can look to the Sacred Scriptures to see, throughout salvation history, the great Mercy of the Lord God upon His people. The Lord Jesus told St. Faustina, "Proclaim that mercy is the greatest attribute of God. All the works of My hands are crowned with mercy" (Diary, #301).

Early in salvation history, the Lord God revealed Himself to His servant Moses on Mount Sinai, and spoke of His mercy, "Having come down in a cloud, the Lord stood with him there and proclaimed His name, 'Lord.' Thus the Lord passed before him and cried out,

'The Lord, the Lord, a merciful and gracious God, slow to anger and rich in kindness and fidelity, continuing His kindness for a thousand generations' " (Ex. 34:5-7).

When the chosen people of Israel were brought through the Red Sea, they sang of the mercy of the Lord, Who had delivered them from slavery. King David wrote: "Forever I will sing the mercies of the Lord" (Ps. 89:1). Years later, when King David was dying, his last words spoke of justice and the fear of the Lord; I see this as implying benevolence and mercy as a leader, "He that rules over men in justice, that rules in the fear of God, is like the morning light, the sun shining forth upon a cloudless morning, like rain that makes grass to sprout from the earth" (2 Sam. 23:3-4).

This is the same sentiment that we read about in the Book of Proverbs: "A king's wrath is like the growling of a lion, but his favor is like dew upon grass" (Prov. 19:12). Elsewhere throughout the Old Testament, we hear frequently about the mercy of God, especially upon those who put aside their sinful ways and try anew, to walk a better path with the Lord God, "How great the mercy of the Lord, His forgiveness of those who return to him" (Sir. 17:24)!

The day of our ordination, we priests make a solemn commitment to pray the Breviary each day. It is officially known as the Liturgy of the Hours. During our daily Morning Prayer, we pray the *"Benedictus,"* which were the words spoken by Zachariah, the father of St. John the Baptist, after his tongue had been loosened. There is a phrase in that prayer that goes like this:

> "In the tender compassion of our God, the dawn from
> on high shall break upon us. To shine on those who
> dwell in darkness and the shadow of death, and to
> guide our feet into the way of peace (Lk. 1:78-79).

Over the years, I have had the opportunity to learn several prayers from the Liturgy of the Hours in the Latin language. This is one of them. In Latin, there is a very beautiful translation for the words "Tender compassion of our God" cited above. It reads as *"Per viscera misericordiæ Dei nostri."* If one knows a bit of biological terms, the interior organs are called the viscera, and so this means that the mercy of God is coming "from His gut," from deep down inside of Him, so much does He love us, and want to draw us close to Himself, by means of His great mercy.

When Our Blessed Mother Mary praised the Lord in her "*Magnificat*," she said, "He has mercy on those who fear Him in every generation" (Lk. 1:50). When He called the apostle, St. Matthew, to follow Him, the Lord Jesus said: "It is the sick that need a physician, not the healthy; it is mercy I desire not sacrifice, I have come to call sinners, not the righteous" (Mt. 9:12).

In the Beatitudes, we hear, "Blessed are the merciful, they shall receive mercy" (Mt. 5:7). In the Parables of the Unforgiving Servant (Mt. 18:21-35), the Prodigal Son (Lk. 15:11-31) and in particular, the Good Samaritan (Lk. 10:29-37), Jesus tells us to "Do likewise." He sums it up by telling us, "Be merciful, as your Father is merciful" (Lk. 6:36).

This reminds us of another glimpse of God the Heavenly Father through the words of the Lord, "So be perfect, just as your heavenly Father is perfect" (Mt. 5:48). This is sometimes translated as "Be holy as your Father is holy." For me, it leads one to see the parallelism between mercy as an attribute of the Father, and holiness and perfection as well. The path to a holy, perfect life, which is the invitation of the Lord to us, can be achieved through being merciful.

The experience of working with the Mercy Congress has enhanced my life more than I ever could have imagined, and has been a source of great blessings for me. In my priesthood, I now am able to consider it as a "Vocation within a vocation" to quote Blessed Mother Theresa of Calcutta, whose religious life found a new impetus and an enhanced dimension, when she began to work with the poorest of the poor.

I am truly humbled that the Lord chose me, an unworthy servant, to be one of the many who can serve as His instruments, in order to better promote His wonderful message of Love and Mercy to others. I hope and pray that my efforts, along with the great committee with whom I work, will be able to help many others to grow in the understanding of the Lord's mercy for them. May the faithful never be hesitant to approach the Merciful Lord, and grow in His love and friendship, with the ardent desire to be with Him one day in the kingdom of heaven.

# Living Mercy

There is a story about two gentlemen who died, and are met by St. Peter at the "pearly gates" in heaven. St. Peter greeted them both, and asked that they join him, as he showed them to their respective mansions. The three of them arrived at the first mansion and St. Peter told one of the gentlemen to enjoy his stay there. It was a magnificent home, with a large and imposing façade, many bedrooms and a reflecting pool. The other man continued with St. Peter, until they arrived at a more modest home. When St. Peter told the second gentleman to enjoy his stay there, he asked St. Peter why his mansion was more modest than that of the first gentleman. To that St. Peter replied, "You see, we can only build your mansion with the building materials that you send up to us, from when you are still on earth."

The Lord Jesus tells us "Do not store up for yourselves treasures on earth, where moth and rust destroy, and where thieves break in and steal, but store up for yourselves treasures in heaven, where moth and rust do not destroy, and where thieves do not break in and steal" (Mt. 6:19-20). Some of the best building blocks that we can send up to heaven, to get our mansion ready are Acts of Mercy.

Mercy is a gift that we receive; it is not to be put in our pockets, or the bank, but to be given away to others. The Mercy Congress is giving us the opportunity to revisit this great treasury of the mercy of the Lord, and help to deepen our understanding of it throughout Sacred Scripture. It also allows us to look at the Corporal and Spiritual Works of Mercy. These are the ways that we can live mercy, by being merciful to others, and not just learn about it. This has been a constant goal of the First World Apostolic Congress on Mercy: to learn about the Mercy of the Lord, but especially to live it, by being merciful. The Lord Jesus encourages those who bear His Name as a Christian to be merciful:

> But rather, love your enemies and do good to them, and lend expecting nothing back; then your reward will be great and you will be children of the Most High, for He Himself is kind to the ungrateful and

the wicked. Be merciful, just as your Father is merciful (Lk. 6:35-36).

We hear reminders from throughout the centuries that invite us to be the instrument of the Mercy of the Lord. The great Spanish mystic and Carmelite reformer and founder, St. Teresa of Avila (1515-1582) wrote, "Christ has no body on earth now but yours, no hands but yours, no feet but yours. Yours are the feet with which He is to go about doing good, and yours are the hands with which He is to bless us now." We are invited to continue His work. Jesus Christ was the perfect image of His Heavenly Father. He has come to this world to show us the way to share in His divine life of grace and He taught us, by both His words and example.

When I offered my First Mass as a priest, the homilist was my spiritual director, Fr. Arthur, who is now a bishop. That day, he told the story about a beautiful painting by the Italian artist, Guido Reni, (1575-1642) a member of the Bolognese school of painters. The famous painting, "Aurora," which was painted in 1614, is considered his masterpiece, and is on the ceiling of the main salon in the Palazzo Ruspigliosi in Rome. It is located so high up, that one has to bend far back in order to appreciate its beauty. Often, when leaning back, many people have bumped into a large table in the middle of the room. They soon then realize that the top of the table is fitted with a mirror. Now, they need not look high up to the ceiling, since the mirror has the perfect reflection of the painting.

So it is with Christ. He is the perfect reflection of His Heavenly Father. The attributes of compassion, love and mercy we see in Christ are attributes of the Father. Pope St. Clement of Rome wrote, "Through Christ, we see as in a mirror, the spotless and excellent face of God." As mentioned earlier, Jesus tells us, "Be merciful, as your Father is merciful" (Lk. 6:36). Jesus practiced what He preached. He showed compassion for those who were in need, performing miracles to assist them.

We see mercy of the Lord, when He was moved with pity and compassion, and raised to life the dead son of the widow of Nain, "Soon afterward He journeyed to a city called Nain, and His disciples and a large crowd accompanied Him. As He drew near to the gate of the city, a man who had died was being carried out, the only son of his mother, and she was a widow. A large crowd from the city was with her. When the Lord saw her, He was moved with pity for her and said to her, 'Do not weep.' He stepped forward and touched the coffin; at this the bearers halted, and He said, 'Young man, I tell you, arise!' The dead man sat up and began to speak, and Jesus gave him to his mother" (Lk. 7:11-17).

We hear in the Book of Daniel, "The Lord our God is merciful and forgiving, even though we have rebelled against Him" (ch. 9:9). Our Savior not only taught about forgiveness, He also demonstrated it as well. These are a few examples of Jesus' tremendous Love and Mercy toward mankind, His willingness to forgive, and that same forgiveness applies to us today. The Lord's compassion can be seen when He fed the multitude, "When He disembarked and saw the vast crowd, His heart was moved with pity for them, and He cured their sick" (Mt. 14:14-21).

There is also the occasion when some men brought to Him a paralytic, lying on a mat. When Jesus saw his faith, He said to the paralytic, "Take heart, son, your sins are forgiven" (Mt. 9:2). The Lord showed His mercy with the woman caught in adultery, after the Pharisees and the teachers of the law had brought her to stand before Him, and the group gathered there, and made the accusation as we hear,

> "Teacher, this woman was caught in the act of adultery. The Law of Moses commanded us to stone such women, now what do You say?" They were using this question as a trap, in order to have a basis for accusing Him. When they kept on questioning Him, He straightened up and said to them, "If any one of you is without sin, let him be the one to throw the first stone at her." At this, those who heard began to go away first, the older ones first" (Jn. 8:3-9).

The Lord Jesus showed His mercy to one of the criminals, who professed his faith in Him,

"One of the criminals who hung on the cross near Jesus was insulting the Lord saying, 'Aren't you the Christ? Save Yourself and us!' But the other criminal rebuked him saying, 'Don't you fear God, he said, since you are the under the same sentence. We are punished justly, for we are getting what our deeds deserve. But this man has done nothing wrong.' Then he said, 'Jesus, remember me when You come into Your kingdom.' Jesus answered him, 'I tell you the truth, today you will be with Me in paradise' " (Lk. 23:39-43).

Most of all, I believe that we see the Lord's mercy and forgiveness as He suffered, after being nailed to the cross. He said of those who had betrayed Him, had yelled, "Crucify Him" and had executed Him, "Father, forgive them, they know not what they do" (Lk. 23:33). The Lord Jesus practiced what He preached. We are called to follow His example. We are all sinners, and have offended the Lord and perhaps our sufferings can even serve as a means of reparation for the sins we have committed. However, the Lord, Who was innocent and sinless, underwent a horrible ordeal for the salvation of the world. He was forgiving to the end, and showed mercy to others, even during His unbearable pain, while He was nailed to the cross. The Lord Jesus told us to "Love your enemies and pray for those who persecute you" (Mt. 5:44) and indeed, He has done just that.

In fact, the Lord Jesus in that same discourse, tells us to "Turn the other cheek," (Mt. 5:39) and He admirably followed His own advice, thereby giving us good example, inspiring us to do the same. This is a response of strength, saying, "I will not retaliate or seek revenge, but return good for evil." When the Lord Jesus was afflicted, He did not open His mouth to His oppressors, but was silent, "Like the sheep before the shearers" (Is. 53:7).

This is part of our Christian calling to be transformed into "Another Christ" so that our thoughts, words and actions can reflect His ways, and not our ways. There is an expression that many of us have heard over the years, "You are what you eat." Well, I like to phrase it differently in terms of our spiritual lives: "You are what you think, say and do."

Our thoughts, words and deeds are to give an insight to others that we are trying to live a Christ-centered life. We need to work on the inside first and foremost, so that the exterior actions of love and mercy can flow naturally from there. There is an expression, "No one gives what he does not have" which is a legal term, referring to ownership and is expressed in Latin as *"Nemo dat quod non habet."* This reminds us that we are to be united with Christ, and filled with His love and life first, before we can bring His love and mercy to others.

I once heard a story that during World War II, there was a small church in Belgium that a soldier returned to see, after it had been bombed. After the war, he wanted to return to see his favorite statue of the Sacred Heart of Jesus and offer a prayer there. He found it there intact, except that the hands had been blown off and never found. Someone wrote a sign and put it around the neck of the Lord that said, "I have no hands but yours."

We are invited to be merciful as the Lord is merciful. The origin, or etymology, of the word, mercy is the Latin word, *"Misericordia."* This can be broken into two words, *"Miseria,"* which means misery, and *"Cordia,"* which means heart. Thus, the word mercy means "To feel the misery of another person in your own heart." Sometimes there is another translation for the word mercy. In Psalm 33, for example, the term "Loving kindness" is used. "The loving kindness of the Lord fills the whole earth," (vs. 5) or in Latin, *"Misericordia Domini plena est terra."* This helps to reinforce the sense that a merciful act is a compassionate or kind one, done with love for another.

When we, the members of the International Executive Committee were planning the First World Apostolic Congress on Mercy in 2008, we had the opportunity to gather together in Ars, France, in September 2007 for a series of meetings. One morning, His Eminence, Cardinal Philippe Barbarin, the Archbishop of Lyon, France, addressed us on the subject of the Mercy of God. He told us that sometimes mercy can be construed as a "Sweet" word, but it is actually a "Strong" word. It is a strong word, since we see God's engagement in history, wherein He reveals Himself. His Eminence told us that "Mercy is the first supreme action of God, His first attribute." God has heard the cry of the small, and allowed the proud to be humbled so they can return to Him.

These comments brought mind the opera by Mozart, (1756-1791) entitled "*La Clemenza di Tito*," (The Clemency of Titus) wherein the plot line involves love, betrayal and an attempted assassination of the Emperor Titus. After the Senate finds the perpetrators of the crime guilty, all that remained was for the Emperor to sign the death sentence, in order to condemn all those involved. In my eyes and that of the audience, that would have been the simple and most expedient thing to do, and operas have many times ended with a main character dying on stage, or a few of them, at that! However, the strong action was for the Emperor to show mercy, and he did, in fact, pardon all those involved in the plot to kill him. The opera concludes with all the subjects raising their voices in song, praising the extreme generosity of the Emperor Titus.

On the opening day of the World Apostolic Congress on Mercy, April 2, 2008, His Eminence, Cardinal Schönborn gave the opening talk to the participants assembled in the Basilica of St. John Lateran in Rome. He told all of us that The Old Testament is the "Great school" of the Mercy of God (Catechism, no. 210). We hear, "Yahweh, a God merciful and gracious, slow to anger, and abounding in steadfast love and faithfulness;" Moses then confesses that the "Lord is a forgiving God" (Ex. 34:6).

The cardinal reminded all of us that Jesus, in the parable of the Good Samaritan, showed us that mercy is a concrete action. When He asked His listeners which, of those who passed by the man who had been attacked by the robber, had acted as a neighbor, the answer was, "He that showed mercy on him. And Jesus said unto them, "Go, and do thou likewise" (Lk. 10:37). His Eminence reminded us of Psalm 95, which we begin each day in the Liturgy of the Hours, with the Invitatory,

> "Come, let us sing joyfully to the Lord; cry out to the
> rock of our salvation. Let us greet Him with a song of
> praise, joyfully sing out our psalms" (vs. 1-2).

The same psalm continues, "Oh, that today you would hear his voice: do not harden your hearts as at Meribah, as on the day of Massah in the desert" (vs. 7-8). The hardness of heart is contrary to mercy; one's heart becomes like stone, and can be the cause of so much hurt and pain among us. We need to allow the love of the Lord, Who died on the cross for us, to soften our hearts, and thereby we can bring that mercy of the Lord to others.

The Lord Jesus revealed to St. Faustina, "My mercy works in all those hearts which open their doors to it... Conversion, as well as perseverance, is a grace of My mercy" (Diary #1577). The Lord Jesus dictated the following to St. Faustina, regarding His desire for the faithful to show mercy to others,

> "I demand deeds of mercy, which are to arise out of love for Me. You are to show mercy to your neighbors always and everywhere. You must not shrink away from this, or excuse or absolve yourself from it. I am giving you three ways of exercising mercy toward your neighbor: the first – by deed, the second – by word and the third – by prayer. In these three degrees is contained the fullness of mercy and it is an unquestionable proof of love for Me. By this means a soul glorifies and pays reverence to My mercy" (Diary, #742).

St. Thomas Aquinas taught "Mercy signifies grief for another's distress." We can respond to the distress of another, and try to relieve it. This is to show compassion and mercy for another in our hearts and to put this into action, by practicing the Corporal and Spiritual Works of Mercy.

*The Corporal Works of Mercy are:*

*To feed the hungry*
*To give drink to the thirsty*
*To clothe the naked*
*To give shelter to the homeless*
*To visit the sick*
*To ransom the captive*
*To bury the dead*

*The Spiritual Works of Mercy are:*

*To instruct the ignorant*
*To counsel the doubtful*
*To admonish sinners*
*To bear wrongs patiently*
*To forgive offenses willingly*
*To comfort the afflicted*
*To pray for the living and the dead*

St. John of the Cross, (1542-1591) the Spanish Carmelite priest, mystic and reformer wrote, "In the evening of life, we shall be examined on love." The Lord Jesus tells us, "Love one another, as I have loved you" (Jn. 13:34). This is brought home to us when we hear the account of the King, Who separated the sheep from the goats. Those who showed compassion to the least of their brothers, were invited to share in the joys of the kingdom,

> "Then the righteous will answer him and say, 'Lord, when did we see You hungry and feed You, or thirsty and give You drink? When did we see You a stranger and welcome You, or naked and clothe You? When did we see You ill or in prison, and visit You?' And the king will say to them in reply, 'Amen, I say to You, whatever You did for one of these least brothers of mine, You did for me' " (Mt. 25:31-46).

Those who showed mercy received the reward for their compassion and heard the beautiful words, "Come, you who are blessed by My Father. Inherit the kingdom prepared for you from the foundation of the world" (Mt. 25:34). For me, and hopefully for many, these are the most important words we ever want to hear, when at the end of our earthly pilgrimage, the King of Heaven and Earth welcomes us with these long hoped for words, to invite us to join Him into the glory of the kingdom of heaven.

# Crosses

There are two memorable events in my fond recollections of the First World Apostolic Congress on Mercy. The first of these took place in late July 2007. Since I served as the president for the North America Committee, and a member of the International Executive Committee, I was invited to participate in a series of preparatory meetings in Rome, Italy, from July 24 to August 3. This involved such large items as the schedule of events for the Mercy Congress, logistics, accommodations and such smaller items as input on the official logo for the congress.

Rome was rather hot, as it usually is that time of the year, and so, between the indoor meetings, I tried my best to stay out of the sun. Mr. Brendan Gleeson had been assisting me with financial matters for the North American Committee, and since he was doing a very competent job, was invited to oversee the entire financial team of the Mercy Congress by Cardinal Schönborn, the President of the Congress.

One afternoon, after our various meetings, we decided to go offer a prayer at the tomb of the Venerable Pope John Paul II, since we did not previously have the opportunity to do so, during our stay in Rome. It looked like there was not too long a line to pass the tomb, however, when we got into the grotto, it was stalled. Brendan felt warm and decided to turn back, and said he would meet me outside.

As soon as he departed, the line started to move, and although I called for him, he had already left. I offered my prayer at the tomb and met up with Brendan sooner than we had expected. With that, I told him that there was no more delay in the grotto, and we should go back there, so that he too could offer his prayers.

We returned to the Holy Father's tomb, I believe it was truly the goodness of the Lord that we went there again, so that we could be there at that very moment. Directly in front of Brendan and me, there was a family accompanying a young lady in a wheelchair. She was in her early twenties, and had a beautiful and sweet face, and long blonde hair. However, she had both legs amputated at the knees, as well as her left arm to the elbow area. All she had left on her right arm was one finger, the pointing finger, next to her thumb.

We watched as the guard took away the velvet rope that marked off the area of the tomb, and then rolled the wheelchair close to it. It took her three attempts, but she finally touched the grave, and she had a big smile on her face. Her parents began to cry and said, "She is happy." Later, they explained to us that he had been afflicted with the terrible flesh-eating bacteria.

They had come from Holland, to ask strength for her to deal with this cross, at the tomb of Pope John Paul II. With some emotion in my voice, I gave the young lady and her family a blessing, and offered a few words to promise that I would remember them in my prayers. Then I turned to Brendan and said, "And we think that we have our own crosses? They are nothing compared to this." That moment is now indelibly marked in my mind. It was a true gift of the Lord, to help me realize how much worse things could be, when we see the difficulties that other people must endure.

The second of the memorable events actually occurred during the proceedings of the Mercy Congress, on Friday, April 4, at the Basilica of St. John Lateran in Rome. One of the speakers was Sister Elvira Petrozzi, who, in 1983, founded the "*Comunita` Cenacolo*," the "Community of the Cenacle" in Bosnia. She explained that its purpose has been to help people with drug addiction problems who were completely lost. She called her center the "Hill of Peace," the place where her community is located. The young people are offered a radical change of lifestyle, based on prayer, faith and work, but most important, a renunciation of their old ways, which had put them on the path to self-destruction. Sister Elvira was born and raised south of Rome, near Frosinone, the section called the "*Ciocaria*" area.

She told the participants about the Providence of the Lord and how in almost twenty-five years, they never had to go to the market to shop for food, since many of the local people knew of the good work of rehabilitating those who were suffering. They would bring donations to the door out of generosity, kindness, love and mercy. She told us the story that one day, when they were preparing lunch for those in the community, there was nothing to put in the spaghetti to flavor it, just a drizzle of olive oil. She told those who were helping her to cook, that it was too bad there were not just a few tomatoes in the pantry, to make a quick sauce, but that within about ten minutes the door bell rang, and a local farmer delivered two bushels of beautiful, ripe tomatoes.

Her most touching story, in my opinion, was about her days at home with her parents in her youth. We learned of the cross that her mother had to bear, since her father had an unfortunate drinking problem, and from time to time would be without work. Sister Elvira told us not to have anger in our hearts against anyone, especially our parents, but appreciate the sacrifices that they made. They did the best they could, and sometimes made mistakes, like all human beings. We are to forgive, as the Lord forgives us.

She urged us to love our parents and when we see them say, "Mom, I love you" or "Dad, I love you" and hug them tightly, and to count to seven and do not let go until then, and both of you would be crying by the end of the hug. She told us that when her mother would get frustrated, she would say, "*Croce di Cristo, no mi abandonà*" This was the southern Italian dialect way of saying, "Cross of Christ, do not abandon me." This is the same sentiment in the fourteenth century prayer, *Anima Christi*,

> *Soul of Christ, sanctify me*
> *Body of Christ, save me*
> *Blood of Christ, inebriate me*
> *Water from Christ's side, wash me*
> *Passion of Christ, strengthen me.*
> *O good Jesus, hear me*
> *Within Thy wounds hide me*
> *Suffer me not to be separated from Thee*
> *From the malicious enemy defend me.*
> *In the hour of my death call me*
> *And bid me come unto Thee*
> *That I may praise Thee with Thy saints*
> *and with Thy angels forever and ever*
> *Amen.*

Many people want to escape from the cross, since suffering is difficult and unpleasant. However, we can take comfort and strength in the sufferings of Christ as the prayer states, "Passion of Christ, comfort me." When we realize all that the Lord underwent to redeem the human race, and bring us back to the divine life of grace, we can put our own sufferings in proper perspective.

I recall visiting the tomb of St. John Nepomucene Neumann, (1811-1860) who was the bishop of Philadelphia, and canonized in 1977. He was a humble priest, who worked tirelessly, and never expected to be named a bishop. The motto he chose for his coat-of-arms at the time that he was elevated to the episcopacy, on his 41ˢᵗ birthday in 1852, was: "*Passio Christi Conforta Me*" and was taken from the Anima Christi. "May the Passion of Christ give me strength or comfort."

The well-known spiritual writer, Thomas à Kempis, the author of *The Imitation of Christ*, tells us, "There is no other road to peace, but the road of the cross" (Bk. 2, ch. 12). There is a peace and blessedness that one receives from the Lord in accepting the cross, not merely in a passive acceptance of suffering, but actively and willingly acknowledging that, what I cannot change, I must accept, along with all of the suffering that it entails, to unite myself to Christ.

When we are weary from the cross, we go to the Lord, Whose invitation for refreshment is perennial, "Come to Me, all you who are burdened and I will give you rest" (Mt. 11:28). This is, for us, the opportunity to be like a child, and trust and rest in the Lord, like a baby that is asleep in the arms of its mother. If we are united with Christ in His sufferings and cross, may we also be united in His glorification, and one day participate with Him in glory. When we do not resist, but accept our cross as the Will of the Father, we find serenity, peace and love, and are readied for the sacrifices entailed. We readily accept them with cheerfulness and even joy.

However, some people do not want to be saved "By the cross, but from the cross." We can think of the words of St. Paul who invites us to "Rejoice in sufferings" (Rom. 5:3) and "Make up for what is lacking in the sufferings of Christ" (Col. 1:24). St. Peter's sentiments are very similar, "But rejoice to the extent that you share in the sufferings of Christ, so that when His glory is revealed, you may also rejoice exultantly" (I Pet. 4:13). In this way, we become collaborators and associates of the Lord Jesus in the work of our own salvation.

I remember the story of an Archabbot, who I got to know quite well. In part, his own writings were an inspiration for me to write this book. He told me that he had been very ill with cancer, and at one point, spoke with Blessed Mother Theresa of Calcutta, asking her to pray for him, in his recovery. She told him "Your illness is a kiss from the Lord, but if you want, I can ask Him to remove this kiss." He told her that he would accept the kiss and all that it entailed. He did, in fact, recover and I heard this story from him several years later. This reminds me of the quote from the Book of Hebrews,

> "My son, do not disdain the discipline of the Lord
> or lose heart when reproved by Him; for whom the
> Lord loves, He disciplines; He scourges every son
> He acknowledges. Endure your trials as 'discipline;'
> God treats you as sons" (Heb. 12:5-7).

We need to collaborate with the Lord, and not resist His plans even when they are difficult or irksome. St. Augustine wrote, *"Deus Qui Creavite Sine Te, Non Salvabite Sine Te"* which means, "God created us without our cooperation, but He will not save us without it." (Sermon 169 / 11, 3) Let us cooperate to the best of our ability, even if it means there is a cross we must bear. If done with love, it will help us in achieving our goal, which is our union with the Lord in His friendship here on earth, and union with Him forever in the kingdom of heaven.

# Congress Blessings

In preparation for the Mercy Congress to be held in April 2008 in Rome, I was invited to participate in an additional series of meetings, once again in Rome, where the Congress was to take place. On September 24, 2007, the entire International Executive Committee met at the Lateran Palace with our Episcopal moderator, Cardinal Schönborn. This meeting was after a series of logistical meetings at the Vatican Bank, to discuss the financial matters that had been determined during the previous few days.

After the meeting, as he was walking to his car, the Cardinal gave a few words of admonition to us. He told Brendan and me, "Be prepared, the devil will throw sticks in your path. He does not want the work of spreading the message of the Lord's Mercy to flourish!" Yes, there have been sticks and obstacles put in our path, most likely there are still more sticks to follow, but the blessings have outnumbered the sticks by far.

The day after the meeting at the Lateran, the entire committee departed for a four day Spiritual Retreat, which was a time of prayer and reflection. This was held at the Seminary of the Diocese of Belley-Ars, in France. This is the small village where the patron of parish priests, St. John-Marie Vianney (1786-1859) had served. He was the pastor of the parish church of Ars from 1818 until his death. There is an entire chapter dedicated to him later in this book. Since my Ordination to the Priesthood in 1988, I had always hoped that I might have the opportunity to visit his tomb, and to ask his intercession on my behalf, that I serve the Lord and his Church as a dedicated priest. So, this visit to Ars was like a dream come true for me.

A group of us arrived early in the day, before the retreat began later that afternoon, and so we went to the picturesque village of Paray-le-Monial, about ninety minutes from Ars. That is where Our Lord Jesus Christ revealed His Sacred Heart to St. Margaret Mary Alacoque. Jesus confided to her the mission to promote Devotion to His Sacred Heart. This led to the establishment of the Solemnity of the Most Sacred Heart of Jesus as a perpetual reminder of the Lord's great love for us.

We had the opportunity to visit her tomb in the Chapel of the Apparition, and also visit the tomb of her confessor, St. Claude de la Colombiere, (1641-1682) in a chapel nearby. On June 16, 1675, Jesus had revealed His Heart to St. Margaret Mary and said, "Behold the Heart that has so loved men, instead of gratitude I receive from the greater part of mankind only ingratitude." He asked St. Margaret Mary that a Feast day be established, to be held in reparation, on the Friday after the Octave of Corpus Christi. Our Lord had also told her, "Sinners shall find in My Heart, an infinite ocean of mercy" and, "I will bless those places where the image of My Sacred Heart shall be exposed and honored."

The retreat progressed well, and it served as a wonderful opportunity to grow in our knowledge of the Mercy of God. On the very last day of the retreat, our speaker was the current pastor of the parish church of Ars, who is the successor to the saint now entombed in the church where he had served. After his presentation, one of those attending the retreat asked him a question, "What was the principle theme of the preaching of the Cure` d'Ars?" The answer was simple, "Do not allow the folly of sin to prevent your soul from glorifying God." I thought to myself, "Wow, this was just the answer I need to hear." It truly helped to redirect my own life and preaching on another course.

At that retreat in Ars, there was a delegation of several representatives from Dublin, Ireland, who were involved with the preparations for the Mercy Congress in Rome. For the past seventeen years, they have held an annual conference in Dublin, on the Divine Mercy of the Lord. They told me that the next one would be March 1-2, 2008, in the Royal Dublin Society Hall and that approximately 4,000 to 5,000 people usually attend it every year. Toward the end of our stay, they asked me if I would consider being one of the speakers at this conference, and I was truly honored to be asked and happily accepted.

When I arrived in Dublin, I was told that there was a spiritually gifted man, Mr. Eddie Stones, who was coming from Clonfert, about two hours north of Dublin. He had been a butcher and a man of prayer. The Lord had spoken to his soul, telling him that he was chosen to be an instrument of God's healing. After several years of investigation by the local bishop, Eddie was made the administrator of a Retreat House in Clonfert, and his Healing Ministry received the approval of the bishop. When I learned that Eddie was to be at the conference, I hoped to have a word with him, to ask him to please pray for me to persevere, so I might serve the Lord to the best of my ability.

Shortly after lunch, I had the opportunity to introduce myself to him, and ask for a prayer for my priestly work. He offered to pray right then and there with me, and he told me the Lord wanted me to have a message, "Tend to the garden of your soul, get rid of the weeds, so that the beautiful roses can grow and flourish and give glory to God." This was another "Wow," in my thoughts; since it struck me how similar it was to the preaching of the Cure` d'Ars. This is the same idea I learned from *The Imitation of Christ*, "But let us lay an axe to the root, that being purged of our passions, we may possess our minds in peace. If, every year, we rooted out one fault, we should soon become perfect" (Bk. 1, ch. 11).

After this, I spent the rest of the season of Lent that year examining my life, and looking into the depths of my soul even better, to see where these weeds are located, and how to get rid of them. The time had now come to truly eradicate them, right from the roots, in order to make progress and recommit myself to "Doing good and not evil." This was the best means: to weed the garden and make the choice to eliminate anything that is preventing the Lord's grace from flowing in me.

Over the years, I have come to believe that we are all "Masterpieces in Progress." The Lord has a beautiful plan for each of our lives, and we are to cooperate with Him, in bringing about our sanctification and salvation. At this point in our lives, that plan of God is hidden from our eyes, but we do get to see glimpses of the master plan of the Lord, just a little at a time. I recall an analogy of life that I once heard,

> *Life is like a tapestry. The bottom faces the earth and the top faces heavenward. God can see the beauty of the work He is doing and the picture as it is completed. All that we on earth can see are the knots*

*and loops on the back side. When we get to heaven,*
*we can then look down on the tapestry and see it all*
*complete and it will be very beautiful. It takes faith*
*in Christ to be able to live with the knots down here.*

There is a similar version that is more poetic. I saw it printed on the front of a note card in the bookshop in the Catholic Cathedral of Westminster. It is entitled "Then shall I know" and goes like this,

*Not till the loom is silent*
*and the shuttles cease to fly,*
*shall God unroll the canvas*
*and explain the reason why*
*the dark threads are as needful*
*in the weaver's skillful hand,*
*as the threads of gold and silver*
*in the pattern He has planned.*

We need to remember that both the knots and the dark threads are not the end of the story. They help to comprise those twists, turns and sorrows that join with the joys, and are a part of each day. Of course, we are to be careful not to add even more knots and dark threads to the big picture. We can do this by our disobedience to the Lord's plan for our growth in holiness. However, we can always look to the Lord for that serenity and faithfulness we need amid trials, asking Him that they will help lead to our sanctification.

While we spend the majority of the days on this earth working on untangling the knots, it is good to keep in mind that they are necessary to form the masterpiece of our lives. One day, as the above poem states, it will all make sense. We will be let in on the master plan that the Lord God has for each of our lives. Until then, let us try our very best to tend the garden of our souls, get rid of any and all weeds, and glorify the Lord with our lives. Then, if we are faithful to Him on earth, we will see Him as well as the front side of the beautiful tapestry one day in the kingdom of heaven.

## Another Congress Blessing

The last of the many blessings which I received during the Mercy Congress, was the wonderful opportunity to get to know a truly kind and Christ-like person. This was our beloved President for the World Apostolic Congress on Mercy, Cardinal Schönborn. As members of the International Executive Team, we all resided at the Clergy Residence on Via della Traspontina, just a few blocks from the Basilica of St. Peter. On April 1, the night before the opening of the Congress, there was a pre-Congress meeting of the team. Earlier that day, I had visited a dear family that I know in Rome, and they gave me a bottle of their homemade *limoncello*, which is a lemon-flavored liqueur.

I thought it might be a good idea to share it with the team, so I brought it to the meeting, along with some small plastic cups, and we had a toast to wish us much success for the days ahead. The cardinal was scheduled to arrive at the residence after the meeting, and just as I was heading to my room, he was checking in at the front desk. He looked a bit tired after a long day of traveling from Vienna, Austria, so I offered him the remainder of the bottle of *limoncello*, and a few of the cups, and suggested that perhaps a drink before bed might help him to get a good night's rest.

He presided magnificently as the President of the Congress, and was always poised in what he said and did. He never seemed rushed, but always gave his best attention to everyone. When we were at meals, he was solicitous and friendly toward all, participating in the sometimes animated conversation. He truly became a "*Pater Familias*" a gentle and loving father to all of the team, which had indeed become more like a family, throughout the last year of working together.

During lunch on the first day, when the server was about to give the second course to the cardinal, he asked that they might please take away half of the portion, saying that he is not used to eating so much. The desserts had already been placed on the table, one at each place, which was an apple tart. Someone then offered to remove it from his place setting, since he appeared to be cautious in what he was eating, and he stopped them, saying, "Oh no, always dessert!" We all laughed at this, as did he. I thought to myself a short, almost comical prayer, that I once heard, that fit the occasion. "Lord, grant us always the luxuries in life, and we will gladly give up the necessities."

The events of the Congress culminated with the beautiful closing Mass on Sunday, April 6, 2008 in St. Peter's Basilica. The cardinal was the principle celebrant, as well as the homilist. Since it was the Third Sunday of Easter, the Gospel reading was the story of the two disciples that met Jesus on the road to Emmaus (Lk. 24:13-35). In his homily, he told us: "Now that we are departing from these blessed days of the Congress, we are putting ourselves on the road, with our hearts burning, to bring the message of the Lord's immeasurable mercy."

At the conclusion of the Mass, we all went to St. Peter's Square, and listened to the Angelus Message of Pope Benedict XVI, and received his Apostolic Blessing. During his message, the Holy Father greeted all the participants of the World Apostolic Congress on Mercy, and said: "I address my cordial greeting, which now becomes a mandate: Go forth and be witnesses of God's Mercy, a source of hope for every person and for the whole world. May the Risen Lord be with you always!"

That afternoon, at two o'clock, there was a gathering of the representatives from the many dioceses that were represented throughout the world, who had attended the Congress. At that meeting, there were approximately two hundred participants, from throughout Europe, Africa, North and South America, and the Philippines. Together, we set the course for the future, to bring the wonderful spark of the message of God's Mercy across the seas, so that the good work, which was begun in Rome, might continue. This would be through the various Congresses, to be held on the different continents. With God's help, there would be a Second World Apostolic Congress on Mercy in 2011, in Cracow, Poland.

After that meeting, my good friend, Brendan, who serves as a member of the International team, and I, walked back to the residence together. We had no sooner arrived, and Cardinal Schönborn walked through the door right after us. He gave us a big, friendly smile, when we wished him a very safe trip home. We also thanked him for all that he had done in making the Mercy Congress such a great success. Then, with a sparkle in his eye, he said to the both of us, "I have some very nice *limoncello* and some "elegant" cups in my room, would you like to join me for some?" He was referring to the plastic cups that I had given to him. With all he had to do, pack his bag, and make his flight back to Vienna, how thoughtful it was of him to give us even a few minutes of his time, after a busy day, in fact, a busy week.

While visiting in his room, he thanked both of us for the work we did in the preparations for the Mercy Congress and he wished us well. Our few minutes with the cardinal were like a warm embrace from a loving father. As I had already observed, the cardinal had become the father of the family. However, this was not limited only to the committee members, but to all the participants at the Mercy Congress. For Brendan and me, this impromptu visit was a little gift from the Lord, Who gave us this opportunity for a little relaxation, together with our beloved father of the team, after a week of hard work. It was the perfect conclusion to a truly spectacular week.

My friend Brendan has a personal motto, almost like a war cry, "Never Surrender!" When he asked me to give him the translation in Latin, I came up with, *"Numquam Summittere."* It means do not give up, but to fight the good fight and run the course, just as St. Paul wrote, "I have competed well; I have finished the race; I have kept the faith" (2 Tim. 4:7). The three of us finished our *limoncello* and we said *"Arrividerci,"* meaning, "Until we meet again," with the hope of working together in the future. The words "Never Surrender" were Brendan's final words to him. The cardinal stood upright, took a deep breath, clenched his fists, and with a big smile said, "Never!"

And indeed, we hope to not surrender, but persevere in fighting the good fight, with God's grace, and continue our work of spreading the message of the Lord's love and mercy. May our work be an instrument to invite others to "Taste and see the goodness of the Lord" (Ps. 34:8) and live in His abundant life of grace in this world and one day with Him forever in the kingdom of heaven.

# Mercy, Our Hope

After the beautiful First World Apostolic Congress on Mercy, all of us, both the committee members as well as participants, were given the commission to bring the message of the Lord's Great Mercy back with us, to our various continents, countries, dioceses and parishes. Our work in the North American Committee began right away, after we returned from the Congress in Rome and had sufficient time to get over jet lag!

Together, we looked over the calendar, and proposed that the North American Congress on Mercy would be held, with the help of God, at the Basilica of the National Shrine of the Immaculate Conception in Washington, D.C. on the weekend of November 14-15, 2009. The Second World Apostolic Congress on Mercy will be held in Cracow, Poland on October 1-5, 2011. This is in the same diocese where the Venerable Pope John Paul II had served as the Archbishop, prior to his election to the Papacy. The current Archbishop is Stanislaw Cardinal Dziwisz, who had served as the secretary of Pope John Paul II.

Our Holy Father, Pope Benedict XVI, had recently visited the United States, and the theme of his Papal Visit was, "Christ, our Hope." We tried to incorporate this same theme and had been seriously considering two possibilities as the themes for the North American Congress: "Mercy, our Hope" or another possibility, "Mercy: Learn it and Live it." In the end, the committee decided to incorporate both ideas, and we made the official theme: "Mercy, our Hope: Learn it and Live it."

I have a dear friend in New Jersey, who was in the seminary with me, Fr. Anthony Dandry, and I was inspired to ask him to help me write the lyrics for the "Official Hymn" for the North American Congress on Mercy. We got together and with a pad, pencil, the Holy Word of God, along with our imaginations, and we sat down and brainstormed to come up with the lyrics for the Mercy Congress Hymn. It was our desire to trace the Mercy of the Lord throughout Salvation History, based on the Sacred Scriptures, as well as Sacred Tradition. The lyrics of the hymn are sung to the tune, "O Jesus we Adore Thee" and are as follows,

*Mercy, Our Hope*

*Refrain:*   *Lord Jesus, King of Mercy*
           *We place our Trust in Thee (1)*
           *Our Hope and our Salvation,*
           *Please hear our humble plea.*

*Verses:*

*1. You saved Thy chosen People,*
*Their foes went in the sea (2)*
*Thy Mercy was upon them, (3)*
*And set the captives free. (Refrain)*

*2. Our Light and our Salvation,*
*No peril shall we fear (4)*
*Our Hope in times of danger*
*Shows proof that Thou art near. (Refrain)*

*3. You give us strength (5) to prosper (6)*
*There's nothing without You. (7)*
*Your Gospel gives us guidance*
*In what we say and do. (8) (Refrain)*

*4. You reach out to the sinner*
*When they are far away (9)*
*Bring back into Thy Sheepfold (10)*
*All who have gone astray. (11)*

*5. We sinners need Thy mercy*
*We give as we receive (12)*
*By deeds done with compassion*
*We show that we believe. (13) (Refrain)*

*6. Dear Mary, Queen of Mercy (14)*
*O, please our Mother be*
*Our Advocate and Helper*
*We give our Hearts to thee. (15) (Refrain)*

*Notes:*
*1: Ps. 37:3, Ps. 115:9, Prov. 3:5 "Trust the Lord with all your heart."*
*2: Exodus 15:1 "Let us sing to the Lord, Who is gloriously triumphant."*
*3: Ps. 136:1 "Give thanks to the Lord, for He is good."*
*4: Ps. 27:1 "The Lord is my Light and my Salvation, whom shall I fear?"*
*5: Phil. 4:13 "I can do all things in Him, Who gives me strength."*
*6: Ps. 1:3 "The tree planted by water will flourish"*
*7: Jn. 15:5 "Without Me, you can do nothing."*
*8: Jn. 14:15 "If you love Me, keep My commandments."*
*9: Lk. 15:20, Jn. 8:3-11 Parable of the Prodigal Son.*
*10: Jn. 17:21-22 "That all may be one."*
*11: Lk. 15:4-5 The Good Shepherd*
*12: Mt. 5:7, Mk. 4:24 "Blessed are the merciful."*
*13: Jas. 2:26 "Faith without deeds is dead."*
*14: Prayer: Salve Regina*
*15: Act of Entrustment of Pope John Paul II of October 8, 2000*

One of the main purposes of both the First World Apostolic Congress on Mercy, as well as the North American Congress on Mercy was to make the message of the bounteous Mercy of the Lord become more universally known. The humble sister, St. Faustina, served as the person to whom Jesus entrusted His message of mercy. He told her: "Mankind will not find peace until it turns trustfully to divine mercy" (Diary, #300). The day of the Canonization of St. Faustina, on Sunday, April 30, 2000, Pope John Paul emphasized this point in his homily. It has been the earnest hope of the organizers of both the World and National Congresses, that the Mercy of the Lord will be given greater appreciation, and not limited to the devotional aspects such as the Chaplet and Novena, or to the devotees of St. Faustina alone.

Another opportunity to reflect upon the message of the mercy of the Lord is through the World Apostolate of Fatima. The message that our Blessed Mother gave to the three children in 1917 was that of prayer and reparation, and to ask the pardon and mercy of the Lord for many offenses against Him. Several years before the image of the Merciful Jesus was revealed to St. Faustina, on February 22, 1931, there was an apparition to the Servant of God, Sr. Lucia dos Santos, who was one of the visionaries at Fatima.

This took place in the chapel of a convent in Tuy, Spain on June 13, 1929, where Sr. Lucia was residing, and this has been referred to as the "Last Vision of Fatima." In this vision, the Holy Trinity appeared to Sr. Lucia, and under the left arm of the Crucified Lord Jesus, there were large letters spelling "Grace and Mercy." In her own words, Sr. Lucia described the vision,

> "Suddenly the whole Chapel was illumined by a supernatural light, and a cross of light appeared above the altar, reaching to the ceiling. In a bright light at the upper part of the cross could be seen the face of a man and His body to the waist (God the Father). On His breast there was a dove also of light (the Holy Spirit) and, nailed to the cross, was the body of another man (God the Son). Somewhat above the waist, I could see a chalice and a large host suspended in the air, onto which drops of blood were falling from the face of Jesus Crucified and from the wound in His side. These drops ran down onto the host and fell into the chalice. Our Lady was beneath the right arm of the cross (it was Our Lady of Fatima with her Immaculate Heart in Her left hand, without sword or roses, but with a crown of thorns and flames). Under the left arm of the cross, large letters, as of crystal clear water which ran down over the altar, formed these words: Grace and Mercy."

When considering those who have promoted the great Mercy of the Lord, we also need to look at the work of the Venerable Mother

Speranza, (1893-1983) who founded the Institute of Merciful Love. She was born in Spain at Santomera, near Murcia, and became a sister in a convent of the "*Hijas del Calvario*" (Daughters of Calvary) at the age of 21. She founded the Congregation of the Handmaids of Merciful Love at the age of 37, and in July 1936, she opened her first community in Rome, Italy. The men's religious Congregation, called Sons of Merciful Love was founded shortly thereafter.

The new Congregation was erected as a Congregation of diocesan right in July 1968, and papal right in August 1982. In order to spread the concept of the great and unlimited love of our Lord Jesus Christ, in 1951, she established the Sanctuary of Merciful Love at Collevalenza, near Perugia, in central Italy. The Venerable Mother Speranza died in 1983, at the age of almost ninety. Her religious community aims to attend to the assistance and sanctification of the diocesan clergy, especially by building links between them and the religious order. Her cause for beatification began, and she was declared Venerable in 2002.

The Venerable Pope John Paul II has been called the great "Mercy Pope." After the assassination attempt in the Piazza of St. Peter's Basilica, on May 13, 1981, the first pilgrimage, outside of Rome, of the Holy Father was on November 22, 1981, to celebrate Holy Mass at the Shrine of Merciful Love in Collevalenza.

During his homily on that day, the Holy Father reaffirmed the importance of the Mercy of God, both its message and devotion, and told the listeners that this was his "Special task" given to him by God "In the present situation of man, the Church and the world." The dedicated work of Mother Speranza, along with the messages entrusted to St. Faustina and Sr. Lucia, have been given to humanity as God-given opportunities, to deeper and further consider the Mercy of God.

The goal of the congress was that there might be a wider and more ample appeal, as well as an outreach, to a greater multitude of the faithful, especially even beyond the congress participants. They are perhaps those who are most in need of the mercy of the Lord, those who are farthest from Him, and need to be called back into His friendship in this life, so they can enjoy His intimate friendship in this world and His presence forever in the kingdom of heaven.

# The North American Congress on Mercy

The first North American Congress on Mercy was a great success. It was held on Saturday and Sunday, November 14-15, 2009 in the Basilica of the National Shrine of the Immaculate Conception in Washington, D.C. More than 700 pilgrims had the opportunity to learn about the abundant mercy of the Lord Jesus Christ. The participants had arrived from throughout the United States, Canada and Central America. They were from various locations in California: Oakland, San Francisco, Los Angeles and San Diego, as well as Middle America: Chicago, Louisville and various towns in Ohio.

Pilgrims for the Congress also arrived from various parts of the East Coast: Massachusetts, New Jersey and places in Florida such as Tampa and Miami. We, the members of the committee, had the opportunity to meet participants from Ottawa in Canada, San Juan in Puerto Rico, as well as Nicaragua, Spain and France. They all came to learn more about the mercy of the Lord, and to bring the message and wonderful experience of the Mercy Congress back home and share it with others.

The participants had the opportunity to listen to a variety of speakers, among whom was Theresa Bonopartis, who is the Director of Lumina / Hope and Healing after Abortion. In her powerful talk, she described her desolation and distance from the Lord, at one point in her life. As a teen, she had aborted a baby boy. Although she had kept this a secret for many years, it ate away at her, until she finally turned to the merciful Lord for healing and forgiveness. This led her to dedicating her life work to help other women who are seeking healing after having an abortion.

Throughout the proceedings of the day, we heard heartfelt talks from the various speakers, who each focused on the theme of the Mercy of the Lord. Dr. Scott Hahn, a well-known author, gave the keynote address. Dr. John Bruchalski, MD, gave the first of the "Witness talks." He is the founder and director of Divine Mercy Care, which performs spiritual and corporal works of mercy in Northern Virginia, Maryland, and the District of Columbia.

We also heard from Kellie Ross, who is the co-founder and director of Missionaries of Our Lady of Divine Mercy in Manassas,

Virginia. In her talk, she explained her work with the poorest of the poor in the Ivory Coast in Africa, and told of her experiences there. Fr. Donald Calloway, M.I.C., the Vocations Director for the Marian Fathers of the Immaculate Conception in Steubenville, OH, was the principle speaker in the afternoon, and he focused on the role of Mary as Mother of Mercy.

Father Patrice Chocholski, of the Archdiocese of Lyon, France, who serves at the General Secretary of the World Apostolic Congress on Mercy, gave the concluding reflection. He came to lend us his support, as he has done in the various National Congresses, which have taken place as the fruits of the World Mercy Congress. His travels have brought him to Samoa, Hong Kong, and the Philippines, as well as throughout Europe.

The Most Rev. William Lori, Bishop of Bridgeport, CT, who has served as the episcopal adviser to the North American Congress on Mercy, was the principal celebrant and homilist at the 5:15 pm Holy Mass that concluded Saturday's schedule. His Eminence, Cardinal Justin Rigali, the Archbishop of Philadelphia, Bishop Thomas Paprocki, who was then the auxiliary bishop of the Archdiocese of Chicago, and the auxiliary bishop of the Archdiocese of Los Angeles, Bishop Gabino Zavala, also concelebrated.

In his homily, Bishop Lori remarked that the listeners were probably wondering if the committee had considered the readings of the day, when scheduling the date of the North American Congress on Mercy. Since it was the Thirty-Third Sunday in Ordinary Time, soon approaching was the Solemnity of Christ the King, and the Gospel reading was from St. Mark, ch. 13:24-32. It spoke of the coming of the Son of Man at the final judgment, when there will be "Tribulation when the sun will be darkened and moon will not give its light" (vs. 24).

As the congress came to its conclusion, the speakers commented to us, the organizers, that their experience in participating in the Congress had been very joyful and profound. They told us that they were enthused and better equipped to share the Lord's Mercy with others, both in word and in action. One of those who spoke at the congress told the listeners, "Mercy is not noun, but a verb."

For my own part, as the president of the Congress, I had the privilege to serve as the Master of Ceremonies throughout the proceedings of the day. Moreover, I had been scheduled to speak on three occasions, besides my role in introducing the individual featured speakers and witness talks. As the first person to welcome the participants, at 9:00 am punctually, and after introducing myself, I led them in the Opening Prayer and message of welcome. I told the listeners that it is appropriate that the Congress is taking place during the Year of the Priest, since it is through the instrumentality of the priest, that the Lord dispenses His Mercy through the Sacrament of Reconciliation. When Jesus was criticized for eating at the house of St. Matthew, he responded, "The healthy do not need a physician but the sick do, I have not come here for the righteous, but for sinners, it is mercy I desire, not sacrifice" (Mt. 9:13). I told them that the church is not a museum for saints, but a clinic for sinners.

In the opening talk, I had the opportunity to explain to the participants that the word mercy comes from the Latin word "*Misericordia*" and also spoke about its application as compassion. The compassionate person participates with another, in suffering with another in their pains. This should then spur us on to action.

I reminded them that Our Lord spoke about charity and compassion for others in the Gospel of St. Matthew (ch. 25:31-46) when He spoke about the final Judgment when the King says, "Come, blessed of My Father, enter the kingdom prepared for you. For I was hungry and you gave Me to eat, thirsty and you gave Me to drink." and the list continues. The just then reply: "Lord when did we see You hungry and feed You or thirsty and give You to drink or attend to You in Your needs?" And the King will reply, "Whenever you did it to one of the least ones, you did it to Me." This is what we are called to do: to learn about and imitate the Merciful Lord and put it into practice in our lives. This was the purpose of the Congress, to which so many of them had come, from both far and near.

The next opportunity for me to address the participants was during a spiritual reflection during the Eucharistic Holy Hour at 3:00 pm. At that time, I reminded the participants that we are in the month of November, in which we honor all the Saints. This is our ultimate destiny: to live our lives in the love and friendship of the Lord, and to be joined to Him one day in heaven.

I asked if perhaps they recalled a particular Catechism question from when they were studying for their First Holy Communion. The question was: "Why did God make you?" The answer is "God made me, so that I can know Him, love Him and serve Him in this world and be happy with Him forever in heaven." This is the goal as Christians: to live a holy life throughout this earthly pilgrimage, and arrive at the destination in heaven. I told them that my personal goal is to be a "canonizable" saint. No, I certainly do not want to be recognized by the Church, but rather, want to live a life of heroic virtue, to do good and avoid evil the best I can, and abide in the grace of the Lord. So many people have done it throughout the centuries and "God shows no partiality" (Acts 10:34) as we hear in Sacred Scripture. We are all invited to holiness. We need heroic virtue to do this, since it is one of the main ingredients of sainthood.

My reflection continued as I reminded them that Jesus tells us in Chapter 15 of the Gospel of St. John that He is "The True Vine and we are the branches" (vs. 5). We need to be connected to Him, so as to have His life within us. He invites us to "Abide in Me" (vs. 4) and tells us, "Apart from Me, you can do nothing" (Jn. 15:5). This is the way to grow in holiness. Is it easy? No, it is not, but it is possible. Many saints have done it throughout the centuries. In St. Paul's Letter to the Philippians, he wrote, "I can do all things in Him, Who gives me strength" (ch. 4:13). The themes of my talks at the Congress were almost like a condensed version of my thoughts that are found in this book.

I told the participants that this day, in this holy place, in the presence of Our Lord truly present, Body, Blood, Soul and Divinity, we are like the apostles, Peter, James and John on Mt. Tabor. We say, as they did, "Lord, it is good to be here" (Mt. 17:4). The Lord Jesus had given them a foretaste of heaven on that mountaintop. He was going up to Jerusalem to undergo His suffering and death, but wanted to give them courage, assuring them that all would be well. They saw, in advance, the glorification of His triumph.

However, just like the chosen apostles, who wanted to build three booths there, we too must go down the mountaintop, and resume our lives, with our own crown of thorns and crosses. Yet, we have had a glimpse and foretaste of heaven, in the presence of the Eucharistic Lord, and still can do so at every Holy Mass, when we unite ourselves to Jesus, the Way the Truth and the Life. His victory is ours as well, and with Him and His grace, all things are possible. He can help us live an abundant life, united to Him in this world, to aid us on focusing on our true goal of becoming saints, and be with Him in the kingdom of heaven.

The third opportunity for me to address the participants was at the conclusion of Holy Mass on Sunday, November 15th in the Crypt Chapel of the Basilica. As the President of the Congress, I was selected to be the principle Celebrant of the Mass. The committee and I had invited Fr. Seraphim Michalenko, M.I.C., who had dedicated many years to the study of the Mercy of the Lord, to be the homilist. As the Mass was drawing to a conclusion, and before the final blessing, I addressed the participants with these words of gratitude.

First and foremost, I offered words of thanksgiving to the Lord for His aid in promoting the work of spreading the message of His bountiful Mercy. We, of the committee, had asked the Lord not to be impediments, but rather, to serve as His unworthy instruments, in spreading the message, "Mercy Our Hope: Learn it and Live it." In my remarks, I gave thanks in particular to the Blessed Mother Mary. We put all our work under her mantle and maternal protection, and had asked her to help us in promoting the message of her Son's love and mercy.

Continuing, in the name of the committee and participants, I expressed our gratitude to our Holy Father, Pope Benedict, for continuing the work of his predecessor, the Venerable Pope John Paul II, the great mercy pope. In Rome, at the World Apostolic Congress on Mercy April 2-6, 2008, Pope Benedict told us to continue to spread the message of the Lord's mercy. It is like we had brought a lit torch, just like the Olympics, which was ignited in Rome, to accompany us here in North America, then from the North American Congress on Mercy in Washington, DC, and finally carry that flame of the message of the Lord's Mercy to each diocese and parish.

In the name of all, I thanked Cardinal Schönborn, the President of the World Mercy Congress, who sent us a letter of his support and blessings. I expressed our very special thanks to Fr. Patrice Chocholski, the General Secretary for the World Apostolic Congress on Mercy, who had come from Lyon, France, to support us and address us. In the same way that Fr. Patrice offers his support and presence throughout the world, as the North American Coordinator, I offered my own presence, when possible, to help in regional and local conferences and congresses to be held on the Mercy of the Lord.

In particular, I thanked the great support system of the Marian Fathers of the Immaculate Conception in Stockbridge, Massachusetts, and all the dedicated workers who, with their talents, pulled together the many details of the Congress. I quoted the phrase, "When a woman is in labor, she is sad that her time has come. But when she gives birth to a child, she forgets the pain, since a child has been born into the world" (Jn. 16:21). We of the committee had a few struggles and difficulties to pull the work of the Congress together, but it had all been worth it, to see the final result.

Nearing the conclusion of my comments, I told the participants that they may feel free to use the hymn, "Mercy our Hope," which served as the official hymn of the Congress, as a means to help to dissipate the message of the Lord's mercy throughout salvation history.

The phrase that continually came to my mind was that found in St. Paul's Letter to the Romans, *"Omnia cooperuntur in Bonum"* (8:28) in which we hear, "All things work unto good, for those who love God." We, of the committee, had placed the entire planning of the North American Congress on Mercy to the good Lord and placed our Trust in Him. It was not our work to spread the message of mercy; we were just serving as ambassadors to bring that spark, which had been lit in Rome at the World Congress, to be ignited in our own land.

The entire motivation for the Congress was that the message of the Mercy of the Lord will take root, and spread in the hearts of many who were at the Congress. Hopefully, it served as a help for them to live the message of mercy. In this way, they can grow in their friendship with Christ the Lord, and keeping their eyes ever fixed on the true goal, to be with Him forever in the kingdom of heaven.

# Mother of Mercy

As I was coming to the conclusion of this section of the book, I telephoned one of my dearest priest friends from my seminary days, Fr. Anthony, who lives in New Jersey. We discussed my desire to bring to others this written gathering of my experiences and reflections on the mercies of the Lord in my life, as well as His mercy in the lives of others. I asked for his prayers in this endeavor, since I was about to conclude the first section. He assured me of his prayers, and as we were nearing the end our conversation, he suggested that I write about the Blessed Mother Mary as "The Queen and Mother of Mercy." What a fitting way to end the first part of the manuscript, by paying tribute to the Blessed Virgin Mary, at the end of this section on the Mercy Congress?

The title, Mary, Queen and Mother of Mercy, could possibly be misunderstood. Our Blessed Mother Mary is a creature just like you and me, and she cannot have mercy upon us. That is reserved to the divine power of God alone. We can go to her, and humbly ask her help and intercession. Many centuries ago, the prayer we know as the "Hail Mary" consisted of only the angelic salutation, which was the greeting of the Archangel Gabriel to Mary. Soon, the words of St. Elizabeth, "Blessed are you among women and blessed is the fruit of your womb" (Lk. 1:42) were added.

Then, according to tradition, the prayer: "Holy Mary, Mother of God, pray for us sinners, now and at the hour of our death, Amen" were also added by the great preacher, St. Bernardino of Siena, (1380-1444) in the middle of the fifteenth century. We ask for Mary's help before the throne of the Lord. The author Dante Alighieri, (1265-1321) in his well-known work, "The Divine Comedy," wrote of Mary's power of intercession:

*Lady, so great art thou, of such avail,*
*That one who wishes grace and seeks not thee,*
*Lo, his desire essays flight without wings.*
*Not only does thy bounty succor him*
*Who asks of thee, but oftentimes also*
*Foreruns the prayer, in liberality.*

*In thee is mercy, pity dwells in thee,*
*And all magnificence and every good*
*That anything created may possess.*
                    *(Paradiso, Canto 33, n.13-21)*

This helps to underscore that Mary goes on our behalf to her Son, Our Lord and Savior, Jesus Christ, and asks Him to have mercy upon us. Mercy is to be asked of the Almighty and Merciful God, the Most Holy and Undivided Trinity, Father, Son and Holy Spirit. It is through the power of the Lord Jesus that we receive mercy, through the forgiveness of our sins. On the same evening after He rose from the dead that morning, the Lord stood among the apostles in the Upper Room, and gave them the power to forgive sins,

> "Jesus said to them again, 'Peace be with you. As the Father has sent Me, so I send you.' And when He had said this, He breathed on them and said to them, 'Receive the Holy Spirit. Whose sins you forgive are forgiven them, and whose sins you retain are retained'" (Jn. 20:21-23).

Mary is called the Mother of Mercy, because of her collaboration in the Divine Plan of God, specifically in her unique role in giving birth and nurturing Jesus Christ, Who is the King of Mercy. She had a deep understanding of the mercy of God. When her cousin Elizabeth greeted her, Mary proclaimed her song of praise, called the "*Magnificat,*" in which she recalled the mercies of the Lord throughout salvation history, and spoke these words, "His mercy is for those who fear Him from generation to generation" (Lk. 1:50) and "He has helped His servant Israel, in remembrance of His mercy, according to the promise He made to our forefathers…" (Lk. 1:54-55).

As Jesus "increased in wisdom and stature," (Lk. 2:52) Mary was there. She heard Him preach during His public ministry, and most likely, she was present when He stood in the synagogue at Nazareth, and there spoke of the favor of the Lord, "The Spirit of the

Lord is upon me, because He has anointed Me, to proclaim a year of the Lord's favor" (Lk. 4:18-19).

We can see that Mary was present during the public ministry of her Son since the Scripture tells us this,

> "While He was still speaking to the crowds, His mother and His brothers appeared outside, wishing to speak with Him. Someone told Him, 'Your mother and your brothers are standing outside, asking to speak with you.' But He said in reply to the one who told Him, 'Who is My mother? Who are My brothers?' And stretching out His hand toward His disciples, He said, 'Here are My mother and My brothers. For whoever does the will of My heavenly Father is My brother, and sister, and mother' " (Mt. 12:46-50).

While some can see this statement of the Lord Jesus as a way of minimizing the importance of Mary, His mother, it really is an elevation of her role. She is not to be elevated only because she was His biological mother. Rather, she was included in the group of believers; in fact, she is the first and the greatest among all the believers. A woman in the crowd said: "Fortunate is the womb that bore you." The Lord answered, again, to elevate his mother from mere family ties to discipleship, "Rather, blessed are those who hear the Word of God and keep it" (Lk. 11:27-28). So that is why Mary, too, is blessed, because she heard the Word of God and kept it. In fact, she was the very first to do so at the Annunciation, when by her consent, she conceived the Son of God.

We look to the venerable Fathers of the Church, throughout the centuries, and thereby can come to appreciate the discipleship of the Blessed Mother through their writings. St. Augustine wrote, "Holy Mary clearly carried out the will of the Father, and therefore it is a greater thing for her to be a disciple of Christ, than to be His mother" (Sermon 72/A, 7).

This is why Mary has been considered the "Model and exemplar" for all believers, for the entire Church, since the time of the

Apostolic Fathers. St. Ambrose, Archbishop of Milan (340-397) wrote, "The Mother of God is a type of the Church in the order of faith, charity, and perfect union with Christ" (Expos. Lc. II. 7). The Blessed Virgin Mary conceived the Lord in her heart, before in her body, since she gave her consent to the plan of the Heavenly Father when she said a complete "Yes" to God's plan for her at the Annunciation.

Mary's cooperation continued through the earthly life of her Son. We call her *"Socia"* which is translated as Associate or Collaborator of Her Son, in the work of our Redemption. She intercedes for us still. Many times over the centuries, we learn of apparitions, wherein Mary has reinforced the message of her Son. She encouraged people to stop offending the Lord and to live in His love and friendship. At Fatima, in 1917, she taught the three children to add this prayer to the Rosary, "O my Jesus, forgive us our sins, save us from the fires of hell and lead all souls into heaven, especially those in most need of Thy mercy."

Over the centuries, Mary has been referred to as "Mother of Mercy." This title has been attributed to St. Odo, (878-942) the Abbot of Cluny, in France, in the tenth century. The prayer *"Salve Regina,"* known as the "Hail, Holy Queen," which was developed in the eleventh century, incorporated this idea that Mary is our "Mother of Mercy, our life, our sweetness and our hope." We join our voices in the prayer attributed to St. Bernard of Clairvaux, "Pray for us, O Holy Mother of God, that we may be made worthy of the promises of Christ." Perhaps the oldest Christian prayer was found on a fourth-century papyrus in the Greek language. It is the *"Sub Tuum Presidium,"* asking Mary's intercession, "We turn to your protection, Holy Mother of God. Listen to our prayers and help us in our needs, Glorious Blessed Virgin!"

Many have heard the beautiful expression, *"Ad Jesum per Mariam"* which means "To Jesus through Mary." This expression was made popular through the preaching of St. Louis Marie Grignon de Montfort (1673-1713). He recommended the Act of Total Consecration of oneself to Jesus, through the hands of Mary. The motto, *"Totus Tuus,"* was the one selected by the Venerable Pope John Paul II when he was named a bishop in 1958. It is taken from the prayer in the Act of Consecration, "I am all thine, Immaculate One, with all that I have: in time and in eternity" as a sign of this commitment.

A dear priest friend, Fr. Tommaso from Rome, once told me of a story that he heard. It is the analogy of being an ailing child, and placing our needs before the Lord, through a loving mother's help. He reminded me that when we were children, and were ill, our mothers would take us to the doctor's office. She, in turn, would then explain all our symptoms, such as a tummy ache, to the nurse. We would just sit there, and open our mouth to say "Ah" and the like. The nurse would then explain all to the doctor, who would then help us to feel better. This is like Mary. We ask her to please go to Jesus, and put our needs before Him. We may not even know what ails us, we may be down, discouraged, or even at times, battle weary, but we implore her to kindly beseech her Son, the Divine Physician of souls, to heal us and help us in our needs.

This reminds me of the passage of Sacred Scripture from St. Paul, which reminds us of our total dependence on the Lord, in particular when we are weakest,

> "The Lord said to me, 'My grace is sufficient for you, for power is made perfect in weakness.' I will rather boast most gladly of my weaknesses, in order that the power of Christ may dwell with me. Therefore, I am content with weaknesses, insults, hardships, persecutions, and constraints, for the sake of Christ; for when I am weak, then I am strong" (2 Cor. 12:9-10).

In his encyclical *"Dives in Misericordia,"* (Rich in Mercy) which was promulgated on November 30, 1980, the Venerable Pope John Paul II wrote about the Blessed Virgin Mary as the Mother of Mercy,

> "Mary is also the one who obtained mercy in a particular and exceptional way, as no other person has… she made possible with the sacrifice of her heart her own sharing in revealing God's mercy…In this sense, we call her the Mother of mercy: our Lady of mercy,

or Mother of divine mercy; in each one of these titles there is a deep theological meaning, for they express the special preparation of her soul, of her whole personality, so that she was able to perceive, through the complex events, first of Israel, then of every individual and of the whole of humanity, that mercy of which "from generation to generation" people become sharers according to the eternal design of the Most Holy Trinity" (no. 9).

At the very beginning of this work of my reminiscences on the goodness and mercy of God in my life, and in the lives of others, there is the page of Dedication. On it is the expression, "My Mother, My Confidence." There also is a beautiful painting of Mary and the Child Jesus, which was painted by Carlo Maratta, (1625-1713) during the High Baroque period of art. The original was in a convent of nuns, called of the Poor Clares in Todi, Italy. Along with the other sisters, there lived Blessed Chiara Isabella Fornari, (1697-1744) who was particularly drawn to the beautiful image.

It is said that the Blessed Mother told her that she was pleased with the image and its tenderness, and Mary promised to grant her tender love and care to those who venerate this image under the title of "Our Lady of Confidence." Subsequently, the short prayer or aspiration, "*Mater Mea, Fiducia Mea*" meaning, "My Mother, my Confidence" has developed over the years.

This was the favorite image of Blessed Pope John XXIII, because a small copy of it has been venerated in the Chapel of the Major Seminary of Rome, located near the Lateran Basilica. It was in that very chapel that he celebrated his First Mass in 1904, and had returned there many times. This simple oval-shaped image depicts Mary holding the Child Jesus, as He points His finger to His mother. They both look lovingly at the viewer, and the impression that comes to me, when I see this touching painting, is that they are inviting us to have great confidence in both of them. We are invited, each and every day, to have complete trust in Jesus and Mary; who will give us their aid in all our needs and help us to persevere.

This is particularly the case when the path is perilous, or we have challenges, especially in the difficult times in which we live. May these beautiful words of St. Bernard help to inspire us,

> *"If you find yourself tossed about the storms of life, if the winds of temptation rise, if you fall among the rocks of tribulation, look to the star, call upon Mary. In dangers, distress, perplexities, think on Mary, call on Mary. Following her, you will never go astray, under her patronage you will never waver, if she is your guide, you will never weary; if she is your star, you will arrive safely in port."*

The morning of my Ordination to the Priesthood on January 11, 1988, I went to see Bishop Juan Torres, who was to ordain me later that evening. I had asked him to bless the chalice that I was to use the next day at my First Mass. We had a few minutes together and he told me, "Tonight I will ordain you to the Holy Priesthood, do you know the secret to being a good priest?" The bishop was happy with my answer. "Stay close to Jesus and Mary" was my reply. This has been my goal in life as a priest, to serve as one of the many beacons, who help to bring the Light of Christ to souls, amid the darkness that the world sometime offers.

Several years later, during my spiritual reading, I a quote by St. Maria Mazzarello, (1837-1881) who was the co-founder, along with St. John Bosco, (1815-1888) of the branch of the religious sisters in the Salesian Order called the Daughters of Mary, Help of Christians. She would tell others, *"Che ama Gesù e Maria contento sarà."* This means, "Whoever loves Jesus and Mary will be happy." Of course, this does not guarantee that everything will be perfect. Perfection exists only in heaven, not in this world. However, with all the strife and struggles in our lives, we will be happy, if we are close to Jesus and Mary, and have them accompany us and help us to get through life's ups and downs. In the song that we children would sing for the May crowning, entitled, "Bring Flowers of the Fairest," there is a line in it that states, "How dark, without Mary, life's journey would be."

May each of us help to lead many souls, that are in our care, to the love of Jesus and Mary, who are the King and Queen of Mercy. Together, may we entrust our lives to the providential care of the Lord and the tender love of His sweet and loving mother. She is called the "Cause of our Joy." May we call upon Our Lady throughout life's journey, never hesitating to ask her gracious assistance. There is an expression that I learned when I was in Rome, "*Vergine Immacolata, aiutateci e fateci santi!*" This means, "Immaculate Virgin, help us and make us holy!" May Our Lord and Our Lady help us and lead us in the right paths throughout this life, that we may be eternally in their presence, together with all the angels and saints, in the kingdom of heaven.

# Part Two

# REFLECTIONS

# 7

# Faith Observations

## Perseverance

When I was about nine years old, I was impressed with a wonderful movie that was released in 1965. It was "The Sound of Music," and is still well known to many, for its beautiful music by Richard Rogers and lyrics by Oscar Hammerstein. Many people are familiar with the movie, and recall the spectacular scenery of Salzburg, Austria, and its surrounding countryside. My favorite scene and line from it, is when Maria, the young postulant, returns to the Abbey, after having served as the governess to a family, and the Mother Abbess asked her, "What is the most important thing in life?" Maria answered, "To know the will of God, and to do it with all my heart."

Toward the conclusion of the movie, Maria, her husband, Captain Von Trapp, along with the children, literally had to "Climb every mountain" till they find their dream, in order to do the Will of God. We hear in the Scriptures, "Behold, I come to do Your will, O God' (Heb. 10:7). Once I had the opportunity to meet Maria Von Trapp, (1905-1987) just a few years before her death. She was invited to give a talk in New Jersey, and I was very happy that I could attend. In her talk, she mentioned her favorite line from the movie, which was the same as mine. The second best line in the movie, in my opinion, is, "When God closes a door, somewhere, He opens a window."

Her story is one of triumph in the face of adversity and that is the story of us all. No one has a perfect life; we are sinners, in a sometimes difficult world. We all have our crosses; some people have to bear bigger ones than others. The Lord Jesus tells us, "I have told you this, so that you might have peace in Me. In the world, you will have trouble, but take courage, I have conquered the world" (Jn. 16:33). When I read the autobiography of Maria Von Trapp several years ago, she gave us, the readers, the motto of the family coat-of-arms: "*Nec Aspera Terrent*" which means, "Let nothing difficult frighten you."

We are invited by the Lord to be courageous, hopeful and to persevere, just as so many holy men and women throughout the ages have done. We can have that abiding peace, which comes from trustful surrender to the Lord in all things. Our lives are like a pilgrimage from the cradle to the grave, from the womb to the tomb. It is through accepting the cross, that we can be transformed into another Christ, which is the true goal of every Christian. We do this by putting away our own sinful and selfish ways, and by keeping our focus on our life's goal, which is our abiding friendship with the Lord in this world and the next. St. Teresa of Avila once remarked that our lives are like a pilgrimage, and in an almost comical way, she said, "Life is like a night in a bad inn."

When I was age eleven, I learned how to pray the Rosary. It was during the month of May, which is dedicated to the Blessed Virgin Mary. Our seventh grade class had been praying it every afternoon, and I finally figured it out. There was a wonderful holy card that I saw, which explained the various meanings of the Mysteries of the Rosary; there were just fifteen back then. The Annunciation, for example, helps us meditate on the virtue of humility, since Mary said she was "The handmaid of the Lord" (Lk. 1:38). The Nativity teaches us the attribute of poverty, since the Lord Jesus was born, under poor conditions, in a stable.

The one mystery and virtue that most caught my attention, was the fifth glorious mystery, The Coronation of Mary. The virtue ascribed to it was perseverance. Mary had been faithful to the Lord, and so, she merited the crown of glory in heaven. I decided, then and there, that I would pray the Rosary every day of my life, and always with the same intention, to persevere, and by the grace of the Lord, I have.

Even though one decides to persevere with faith and trust in the Lord, there are always difficulties along the path. The evil one, of course, wants us to give up, and not follow the path that leads us to walk in the light of Christ, but to darkness. I once heard a story that the devil was having a going-out-of-business sale. All of his ugly looking instruments were marked with prices and there was one with a price that was double the others. When asked why it had such a high price, he answered, "That one is discouragement; it is the one that works every time, when I have tried all the others, and they have failed."

Blessed Mother Theresa of Calcutta was once asked if she became discouraged, when she picked up the dying and the poorest of the poor from the streets. She responded, "God has not asked me to be successful, but faithful." I believe that this is the basis of perseverance, that we continue to try to do the best that we can, in fulfilling the will of the Lord. We do this with great faith and trust that we are not alone, but that the Lord will sustain us.

St. Augustine tells us that things are to be done "Not by running but by believing" which is a sort of play on words in Latin: "*Non Correndo sed Credendo.*" We place one foot in front of the other, stay the course, and get the job done, always with the help of the Lord. If it seems there are even impossible or insurmountable difficulties, the Lord Jesus told us, "If you have faith, you can say to this mountain 'Be taken up and cast into the sea,' it will be done. And whatever you ask for in prayer, you will receive, if you have faith" (Mt. 21:21-22). At times, it may take a lot of blood, sweat and tears to "move the mountain." However, through perseverance, it can be done, along with God's help and a strong faith in Him. At times, we may even need to move the mountain one rock at a time, until it has been moved. But the Lord will give us the grace and strength that we need to do it, if we ask Him with faith.

Trusting in the Lord's Providence and believing in His care for me in every circumstance, has helped to give me inner peace, even amid the troubles and turmoil that arose from time to time in my life, as they do in the lives of us all. St. Pio of Pietrelcina, more commonly known as Padre Pio, was canonized in 2002. He often gave the following advice,

> *Pray, hope and do not worry.*
> *Worry does not accomplish anything.*
> *The Lord God is merciful*
> *And will hear your prayer.*

This advice reminds me of the words of St. Paul who wrote, "Have no anxiety at all. But in everything, by prayer and petition, with thanksgiving, make your requests known to God" (Phil. 4:6).

For people of faith, worry is actually incongruous. A few years ago, I heard a great song with a Jamaican beat, "Don't worry, be happy." The Lord does not want us to be worried, anxious or miserable. Even amid afflictions, He is there for us, to give us His strength and comfort, and to help us to persevere. "The Lord is my light and my salvation, whom shall I fear?" We hear this in the Book of Psalms, (Ps. 27:1) and the last verse of that same Psalm states, "Wait for the Lord, be strong, let your heart take courage, yes, wait for the Lord" (vs. 14).

We know, trust and believe that God has a great plan in store for us. Even though, at times, His plan may entail suffering, He will get us through if we put our confidence in His powerful help. We can see just a glimpse of that plan each day, and we can try our best to persevere in the love and friendship of the Lord. In this way, we do not destroy the beautiful plan of the Lord for us by that terrible three letter word: sin.

We can put our faith into action by good works. St. James wrote, "For just as a body without a spirit is dead, so also faith without works is dead" (Jas. 2:26). When I was about thirteen in July 1970, our family went to the State Convention of the Catholic War Veterans. At the time, my father was serving as the president of the local chapter at our parish. It was held in Atlantic City, New Jersey at a hotel called the Shelbourne. It has since then been replaced by one of the casinos.

It was a venerable looking building and emblazoned over the fireplace was its own coat-of-arms, complete with a motto, which read, *"Virtuti Non Verbis."* At the banquet, the state chaplain gave the main address and told us that the motto meant, "Actions, Not Words." That message has stayed in my mind all these years. It is similar to the encouraging words written by St. James, "Be doers of the word, and not hearers only" (Jas. 1:22).

In recent years, I heard it put in a more contemporary version, "Walk the walk, and don't just talk the talk." The crux of the message is to be authentic, as I once heard, "Mean what we say, and say what we mean." Important attention must be given to important things, and what can be more important to us than our eternal destiny? May we persevere each day in trying our best to live a Christlike life, so that we can one day live in the house of the Lord forever in the kingdom of heaven.

## Holiness

As you read this book, most likely by now, you will have noticed a similarity at the end of each chapter. Since I began preaching in 1987, first as a deacon, then as a priest in 1988, I noticed a consistency in the prayers during Holy Mass. They seemed to direct our thoughts toward our goal, which is to be admitted to the company of the angels and saints in the presence of the Lord God in heaven. Whether it was the Sunday Opening Prayer, or the feast day of a saint, the prayers generally had a format that was similar to the following one, taken from the Solemnity of All Saints:

> *God our Father, source of all holiness, the work of Your hands is manifest in Your saints, the beauty of Your truth is reflected in their faith. May we who aspire to have part in their joy, be filled with the Spirit that blessed their lives, so that having shared their faith on earth, we may also know their peace in Your kingdom. Grant this through Christ our Lord. Amen.*

This made an impression upon me, and I believed then, as I do now, that it is both uplifting and elevating to be reminded of the ultimate goal of our lives: heaven. St. Thomas Aquinas wrote that "We should always start with the 'End' in our minds, the goal that we seek, which is the eternal and indescribable peace and light that awaits us in heaven."

It helps us, both priests and people, to persevere in achieving that goal, which is to live a holy life and get to heaven. Each of us has to have a plan, or a goal, to get to our destination. This is part of everyone's life, whether you are a business person, trying to stay in the "Black" rather than the "Red," or a parent, who is planning for your child's education, by helping them to have a bright future. If we have a clear cut goal, we can focus on that, and not get easily sidetracked or distracted. For all of us, our goal and destination is to enjoy eternal life with the Lord in heaven.

So for these past twenty plus years, I have ended all my meditations and homilies, from that time to the present, with words similar to these, which are a reminder that: "We are here in this life to live each day in the friendship of the Lord, so that we can one day be with Him, forever in the kingdom of heaven." So present in my mind are the beautiful words of St. Paul, "Our citizenship is in heaven" (Phil. 3:20). That particular quote had served as a reminder to his flock, which had gotten off track, after he left them to continue his missionary efforts. He was telling them to put away their destructive ways, and not to put their minds solely on earthly things.

It has been said that when a priest dies, all his homilies are collected, and one realizes that over the years he preached just one homily, with many variations on the same theme. This has been my "*Leitmotif*," a German word, meaning "Guiding motive" over the years, to remind the flock entrusted to my care to "Prefer nothing to the Love of Christ." St. Benedict, (480-547) the founder of Western Monasticism, took this expression from St. Cyprian of Carthage, who died in the year 258. St. Benedict incorporated this phrase in his Rule (ch. IV, no. 21) as an aid for the monks'program of life: "*Nihil Amori Christi Praeponere.*"

This immediately makes me recall the passage from Sacred Scripture, "Seek first the kingdom of God and His righteousness, and all these things will be yours as well" (Mt. 6:33). In this way, our earthly endeavors are geared to eternal life and even our temporal well-being is secondary to this.

As priests, we are to be like St. John the Baptist, the precursor of the Savior, who tells us, "Prepare the way for the Lord, make straight His paths" (Mk. 1:3). For both ourselves, and those to whom we minister, this message of St. John the Baptist urges us to remove the obstacles, and sometimes even boulders, that may be blocking the way between us and the Lord. They can be like stumbling blocks, which impede our full commitment to living in the friendship of the Lord. We are invited to give glory to the Lord with the way that we lead our lives.

Once, when I was in Italy and concelebrated Holy Mass, the celebrant dismissed those in attendance by saying, "*Ite in pace, glorificando vita vestra Dominum.*" This was in Latin for, "Go in peace, glorifying the Lord by your life." Not long ago, I learned that these same words were approved to be included in the Concluding Rite of the Order of the Mass, when the new edition of the Missal in the English language is published.

We are pilgrims here on earth, and we have just one opportunity to do things right. This earth is not the destination, just our pilgrimage or journey toward our real goal, which is eternal happiness in heaven. St. Paul tells us, "We have here no lasting city" (Heb. 13:14). We never know the day or the hour that we will be departing from this earth; we are all just one heartbeat away from eternity. None of us is guaranteed that we will see tomorrow in this world.

The great masters of the spiritual life, over the centuries, have given us an insight how to get rid of the stumbling blocks that impede our commitment to the Lord. I read about this in the writings of the great Dominican theologian, Fr. Reginald Garrigou-Lagrange, O.P., (1877-1964) in his book, entitled, *"Three Ages of the Interior Life,"* which was written in 1938. A desire to work on growing in holiness begins with the "Purgative Way" or the *"Via Purgativa."* In a nutshell, it means we are to purge ourselves of those things that hinder our commitment to the Lord, letting nothing, no person, place or thing take away our attention from Christ. We are to purify ourselves from our sins and faults, and put them all behind us, as we seek the road to spiritual perfection. This may take years, or even decades, for some people, but if someone wants to really do it, it can happen, for as the Lord told us, for those "With faith, even the size of a mustard seed, nothing is impossible" (Mt. 17:20).

This is followed by the second stage on the road to spiritual perfection which is called the *"Via Illuminativa"* which means the "Illuminative Way." Here, the Lord in His goodness and mercy sees the soul's desire to love Him above all things, by destroying sinfulness and preferring virtue. That person has preferred nothing to the love of Him. The Lord gives the soul glimpses, insights and direction in the interior of their soul. The person corresponds by continuing their goal of seeking sanctification through purification, docility and humility.

The third step in one's progress toward holiness is called the "Unitive Way" or the *"Via Unitiva."* The word unitive says it all.

The soul of the person is intimately joined to the Lord by bonds of perfect charity and through contemplation. The soul aspires to live in the presence of the Lord and enjoy His friendship, which is better than life itself. St. Catherine of Siena (1347-1380) in her *Dialogues* wrote: "All our way to heaven can be heaven." In his simplicity in preaching, St. Jean Marie Vianney, the patron saint of parish priests, wrote about the intimate union of the soul of a person with the Lord. Each year on August 4, his feast day, we read this in the Office of Readings in the Liturgy of the Hours,

> In this intimate union, God and the soul are fused together like two bits of wax that no one can ever pull apart. This union of God with a tiny creature is a lovely thing. It is a happiness beyond understanding" (Catechism on Prayer, A. Monnin, *Esprit du Cure' d'Ars*, 1899, p.87).

My own understanding of the way that a soul can be united with Almighty God, came to light when I visited the beautiful church of Our Lady of Victory in Rome, Italy. In one of the side chapels is the well known sculpture, "The Ecstasy of St. Teresa of Avila." It was commissioned by the Coronaro family, who entrusted the task to the sculptor, Gian Lorenzo Bernini, (1598-1680) in 1647. The group of figures illustrates the moment of religious ecstasy that was described by St. Teresa,

> "One day, an angel appeared to me, who was lovely beyond compare. I saw in his hand a long spear, the end of which looked like a point of fire. I felt it pierce my heart several times, pressing into my innermost being. So real was the pain to me that I moaned out loud several times, and yet it was so indescribably sweet, that I could not wish to be released from it. No joy in life can give more satisfaction. When the angel withdrew his spear, I was left with a great love of God."

In the sculpture, one can see St. Teresa's mystical experience in which her hanging foot and hand, as well as the flowing drapery of her habit, convey her utter surrender. The smile of the angel and the iron-tipped spear both remind the viewer of its bittersweet agony. The message for us is that through faith and prayer, a real experience of God in this life is possible. Baroque art, which was a product of the Counter Reformation, is known for its exuberance. This statue helps to represent one of the themes of Baroque Religious art, "*Unio Mystica et Terrena*" which means the "Union of God and the World."

We have entered this world with nothing, and we will take nothing with us when we die. We are reminded of this by reading the Book of Job, "Naked I came forth from my mother's womb, and naked shall I go back again" (Jb. 1:21). All we can take with us is our soul, since our body goes back to the dust from which it was formed. *The Imitation of Christ* tells us, "Ever keep in mind your end, and that time passed will not return" (Bk. 1, ch. 25).

The best thing we can do, at the end of our earthly pilgrimages, is to stand before the Lord God during our particular judgment, with a pure and spotless soul. We need to try our very best, throughout the years of our lives, to rid ourselves of any obstacles, and particularly earthly attachments, that could have impeded the Lord's life of grace within us. I have offered hundreds of Funeral Masses and burials over the decades, and I can absolutely, and without any doubt, testify that not once has a moving van, with the person's treasures, followed the hearse to the cemetery, so that their earthly goods could be buried alongside them!

Over the years, I have always been inspired by the following quote from Blessed Columba Marmion, (1858-1923) who was the Abbot of the Benedictine Abbey of Maredsous in Belgium, and considered a great master of the interior life. His many writings have been considered, "A return to what was fundamental." He wrote, "The years, months and days pass, and all that remains is God, and what we have done for Him." The best path, I believe, is in making the committed decision to strive to live a Christ-centered, holy life. Holiness is the goal of every Christian, not just bishops, priests and nuns. We hear, "For this is the will of God, your sanctification" (I Thess. 4:3). A few verses later, St. Paul continues and reminds us,

"God did not call you to uncleanliness, but to holiness" (I Thess. 4:7).

The saints see themselves as sinners because they are closer to the "Light of the Lord" and thus can see themselves more clearly. When Peter came to the realization that Jesus was truly the Christ, the Son of the Living God, he said, "Leave me Lord, I am a sinful man" (Lk. 5:8). The better we get to know God, the better we get to know ourselves, and how we are to live with Him, others and ourselves. We hear, "He chose us, in Christ, before the foundation of the world, that we should be holy and blameless before Him" (Eph. 1:4).

We have a beautiful reminder of our invitation to participate in the holiness of the Lord at every Mass. During the Offertory, the priest pours the wine and adds a little water in the chalice, and he quietly says, "By the mystery of this water and wine, may we come to share in the divinity of Christ, Who humbled Himself to share in our humanity."

When I was nine years old, the Second Vatican Council, which began on October 11, 1962, came to a close on December 8, 1965. In the years that followed, I would occasionally hear comments about the Vatican Council and one phrase that I heard frequently was about the Universal Call to Holiness. As the years progressed, and I actually began to read and study the documents, I saw that this subject had been included in the Council's Document on the Church, "*Lumen Gentium.*" It was the title of Chapter 5, "The Universal Call to Holiness in the Church" and is treated in numbers 39-42 of that document. Below is an excerpt:

> "Thus it is evident to everyone, that all the faithful of Christ of whatever rank or status, are called to the fullness of the Christian life and to the perfection of charity; by this holiness as such a more human manner of living is promoted in this earthly society. In order that the faithful may reach this perfection, they must use their strength accordingly as they have received it, as a gift from Christ. They must follow in His footsteps and conform themselves to His image

seeking the will of the Father in all things. They must devote themselves, with all their being, to the glory of God and the service of their neighbor. In this way, the holiness of the People of God will grow into an abundant harvest of good, as is admirably shown by the life of so many saints in Church history" (no. 40).

It has been recorded that Blessed Mother Theresa of Calcutta frequently stated, "Holiness is not the luxury of the few. It is a simple duty for you and me." We, the clergy, religious and laity are all invited to accept the invitation to pursue a holy life. We do that best by "Falling in love with Jesus Christ" and making Him our best friend and the very center of our lives. We are to try our best to remain faithful to Him, both in and out of season, regardless of the ups and downs that come our way.

I once told my flock that where you are in your lives, is where God wants you to be, and it is there that you can achieve holiness and thereby glorify Him. If you are a carpenter, appreciate your tools and the opportunity to support your family by earning an honest day's wage, and try to glorify the Lord in all you do. If you are a housewife, kiss your iron, because that is your way to glorify God, but please be sure it is turned off first!

We read in the Book of the Acts of the Apostles, "In Him we live and move and have our being" (ch. 17:28). We, both the priests and faithful, are to stay focused and "on message" and let our lives and actions be a reflection of our interior commitment to live a holy life. There is an old expression, "The habit does not make the monk... but it helps." This means that if the monk faithfully wears his habit, it will be a helpful reminder of his status and commitments. He will, hopefully, act accordingly and even think accordingly, and gravitate toward those things that will bring him closer to the Lord and live a holy life.

We hear St. Paul tell us,

> "Finally, brothers and sisters, whatever is true, what-
> ever is honorable, whatever is just, whatever is pure,
> whatever is lovely, whatever is gracious, if there is

any excellence and if there is anything worthy of praise, think about these things" (Phil. 4:8).

We, too, are encouraged to act accordingly, if we follow this further, as well as the even more succinct advice, of St. Paul to "Put on Christ" (Rom. 13:4). This means to deliberately try our very best to act as Christ would act, with compassion, mercy and forgiveness. We can ask Him to help transform us. It is then that the wonderful fruits of the Holy Spirit, described by St. Paul, become evident in our lives, as we hear, "The fruit of the Spirit is love, joy, peace, patience, kindness, generosity, faithfulness, gentleness, self-control" (Gal. 5:22-23). This beautiful idea of being transformed into another Christ is so simply and humbly stated by St. Faustina in her diary, "O my Jesus, transform me into Yourself, for You can do all things" (Diary, #163).

Just about the time that I was writing this chapter, I happened to meet a lovely woman from the parish in Stamford, where I had served about ten years prior. Her name is Louise, she is now in her mid-eighties, and I always found her to be a devout woman. We saw each other at a restaurant, and she told me that she recalled, in one of my homilies, that I suggested a particular prayer. She told me that she went home, wrote it down and has prayed it every day since then. When I asked about it, she then wrote it on a paper napkin and handed it to me. Interestingly enough, I recalled that very homily and prayer, and, although I never had written it down, have expressed it in similar words in my personal prayer life to the Lord many times over the years. It is below,

*Dear Lord,*
*Let my thoughts be Your thoughts,*
*my words be Your words,*
*my actions be Your actions.*
*Do not let me get in Your way.*
*Come and take over my life, so that*
*all my thoughts, words and actions*
*are a reflection of You.*
*Amen.*

Over the years, I have heard that the saints develop a "Holy indifference," in the sense that they do not worry or care about their circumstances or location, as long as they are united to the Lord through His grace and friendship. There is a story about St. Brendan, who is called "The Navigator" (484-577). He deliberately tossed his oars into the water, trusting that the Lord would bring his boat with his small groups of monks to the next location, where they were to evangelize. This is trusting faith at its best, and if the saints can do it, we are invited to follow their example and do the same.

Chapter eleven of the Letter to the Hebrews, delineates the faith of Abel, Abraham, and in particular Moses, who "By faith crossed the Red Sea as if on dry land" (Heb. 11:29). The chapter ends with this quote, regarding reliance on the plan of the Lord, above our own, "Since God had foreseen something better for us" (vs. 39).

There has been a great quote from *The Imitation of Christ* that has been one of my favorites throughout the years. In it, the disciple tells the Lord that he will accept whatever comes his way, and accept all that the Lord sends, abandoning himself to the plans of God, but that he be given the grace of God in all things,

"Lord, You know what is better for me; let this be done or that be done as You please. Grant what You will, as much as You will, when You will. Do with me as You know best, as will most please You, and will be for Your greater honor. Place me where You will and deal with me freely in all things. I am in Your hand; turn me about whichever way You will. Behold, I am Your servant, ready to obey in all things. Not for myself do I desire to live, but for You, would that I could do this worthily and perfectly! Grant me Your grace, O most merciful Jesus, that it may be with me, and work with me, and remain with me to the very end. Grant that I may always desire and will that which is most acceptable and pleasing to You" (Book 3, ch. 15).

If we stay close to our Lord, aspire to live a holy life, and abandon ourselves to His plans for our lives, then we develop a Christ-like mindset, and then even our decisions will be easy. We will readily pursue the pearl of great price, of which we hear in the Gospel, "Again, the kingdom of heaven is like a merchant, searching for fine pearls. When he finds a pearl of great price, he goes and sells all that he has and buys it" (Mt. 13:45-46).

We are all invited, by the universal call to holiness, to make every sacrifice to obtain that pearl. That pearl is our sanctification and our salvation, with the focus on getting to heaven some day. We are not to despise the world, but do the best we can during our stay, and yet, not let the things of this world be a distraction to the final goal. Perhaps the author C. S. Lewis (1898-1963) put it best, when he wrote, "Aim at heaven, and you will get earth thrown in. Aim at earth, and you get neither." This is the Lord's plan for us, and we are collaborators with Him in this, so the best thing we can do is ask His grace, guidance and help to attain our goal which is the "imperishable crown" and to participate, one day, in the glorious triumph that awaits us in the kingdom of heaven.

# Humility

Humility comes from the Latin word, *Humus*, which means dirt. Every year on Ash Wednesday, we have a stark reminder that we have come from the earth, and that we will return to it. When the ashes are imposed on our foreheads, we have a visual *"Memento mori"* or "Remember death." We hear in the very first book of Sacred Scripture, "You are dust, and to dust you shall return" (Gen. 3:19).

Humility is called the "Queen of all the Virtues" and it is usually juxtaposed with pride, which is called the "King of all the Vices," that leads us to the capital sins. Listed in the same order used by Pope St. Gregory the Great, (540-604) in the 6th century, the seven deadly sins are as follows: lust, gluttony, greed, sloth, anger, envy, and pride. Each of the seven deadly sins has an opposite among the corresponding seven holy virtues. In parallel order to the sins they oppose, the seven holy virtues are: chastity, temperance, charity, diligence, patience, kindness and humility.

The great virtue of humility is the product of two things. First of all, we need to fight against pride above all things. That entails the need to crush self-love and our own desires. Secondly, we need to be in the company of Jesus and Mary, and have absolute trust in them. We have to have strong faith in asking that Our Lord and His Mother will assist us, so that we can more and more "Die to self." In doing so, we can love them better and unite ourselves wholeheartedly to their plan for us. We ask the Lord to help us to see ourselves with His eyes, as He sees us, with clarity. St. Teresa of Avila wrote, "God is all truth. Humility is walking in the truth, otherwise we walk in lies."

The Book of Proverbs abounds with invitations for the readers to be humble. We hear, "The reward for humility and fear of the Lord are riches and honor and life" (Prov. 22:4). We also hear, "When pride comes, disgrace comes; but with the humble is wisdom" (Prov. 11:2-3). The results of pride are also denoted in this quote, "The fear of the Lord is to hate evil; Pride, arrogance, the evil way, and the perverse mouth I hate" (Prov. 8:13). We are reminded that pride brings us down a dangerous path, and leads to troubles, but humility brings happiness, "Pride goes before disaster and a haughty spirit before a fall. It is better to be humble with the meek, than to share plunder with the proud. He who plans a thing will be successful; happy is he who trusts in the Lord" (Prov. 16:18-20)!

The Book of Psalms also encourages the reader to reject pride, "Lord, my heart is not proud; nor are my eyes haughty. I do not busy myself with great matters, with things too sublime for me" (Ps. 131:1). It reminds us that the Lord is pleased with those who humble themselves in His sight, "My sacrifice, God, is a broken spirit; God, do not spurn a broken, humbled heart" (Ps. 51:17). The Book of Sirach offers us the perfect advice,

> "My son, conduct your affairs with humility, and you will be loved more than a giver of gifts. Humble yourself the more, the greater you are, and you will find favor with God. For great is the power of God; by the humble He is glorified" (Sir. 3:17-20).

The greatest example of humility for us, is the self-emptying of Our Lord Jesus Christ. This is explained best through the beautiful and moving words of St. Paul,

> "Though He was in the form of God, did not regard equality with God something to be grasped. Rather, He emptied Himself, taking the form of a slave, coming in human likeness. And being found human in appearance, He humbled Himself, becoming obe-dient to death, even death on a cross" (Phil. 2:6-8).

The attitude of the Lord was steeped in humility and willing submission, which showed itself in obedience to the plan of His Heavenly Father. He did this by wholeheartedly doing the Will of His Father, and thereby gave us an example for us to emulate. We hear these words, "Then He says, 'Behold, I come to do Your will.' He takes away the first, to establish the second. By this 'will,' we have been consecrated through the offering of the body of Jesus Christ once for all" (Heb. 10:9-10).

The Lord Jesus invites us to be humble by following His example, as we hear, "Learn from Me, for I am meek and humble of heart, and you will find rest for your souls" (Mt. 11:29). The Lord also taught us about the virtue of humility in His preaching. In particular, in a parable about those who had been invited to a wedding banquet, and were choosing the places of honor at the table. He warned them not to take a seat of importance, as perhaps a more important guest might arrive. Then the host, who invited both of them, may ask that person to give their place of importance to the other one. Then they would proceed, with embarrassment, to take the lowest place. Jesus told them that it would be better to go the lowest place, so that when the host comes to you, he will invite you to a more important place and even the others in attendance would be impressed by that.

The Lord Jesus gave another lesson in humility, when He spoke of the two men who went to the pray in the Temple area. One was a Pharisee and the other a tax collector. The Pharisee's prayer basically praised himself to the Lord, thanking God that he was not like the rest of humanity, or even like the tax collector. He reminded God that he fasted twice each week, and paid tithes on his income.

Jesus told the listeners that the tax collector, however, stood at a distance, without even raising his eyes to heaven, beat his breast as he prayed, "O God, be merciful to me a sinner." Jesus concluded the parable by telling the listeners, "I tell you, the latter went home justified, not the former, for everyone who exalts himself will be humbled, and the one who humbles himself will be exalted" (Lk. 18:14).

The Lord God is pleased with the prayers of the humble, as one sees in the lesson between the pride of the Pharisee and the humble tax collector. We hear in the Word of God, "The prayer of the lowly pierces the clouds; it does not rest till it reaches its goal, nor will it withdraw, till the Most High responds" (Sir. 35:17-18).

St. Peter advises us how to live in this world, "Clothe yourselves with humility in your dealings with one another" (I Pet. 5:5). If we are immersed in the Lord, by being clothed in Him, and trying to live a humble life, we can be transformed. Just like a dry sponge that absorbs water, we can soak in the attributes of the Lord, and seek to do that which pleases Him. This has indeed been the trademark of the saints, to conform themselves to Christ, by humbly accepting the will of His heavenly Father.

There is a book I have kept nearby my Breviary over the years, and have often referred to as spiritual reading, ever since the seminary days. It is entitled, *"Humility of Heart,"* and was written by the Capuchin priest, Fr. Cajetan Mary da Bergamo (1660-1753). There are many beautiful and inspirational thoughts on the great virtue of humility. I have been impressed by the following passage, which gives the reader a correlation between humility and confidence in the Lord, "Humility generates confidence, and God never refuses His grace to those who come to Him with humility and trust" (pg. 93).

There is a story regarding humility that I heard some years back, which made an impression upon me. In 1989, Empress Zita (1892-1989) died. She was the widow of Blessed Karl I of Austria (1887-1922). She was the last Empress of Austria, the last queen of Hungary and had become a member of the Hapsburg dynasty through marriage. On the day of her State Funeral on April 1, 1989, more than 8,000 mourners were present at St. Stephen's Cathedral in Vienna, Austria, and then fell in line behind the hearse, which was drawn by six black horses. Two hours later, the procession arrived at the Capuchin Church, which is traditionally the place of burial for the Royal Family.

There, in keeping with a centuries long custom, a member of the funeral entourage knocked on the door of the church and a priest inside it asked, "Who goes there?" At that point, Zita's titles were read aloud: "Zita, Queen of Bohemia, Dalmatia, Croatia, Slavonia, Galicia, Queen of Jerusalem, Grand Duchess of Tuscany and Cracow." The response from inside the church was, "I do not know her." So they knocked a second time and were again asked the question, "Who goes there?" "Empress Zita," was the more simple reply this time. Yet, still the door remained shut.

The mourners knocked a third time and when they heard the question, "Who goes there?" this time, they simply responded, "Zita, a poor sinner." That was the right answer and the procession was allowed to enter. Zita had been part of history, and she was nobility. However, at her death, all of these earthly glories were meaningless.

She, like everyone else, was just a poor sinner, seeking the Mercy of the Lord. Her grandeurs needed to be put aside. Her titles would not help to grant her entry to the door of the church. It was only by admitting, in humility, that she was a poor sinner, just like everyone else, and in need of the forgiveness of the Lord, that she was allowed to enter. This attribute of humility is what all of us needs the most. The Word of God tells us that the Lord will "Save the humble people" (Ps. 18:27).

Hopefully, meditating on the importance of the virtue of humility in our lives, will help us to keep the proper perspective, that we are mere creatures in the eyes of the Lord, our Creator. We are all just "poor sinners" like Zita, and in need of the help and forgiveness of the Lord. Whenever someone tells me, "Father, I liked your homily" I respond, "The Lord has been good to me." I certainly hope that they get the message, that all I do and say is His gift to me, and I want to give the Lord all the credit.

I recall the words of St. Francis de Sales, (1567-1622) "I fear the good opinion of my family and friends, lest they think me to be in heaven, and leave me to suffer in purgatory." Although this refers to after one's death, but we are better off if we keep that sense of humility, and give the Lord all the honor and glory. The expression in Latin comes to mind, "*Soli Deo Gloria*" meaning "To God Alone be all Glory." Humility will help us to realize we are in need of His great mercy to overcome our human weaknesses, and grow in the grace and the friendship of the Lord, so that we can one day be admitted to the kingdom of heaven.

# Attitude

Over the years, I have increasingly seen the importance of one's attitude in dealing with life and its circumstances. My Mom and Dad are first-generation Italian Americans, meaning that their parents emigrated from Italy, and they were born in the U.S.A. Although we spoke English at home, there were a few idiomatic expressions that we retained in the Italian language. For us, some of those words seemed to roll off the tongue more easily, since we heard them from our grandparents and relatives for decades. For example, we would say "*Salute,*" which means, "To your health," instead of "God bless you" when someone sneezed, in the same way that some people say "*Gesundheit,*" which I have heard comes from German and Yiddish origins.

One Italian expression that has remained with me has been "*Pensate cose buone e fate cose buone*" which means, "Think good thoughts and do good things." My father still tells me this to this very day, when I am leaving my parents' home after my weekly visit on my day off, to return to my parish. It is a way of him telling me: "Be positive and keep up the good work."

We need to be encouraged, and also to be encouraging others. St. Paul was grateful for the encouragement that he received, "For I have experienced much joy and encouragement from your love, because the hearts of the holy ones have been refreshed by you, brother" (Philem. 1:7). How important it is to cultivate an optimistic and positive attitude. The way we do this, I strongly believe, is by trying to surround ourselves with positive people. We also need to realize that the negative people can infect us, damage our inner peace, and bring us down to their own level of negativity, thereby invading our own joy.

We have control over our joy, and are not to let others take it away. We should be careful of pessimistic and argumentative people, and in particular if they are "toxic," we need to be cautious. We must not let it infiltrate our own lives and attitudes, and thereby pull us down. I have also heard that there are scientific studies which show that people with positive, hopeful attitudes help in preventing

Alzheimer's disease, and can aid as a remedy for those in the first stages of it.

In 1973, when I was in the junior year of High School, the school play was the musical, "South Pacific" by Rogers and Hammerstein, whom I consider two true geniuses. My favorite song was entitled "The Cockeyed Optimist," which was sung by the leading character, named Nellie Forbush, a nurse from Little Rock, Arkansas. The tune was bouncy and upbeat and the lyrics made a great impression on me. In it, Nellie sang that when she sees the sky a bright canary yellow color, she couldn't recall ever having seen a cloud. Even though others may be pessimistic, and go on and on how bad the world had become, she refuses to buy into that negativity, and remains an incurable optimist. She concludes by singing that although some may think her a dope, she refuses to get rid of hope. It is firmly planted in her heart, and staying there, right alongside her optimism.

To this day, if I am driving the car and it is sunset, or serving as the chaplain on a cruise ship, and take a few well spent minutes to watch the magnificent sunsets at sea, when the yellow appears in the sky, I cannot help but think of Nellie's song.

A positive and optimistic attitude should be the hallmark of a Christian. For years, we have been told to carry our crosses cheerfully, and this is how we are to do it. I remember hearing an analogy about a duck that seems to glide gracefully in the water, but underneath the water, those webbed feet are paddling away, but you cannot tell.

As the pastor of a parish, I believe that it is integral to try one's best to be a loving father of a family, with the staff as well as the flock. We are to "Put on Christ," (Rom. 13:4) and be His ambassadors, not only while at the altar, but even more importantly away from it, so that people will realize that we are "Real and not Memorex." Over the years, I have tried my best to cultivate a friendly atmosphere, and ask how the employees' weekend went and how their families are, especially if there is a sick member. We all need to be warm, nurturing and caring, and do so genuinely, trying to build up a good rapport. There is nothing worse than working in an atmosphere of tension, animosity or adversity.

I once went out to lunch with a friend and all I heard from him were complaints from start to finish. I recalled the words from the Book of Proverbs as I was driving home, and began to get a bit of a tummy ache, because eating with stress is not good. This is why the Scriptures tell us, "Better a dish of herbs where love is, than a fatted ox and hatred with it" (Prov. 15:17). When I continue to deal with that person, and whenever he begins to talk negatively, I try to say something like, "But just think of all the blessings you have received!"

When dealing with people who are always critical or complaining, I cannot help but recall the words that are attributed to the 16th President of the U.S.A, Abraham Lincoln, (1809-1865) who stated, "It has been my observation that people are just about as happy, as they make up their minds to be."

We read in the writings of St. Paul, "If God is for us, who can be against us" (Rom. 8:31)? This is just a few verses after one of my all time favorites quotes from Sacred Scripture, "For those who love God, all things work unto good" (Rom. 8:28). If we have God on our side, then we are in good company, and He will get us through every circumstance and help us to carry our crosses. Sacred Scripture tells us, "Our help comes from the Lord, Who made heaven and earth" (Ps. 121:2). Several years ago, a promotional brochure from a private school arrived in the mail. I was happy to take note of the school motto that was part of the coat-of-arms; it read, *"Deo Adjuvante Non Timendum"* which translates as, "With the help of God, we need not fear."

I believe that we need to cultivate a positive attitude, and trust in His mercy and goodness, in spite of all that we have to endure. All of our problems will be solved, if we bring them to the Lord with trusting faith. If it entails pain, the Lord will accompany us in that too, if we unite our sufferings to Him, and not abandon Him in times of peril. He is our only hope, and the solution for all our needs. I recall the response of St. Peter to the Lord, "Jesus then said to the Twelve, 'Do you also want to leave?' Simon Peter answered him, 'Master, to whom shall we go? You have the words of eternal life. We have come to believe and are convinced that You are the Holy One of God'" (Jn. 6:67-69).

To sulk and complain helps nothing or nobody, especially our-selves and our attitude, it just serves to bring us down even more. We have to lift ourselves up by the bootstraps, and move on. The best medicine they say is laughter, and right alongside of it, I believe, is exercise. Even though one cannot afford a membership at a gym or sports club or the like, the best thing is to take a brisk walk for 15-20 minutes daily. It is good to let those beautiful chemicals that the human body produces, like endorphins and serotonins kick in, as to give us a physical and mental boost.

Activity helps to relieve the mind of stress. It has been said that stress can be a killer. The more I read about it, the more I see how true that statement is. Stress affects us emotionally, relationally, spir-itually and physically. When we are stressed, our immune system weakens and we are more susceptible to illnesses as well. The Book of Proverbs tells us, "A tranquil mind gives life to the flesh, but pas-sion makes the bones rot" (Prov. 14:30). If we are having difficulty with another person, we are to approach them in a charitable manner to discuss it, so it does not eat at us inside. Even Jesus told us that if you have a problem with your brother to "Go and tell him his fault, between you and him alone" (Mt. 18:15). There is an expression I once heard from my friend Marlane, "Say what you mean, mean what you say, but do not say it mean."

Christians are to be peacemakers and not troublemakers. I truly believe that we should even try to be pleasant and kind to all, espe-cially those who can be troublesome or have spoken ill of us, or even betrayed us. We are to return good for evil and blessings for curses, even though it may be against what we are feeling inside. Hatred is not a valid option for a Christian, since we hear that, "Love conquers all," or as the Latin adage goes, *"Omnia Vincit Amor."* Blessed Pope John XXIII wrote, "Whoever has a heart full of love always has something to give." In this case, one needs to give the gift of forgiveness to those who have wronged them.

This is what the Lord tells us to do, "But I say to you, love your enemies, and pray for those who persecute you" (Mt. 5:44). Perhaps the best reference to this is given to us by St. Paul, "If your enemy is hungry, feed him; if he is thirsty, give him something to drink; for by so doing you will heap burning coals upon his head. Do not be conquered by evil but conquer evil with good" (Rom. 12:20-21).

The Lord Jesus Christ has given us what has been called the "Blueprint for Christian Living" in the Beatitudes, "Blessed are the poor in Spirit..." as recorded in the Gospels (Mt. 5:3-10, Lk. 6:20-23). The characteristics and attitudes that Jesus spoke about in the Sermon on the Mount, such as being meek and merciful, as well as being a peacemaker, were spoken of many centuries earlier by the Prophet Micah: "You have been told, O man, what is good, and what the Lord requires of you: Only to do the right, and to love goodness, and to walk humbly with your God" (Micah 6:8).

Over the years, I have heard that we are to live in the presence of God throughout the day, not just when we pick up the prayer book, and I have often tried to mention this in my preaching. When we are in the supermarket and there is a snag or price check at the check-out line, we can use that extra time constructively. We need not huff and puff and get annoyed, but can use those few minutes to unite ourselves to the Lord Jesus and His Mother Mary.

We can pray a decade of the Rosary, even using one's fingers to count the prayers. It is all about our outlook or our attitude. I have recommended the "Five Finger Prayer" to sanctify waiting time, and use it positively instead of getting irritated. I do this all the time, and all that one needs to do is use the fingers on one of your hands,

> *The thumb – it is nearest to you and you pray for those closest to you, your loved ones, both living and deceased. They are the easiest to remember as we hold them close to our hearts.*
>
> *The pointing finger – pray for those who point the way, such as doctors and teachers, may they point others in the right direction. Ask the Lord to give them wisdom to guide others in the right path.*
>
> *The index or middle finger – the tallest one and we pray for leaders, the Pope, President, leaders*

*in industry and all those who guide the nation and world. They need the guidance of the Lord*

*The ring finger – our weakest finger, as a piano teacher can tell you. We pray for the weakest, those who are in pain or troubled and in particular for the dying, that the Lord will be merciful to them.*

*The pinkie, the smallest finger – we pray for ourselves, as a child of God. We have seen the needs of others and now, in proper perspective, our own will seem so small.*

I once heard an expression regarding our attitude from a wonderful Dominican sister in my formation program in the Seminary in 1977, Sr. Carmel, O.P., who told me, "Matty, what happens to us is 10 percent of the situation, and how we react to it is the other 90 percent." Actually in writing these reflections, I came across a quote just by accident that predates my very dear friend, Sister Carmel by "just a bit." It is by the ancient Greek author, Epititus, who wrote, "We cannot choose our circumstances, but how we respond to them." That short expression has certainly helped me to put things in proper perspective, and hopefully by sharing it, has helped others as well, over the decades.

The famous Austrian author, Viktor Frankl, (1905-1997) was a Holocaust survivor and prisoner in a Concentration Camp during the Second World War. He wrote a book in 1946, entitled, *Man's Search for Meaning.* In it, he wrote how one needs to choose one's attitude and gave, as an example, those whose attitude helped them survive the horrific ordeal of imprisonment.

Over the years, I also recall hearing the expression, "Let our troubles make us better, and not bitter." There is another quote that resurfaces in my memory from time to time, "Let us turn our scars into stars, and our pains into gains." These quotes have definitely inspired me over the years, and have helped many others too. They are pithy aids to help us to overcome obstacles, and to put the pains and hurts we have experienced in the past, and move on better, for having gotten through them.

Our call is to die to self, and live in Christ, and to seek to perfect ourselves. The Lord Jesus Christ invites us to, "Be perfect as your heavenly Father is perfect" (Mt. 5:48). May we grow in trusting faith, knowing that the perfecting of our spiritual growth is the work of the Lord for us, and that we are in His very capable hands.

A few years ago, I attended a Retreat for Priests, and after five days of wonderful talks there was one expression that really hit home for me. The retreat master, who was a priest, told us of the habit of St. Jose Maria Escrivá, (1902-1975) who, whenever he visited the Basilica of St. Peter in Rome, would go to the tomb of St. Peter, and pray the Creed and after it would add in Spanish *"Credo, al pesar de todo"* meaning "I believe, in spite of it all." We have to remember that no matter how tough things may appear, the Lord can and will get us through it all, if we bring all our needs and pains to Him. We hear in Scripture, "For nothing will be impossible for God" (Lk. 1:37, Mt. 17:20).

May a positive attitude help us to have positive thoughts. Our thoughts lead to our desires, and our desires lead to our actions. Then our actions lead to our habits, which lead to our character. Our character leads to our destiny. If we are positive and we think the right thoughts and do the right things, then we will not allow negativity to enter. We will be seen as a loving, kind and Christ-like person by others, and give good example to them as well. May we try our best to do what is pleasing in the sight of the Lord, which will lead us on the righteous paths and fulfill our destiny. Our destination, as pilgrims on this earth, is to be joined forever with the Lord in the kingdom of heaven.

# Compassion

The word compassion comes from two Latin words, *"Cum,"* meaning "With" and *"Passio"* meaning "Suffering." This word reminds us of the sufferings that the Lord endured on Good Friday, which we call Jesus' "Passion." Compassion is when you suffer along with someone else; you are sympathetic to another, amid their pain and sorrow. You put yourself in their shoes, at a difficult time in their lives.

As I frequently say, we are called to "Be peacemakers, not trouble makers." I have used this expression in my various parishes, when I sense there may be tension and a few inappropriate comments are beginning to surface. Peacemakers must first have peace inside themselves. The peace that Christ alone can give as we hear the Lord tell us, "Peace I leave with you; My peace I give to you. Not as the world gives, do I give to you. Let not your hearts be troubled, neither let them be afraid" (Jn. 14:27).

In mid-October 2007, I had my gallbladder removed. There were some complications and my recovery was somewhat longer than I expected. After about six weeks, I finally was back to normal. The day after Thanksgiving is called "Black Friday," as many know, since there is a lot of pre-Christmas shopping on that day, and the stores that are "In the red" make their profits and go "In the black."

As things would have it, I got up that morning and was "bright eyed and bushy-tailed" as the expression goes, and after the surgery and recovery, I was back to the top of my game, thank God! Maybe it was the tryptophan in the turkey in the Thanksgiving meal the day before, which had given me that final push. It was a beautiful, crisp autumn day, so I went to the pool at the local gym for a swim, to get some exercise; it was my first time back there since before the surgery.

Then I had planned to go to the tailor, to pick up an alteration. I kept thinking to myself, thanks be to God, how wonderful I'm feeling: I went back to swimming, am doing my errands, do not feel weak or tired; I am finally better since that October 16ᵗʰ surgery. However, as I continued driving on the road, just a few minutes later, with the wet bathing suit in the trunk and all, there was a seat belt check, and I saw the police officer who was doing it, and came to a stop.

Apparently, the driver behind me did not see the police officer, and plowed into my car at about 30 miles an hour, pushing me into the car in front of me. That person's airbag even went off. My car was "totaled" and I was banged up and shaken up quite a bit, as was the driver behind me. The police were standing right there and witnessed the whole thing, since they were nearby my car, doing the seat belt checks. After I got out of the car, I went up to the driver, who had hit my car, and gave them a hug saying, "These things happen, let's just thank God that we were not injured or worse." I just felt in my heart that was the right thing to do.

The policemen came up to us and asked, "Do you know each other?" I responded that we did not, but I just wanted to assure the other driver that we will get through this. It was just another "Bad blip on the radar screen," and it would not be the first or the last. There is an expression, "That which does not kill you, will make you stronger" and I truly believe this applies on all levels, physically, along with mentally and spiritually.

My rationale was, what good would there have been in getting upset, angry and start making a big fuss? It would just make a bad situation even worse, and it would not help or change anything. The damage was done and could not be changed. Cars are just cars, and can be replaced, but thank God, there was no death or serious injury. It did not hurt to be compassionate and kind, even if it was to the person who did damage to my car and me. St. John of the Cross wrote, "Who has ever seen people persuaded to love God by harshness? Where there is no love, put love and you will find love." Our dear Lord Jesus said it best, when He gave us what is now called the "Golden Rule" which is, "Do to others as you would have them do to you" (Lk. 6:31).

St. Francis de Sales is quoted as saying, "You attract more flies with one drop of honey, than with a gallon of vinegar!" We also read from the beloved disciple, St. John, "God is love, and he who abides in love abides in God, and God abides in him" (I Jn. 4:8). This was the theme of the first encyclical of Pope Benedict XVI, *"Deus Caritas Est,"* (God is Love) that was promulgated on December 25,

2005, and I had just finished reading it again, during my recovery after surgery.

The other person's frown soon became just the slightest smile, perhaps they felt reassured that I was not unduly angry or upset. Of course, I was certainly not happy at all about the accident, just as the next person would not be, but it was an opportunity, given to me by the Lord, to be a peacemaker and not a troublemaker, and to practice what I preach.

Looking back on the accident, I cannot help but think of two events in the lives of the several saints. The first event involved St. Jose Maria Escrivá who was canonized in 2002. There is a story that one day he was traveling, and when he was getting into the car, his hand got caught in the door, when someone else shut it. Since it was badly hurt, those all around him were quite concerned that the Father Founder of their religious community had been seriously injured. They all waited to see if he would reprimand the person who shut the door on his hand. Instead he said, "Thank You, Lord, for this sharing in Your sufferings."

When I first heard that story, I thought that "only a saint" could have such a response, and that is why they are saints. If we strive to be saints too, that is, get to heaven, we need to have the same mindset as they did, and let a response such as his come from our lips too. The second event is when St. Teresa of Avila was once getting out of a carriage, after visiting a convent and she fell in the mud. She looked upward and said, "Lord, if this is how You treat Your friends, no wonder You have so few!"

Being compassionate to others also helps us. It can lift us up out of our own difficulties, when we put the needs of others before our own. The Greek philosopher, Aeschylus (525-456 BC) wrote, "Especially in times of darkness, that is the time to love, that an act of love might tip the balance."

By being compassionate and serving as the instruments of the mercy of the Lord, we not only grow in God's grace by choosing the holier path, but we can get into good habits, that build our character. In tough times, whether our own, or in the difficulties of others, we can show our character, whether we are a compassionate, caring and forgiving person or a bitter, miserable and vindictive one.

Many recall that the late and beautiful Princess Diana (1961-1997) was very involved in charities of many sorts, throughout her short life. I recall a poem that she quoted, although she was not the author. It speaks of being compassionate to those who have a burden or cross, as well as being strong and courageous when you have to carry your own. It was written by the Australian poet, Adam Lindsay Gordon, and was first published in 1867,

*Life is mostly froth and bubble,*
*Two things stand like stone,*
*Kindness in another's trouble,*
*Courage in your own.*

These two quotes from Sacred Scripture, "By their fruits you will know them" (Mt. 7:20) and "The things that come out of the mouth come from the heart" (Mt. 15:18) are reminders that we are Christ's ambassadors as Christians; our words and actions should be in accord with this high calling.

By our Baptism, we were conformed to Him; we are honored to be sons and daughters of the King of Kings. There is a French expression that the aristocracy used, *"Noblesse oblige,"* which means "Nobility obliges," and it was generally used to imply that along with nobility, wealth, power and prestige, also comes the responsibility to act in the appropriate manner. For us Christians, it means that we are obligated to live according to our high calling, as children of God and co-heirs of the kingdom of heaven.

# Prayer

The best way to stay in touch with your best friends is by communicating with them. So it is with the Lord Jesus Christ. We want to draw closer to Him and participate in His Divine Life of grace. *The Imitation of Christ* tells us, "In life and death, keep yourself close to Jesus and entrust yourself to His fidelity, Who alone can help you when all others fail" (Bk. 2, ch. 6). We have a divine promise from Our Lord Himself, which reminds us of that intimate union with Him, that is possible throughout our lives. He tells us, "Whoever loves Me, will keep My word, and My Father will love him, and We will come to him and make Our dwelling with him" (Jn. 14:23).

The very best means to achieve this is through a life of prayer. St. Teresa of Avila said that "Prayer is a close sharing between friends, to be alone with Him who loves us." Prayer is defined by St. John Damascene, (676-754) as the "Lifting up of the heart and mind to God." The Lord Jesus invites us to live in His friendship and love. He tells us, "Come to Me." (Mt. 11:28) and "He who remains in Me, and I in him will bear much fruit" (Jn. 15:5). Unfortunately, there are too many people who see prayer as a parachute waiting in the cockpit of a plane; it is nice to know that it is there and only to be used in emergencies! There is that old saying, "There are no atheists in a foxhole," but why wait till then, the direst of circumstances, to pray?

Prayer is not just about piety and devotions, but it is a real relationship with the Lord. We speak to Jesus from our hearts. Just like anything worthwhile, such as our families, health or careers, one reaps what one sows. The more you invest, the better the return. Mental prayer, humility and purity are the ingredients that help us to grow in holiness. There can be no virtue and holiness without purity, the saints remind us. St. John Vianney tells us, "God does not require of us martyrdom of the body; but only the martyrdom of the heart and will." We are called to die to ourselves and "Put on the new self, created in God's way, in righteousness and holiness of truth" (Eph. 4:24).

I had a former pastor who used to medicate his diabetes with chocolate cake, which was not good for his illness, and led to increased health problems and suffering for him. We get out what we put in. The same is true with our relationship with the Lord. Prayer brings us inner peace, and brings us back to the center of things, in our interior spiritual lives.

We need to spend time with the Lord, and not do all the talking. He will inspire us and give us the answers in our hearts. We are to ask Him to help us see ourselves as He sees us, and as we truly are, and not have spiritual blindness. St. Teresa of Avila said, "All I need is a place to be alone and look within." The well-loved saint, St. Padre Pio, gives us an insight into his own prayer life, when he tells us, "You must speak to Jesus, not only with your lips, but with your heart, and on certain occasions, only with your heart."

When I served as a priest in Puerto Rico, I learned that there was an elderly Capuchin priest in a nearby parish, who, as a young man, had lived in a monastery in Bavaria with St. Conrad of Parzham (1818-1894). This saint was a Capuchin Franciscan Brother, and after his religious profession, was sent to the Convent of St. Anne in the city of Altötting, well known for its Shrine of the Mother of Mercy. Brother Conrad was given the position of porter at this shrine, and retained it until his death. Since there were many people in this city, the duty of the porter at that place was a very difficult job.

However, he was diligent at his work, kind in his words, helped the poor and strangers. Brother Conrad fulfilled the task of porter for more than 40 years, assisting the inhabitants in their needs of body and soul. He was canonized in 1934. A parishioner had asked the priest, who was working in Puerto Rico, what it was like to live with a saint. His response was, "He prayed too much, and was always in the chapel, I hardly ever saw him." To me, it seemed like St. Conrad reaped what he had sowed: by prayer one grows in holiness, and through holiness, one becomes a saint.

We can also aid our prayers by fasting, as it helps to add an important dimension to our prayer life. Of course, it should always be regulated, so as to avoid any physical harm. However, acts such as limiting food and drink can heighten our alertness and awareness before the Lord during our prayer. Some of us know how sluggish we can feel after we overdo it with either food or drink. However, true fasting is not just a matter of reducing our diet, it is spiritual, as well as physical, and is a means to help us be converted in heart and will, to draw closer to the Lord.

St. John Chrysostom, (347-407) the Archbishop of Constantinople and an early Father of the Church, wrote this on fasting, "It means not only abstinence from food but from sins. The fast should be kept not only by the mouth alone, but also by the ear, the eye, the feet, the hands and all the members of the body" (Homily 3 on Statutes).

St. Basil the Great, (c. 330-397) Bishop of Caesarea, in Cappadocia in Asia Minor, what is now Turkey, wrote that it is useless to fast from food if one is critical of his neighbor, "You do not eat meat, but you devour your brother." In the Gospels, we read that the devil is cast out, not by prayer alone, but by "Prayer and fasting" (Mt. 17:21, Mk. 9:29) and we learn that the early Christians also "Fasted and prayed" (Acts. 13:3).

Prayer and fasting is best accompanied by almsgiving. This is love for others, which is expressed in a practical form through acts of charity, forgiveness, mercy and compassion. We need not give only of our money, not just what we materially have, but give from our hearts. Acts of mercy and charity, done for the love of the Lord and others, can give us the opportunity to be Christ-like, and grow in virtue and holiness. There is a touching story about Blessed Mother Theresa. One day, she encountered a dying non-Christian leper, on the streets of Calcutta. She asked him, "Do you want to be saved by Christ?" to which he responded, "Who is Christ, is He like you?" Mother Theresa answered by saying, "No, but I try to be like Him."

The Catechism of the Catholic Church devotes the fourth and final section to Christian prayer, and traces prayer through the Old Testament, through the Gospels, as well as the liturgical life of the church. There are various expressions of prayer: vocal, meditative and contemplative. The Lord's Prayer, "Our Father" is described in the Catechism as the "Summary of the Gospel" and each of the seven petitions is explained in detail. In my own understanding of prayer, I believe that there are four principle components of prayer, which can best be remembered with the word, "ACTS."

The letter "A" stands for "*Adoration*." During the Holy Mass, we express this when we pray together the hymn of praise called the

"Gloria." In it, we pray, "We worship You, we give You thanks, we praise You for Your glory." This is during the Opening Rites of Holy Mass, so we begin our prayer with the acknowledgement of God's majesty. He is the Creator, and we are His holy people who were redeemed by the Blood of the Lamb, and we humbly bow before Him in adoration. It is an opportunity to place ourselves in proper position with the Lord for "In Him we live and breathe and have our being" (Acts 17:28). Otherwise, we are like "dead men walking," without His life of grace within us.

The letter "C" stands for "*Contrition.*" Just as at Holy Mass, we have the Penitential Rite in which we acknowledge our sins, so too, in personal prayer, we remember our faults and ask the Lord's mercy upon us. The psalmist tells us "God does not spurn a broken, humbled heart" (Ps. 51:19). We also know that it is the Lord's Will that we be holy and sanctified. We ask His assistance, to do our very best, to make the right choices hereafter. May we be vigilant, and do nothing to separate ourselves from His life of grace within our souls.

The letter "T" stands for "*Thanksgiving.*" We look upon the goodness of the Lord to each of us in the past, and we raise up our hearts, minds and voices in gratitude for His abundant blessings. The Greek word for thanksgiving is "*Eucharistein.*" The first words of the Roman Canon begin, "We come to you, Father, with praise and thanksgiving through Jesus Christ, Your Son..." There are many opportunities to be thankful, just to realize that the Lord has allowed us to live another day, and be grateful for that opportunity to continue to glorify Him.

The letter "S" stands for "*Supplication.*" This is when we ask the Lord to hear our needs and petitions. The Lord Jesus tells us, "Ask and it will be given to you, seek and you shall find, knock and the door will be opened to you" (Mt. 7:7). The Lord Jesus also assures us, "Therefore I tell you, all that you ask for in prayer, believe that you will receive it, and it shall be yours" (Mk. 11:24, Lk. 11:9, Jn. 16:24). Regrettably, many times we or others might tend to skip over the first few steps of prayer, which are adoration, contrition and thanksgiving, and we jump right to the last step, that of supplication, asking the Lord for His help in all our needs.

Many people have expressed the desire to pray, but do not find the time to do so. The Carmelite religious, the Servant of God, Sister Lucia dos Santos, one of the three visionaries of Our Lady of Fatima in Portugal in 1917, some years later wrote a beautiful letter to her nephew, Fr. Valinho, who was a Salesian priest. In it, she explained to him the importance of finding time for prayer. He gave permission for the letter to be translated and distributed among priests and religious in 1971, in order to help them in their spiritual lives through Sr. Lucia's recommendations. She wrote,

> "Let time be lacking for everything else, but never for prayer and you will experience the fact that after prayer, you can accomplish a lot in a short period of time. I recommend, above all, that you get close to the tabernacle and pray. In fervent prayer, you will receive the light, strength and grace that you need to sustain you and share with others. In prayer, you will find more knowledge, more grace and virtue than you could ever achieve by reading many books."

It is prayer that is the life of the soul. Just as food helps our bodies to grow and flourish, so too, prayer helps us grow in grace and nourishes our interior lives. The only difference is that one can never overdo it with prayer, like with nourishment. It is impossible to "overdose" on holiness and grace. They are the elements that can best fortify us against the attacks of the evil one, and prayer helps us in our goal to "Seek first the kingdom of God" (Mt. 6:33). Since we ask the Lord for so many favors when it comes to the natural world, our health and well-being and that of those we love, we also need to ask the Lord for His generosity in granting us an abundance of grace to help us "Persevere in prayer" (Rom. 12:12).

In November 1991, my sister Suzanne and her husband Pino, which is the nickname for Giuseppe or Joseph, had their first daughter, my niece Francesca. Just over a year later, in December 1992, my nephew Stephen was born. The day of his baptism was just about one year after that of his sister. Shortly after the ceremony, I jokingly made a comment to my brother-in-law and asked if "The baptism of a new baby was going to be an annual event?" His answer made quite an impression upon me, when he responded, "Let us not limit God's generosity." In the same way, let us ask the Lord to be generous to us, but not only with material things. The Lord tells us,

> "Do not store up for yourselves treasures on earth, where moth and decay destroy, and thieves break in and steal. But store up treasures in heaven, where neither moth nor decay destroys, nor thieves break in and steal. For where your treasure is, there also will your heart be" (Mt. 6:19-21, Lk. 12:34).

The way that we store up treasures in heaven is by trying to lead a dedicated life of prayer. In this way, when the difficulties and crosses in life come our way, as they do from time to time, we will be strong with the Lord. We will have built our interior lives on firm rock, anchored firmly to the Lord Jesus, Who will sustain us when difficulties could otherwise make us sink or lose hope. We recall the words of the Lord,

> "Build your home on solid rock. A wise man who built his house on rock, the rain fell, the floods came, and the winds blew and buffeted the house. But it did not collapse; it had been set solidly on rock. And everyone who listens to these words of Mine, but does not act on them, will be like a fool who built his house on sand. The rain fell, the floods came, and the winds blew and buffeted the house. And it collapsed and was completely ruined" (Mt. 7:24-27).

There is the story of St. Thomas More, who was imprisoned in the Tower of London, during the reign of King Henry VIII. He accepted this, and, in fact, gave his all, for something beyond himself, to uphold the decision of the Holy Father and the Church, over the desires of the monarch. While in the Tower, he turned his cell of imprisonment into a cell of prayer. He prayed, "Help me be content to be solitary, thinking about God, and leaning on His comfort." This reminds me of those who are given the news that their own illness, or that of someone dear to them, has no possibility for recovery. Rather than become bitter, they can find their comfort in the Lord by drawing closer to Him through prayer. St. Paul wrote, "Nothing can outweigh the supreme advantage of knowing Jesus Christ" (Phil. 13:8).

The author, Alfred Lord Tennyson, (1799-1892) wrote that "More things are wrought by prayer" than by anything else. He also wrote "Man is never so tall, as when he is on his knees." The United States President, Abraham Lincoln commented on the importance of prayer in his own life and said, "When my own wisdom is insufficient, I am brought to my knees."

A life of prayer gives us the strength from the Lord. If we ask with trusting faith, He will sustain us, and grant us the many graces that we need to persevere in leading a holy life, even with the ups and downs, joys and sorrows that come to us. A holy and prayerful life is the best means to attain our ultimate goal, which is to live in the friendship of the Lord Jesus in this world and forever in the mansion, prepared for us in the kingdom of heaven.

# 8

# J.M.J.L.

## Lucy

The letters above stand for Jesus, Mary, Joseph and Lucy. Since I was in the First grade at St. Joseph School, East Orange, New Jersey in 1962, we students were instructed to put these four initials on the top of each of our homework assignments and tests. Everyone knows who Jesus, Mary and Joseph are, and there is much more about them in this book, for sure.

The initial "L" represents the word Lucy, and refers to St. Lucy Filippini (1672-1732). She was the Foundress of the Religious Teachers Filippini, which was the order of sisters that taught us at that school. She had been a very dedicated catechist in the town of Montefisascone, in the area above Rome, Italy. The bishop at that time was the Venerable Cardinal Marc Antonio Barbarigo, (1640-1706) who was impressed by St. Lucy's dedication. Together, they collaborated in founding an institute of women who consecrated their lives to the service of the Lord as teachers.

When there was an influx of Italian immigrants to the United States, this religious community was invited to teach in the parochial schools here, and arrived in August 1910. With the help of Bishop Thomas J. Walsh of Trenton, NJ, who later became the first Archbishop of Newark, the order grew and flourished on both sides of the Atlantic Ocean and even began missions in Brazil and elsewhere.

While some people have related that they have unpleasant memories of the religious sisters that taught them, I honestly can say that I do not. They were somewhat strict, but then my parents were as well. Some recall being hit by the good sisters with the ruler, but I guess that I had behaved myself, since I never got that treatment. However, what I do vividly recall occurred at Holy Mass for the First Friday of the month. When the sisters were preparing to receive Holy Communion, they would flip up a larger outer black satin hood, called the *"Cuffietto"* over their smaller bonnets, the *"Cuffino"* which were the headpieces of their habits, rather than veils.

After they received Our Lord in Holy Communion, the sisters would then kneel with their two hands covering their faces, and it seemed as if they were totally alone with the Lord Jesus, Whom they had just received as the welcome Guest in their soul. They were in deep conversation with the Lord. I believe that is where they received the strength that they needed to get through each day, and to deal with all of us students, some of whom could be somewhat cantankerous, to say the least!

By the time I graduated from the eighth grade in 1970, those religious habits and bonnets had been modified, after the Second Vatican Council (1962-1965). I truly thank the Lord, with all my heart, for those formative years, and to be associated with those dedicated women of God. As well, I greatly admired the parish priests, and was happy to serve as an altar boy after I received my First Holy Communion in May 1964.

Over the years, I would enjoy visiting the Provincial headquarters of the sisters, called Villa Walsh, in Morristown, New Jersey. The chapel was just beautiful, and decorated in Baroque style, and one felt transported right to a magnificent Basilica in Italy. Over the years, I got to know some of the sisters there, and would visit the elderly sisters in the Infirmary, some of whom had been my teachers. On one visit, before my ordination, I met Sister Rose Fralliacardi, M.P.F. She was living there in retirement, at what the sisters referred to as the "Mother House." Sister had taught Grammar School for many years, and now had taken up oil painting as a hobby. She really painted beautifully, and I admired her work.

After I was ordained to the Holy Priesthood in 1988, I had the opportunity to return to Villa Walsh to offer Holy Mass for the sisters. On that occasion, Sr. Rose presented me with one of her paintings, as an Ordination gift. It was not her usual subjects of flowers and roses, but rather, a lighthouse. She told me something very profound, and in very simple language, just as if she was still a grammar school teacher, who was giving instructions to one of her students, "You are a priest now. You must be a beacon to bring the light of Christ to others, who are in darkness. Just like the ships get tossed around in the rough seas, you are to help guide them to arrive safely into the harbor which is heaven."

Years later, when I was traveling to Italy, I had the opportunity to visit the beautiful hill town of Montefiascione, and went to the crypt of the Cathedral of Santa Margarita to offer a prayer at the tomb of Mother Foundress, as she is called. In particular, I prayed for all the dedicated sisters, who taught me over the years, and whose good example had an influence in my vocation to serve the Lord. May the goodness of the Lord and His mercy be on all of them, who have served Him and His flock so faithfully, and may they be with the Lord, and receive the reward for their labors in the kingdom of heaven.

# Joseph

The second initial, "J" in the heading on our test papers, stands for St. Joseph. He was chosen by the Heavenly Father to be the spouse of the Blessed Virgin Mary, and the foster father of the Lord Jesus Christ. St. Joseph always has had a very special place in my heart, since it was there, at St. Joseph Church, that my parents were married and I was baptized on November 4, 1956, and received the other Sacraments of Initiation. After my Ordination, I also returned to there to offer my First Solemn Mass of Thanksgiving.

The annual feast of St. Joseph, which is celebrated on March 19, was always a time of great celebration in our parish, with the nine-day Novena, which concluded with a Solemn Mass, in honor of the patron saint of the parish. This was followed by a big banquet, called the St. Joseph Dinner. The members of the parish would be busy for the entire week prior, to prepare food, and to set up the tables and chairs in the school gymnasium. Over the years, I also helped in the preparations as well, my specialty became frying the eggplant for the dinner. It would always be an exciting and joyful time, when the vibrant parish family would come together, in great happiness and solemnity, to celebrate its Patronal feast day. It made a very positive impression upon me, and inspired me with the wonderful fellowship that I witnessed between the priest and his people.

Over the years, I had the opportunity to learn more about St. Joseph. He is the patron of the Universal Church, having been given this title by Blessed Pope Pius IX (1792-1868). He also is the patron of fatherhood and purity, and also is invoked as the patron of a happy death. Since St. Joseph is not mentioned in the Gospel accounts throughout the public life of Our Lord, the tradition, throughout the centuries, has been that he died while Jesus was still at the house in Nazareth. The death of St. Joseph has been considered the most beautiful death possible, to leave this world in the presence of both Jesus and Mary at one's side.

This is the way we hope that one day we will end our own earthly pilgrimages, in the friendship of the Lord and His mother, Mary. Ever since the day of my very First Mass as a priest, I have always included St. Joseph's name in the Eucharistic Prayer, right after that of Mary, and done so, with the deliberate intention that my family and myself, as well as those entrusted to my care, would have a holy and prepared death through his intercession.

Unfortunately, throughout the centuries, St. Joseph has been shown to be an old man in paintings and statues. I truly hope this is not the case, but that the Lord God had chosen a vibrant young man to care for His Son. I believe the reason for this depiction as elderly in art, is that he was usually shown as seated and sleeping in the corner of the stable of Bethlehem. This may have given the impression that he was aged and tired, but it may not really be true.

Rather, this is because St. Joseph received several messages through the angel of the Lord, appearing to him in dreams. He was told in a dream not to fear in taking Mary as his wife as "The child she was carrying was through the power of the Holy Spirit" (Mt. 1:24). Again, after the birth of the Lord, the angel again warned him in a dream to flee since "Herod was out to destroy the child" (Mt. 2:13). Finally, the angel told him again in a dream that it was time to return to Israel (Mt. 2:20). In these cases, St. Joseph awoke and did as the angel had instructed him.

I have always been impressed by the wonderful promptness of St. Joseph in fulfilling God's Will. When he was told, "Rise and take the Child and His mother..." we hear that he rose and did so (Mt. 2:20-21). Throughout the four Gospels, we do not have a record of anything that St. Joseph said. He is considered the "Silent saint," whose actions of obedience and fidelity to the plan of God, spoke louder than words.

This reminds me of two expressions, when I was growing up. The first of these I heard from my Mom who would tell me, "Keep your eyes open, your ears open and your mouth shut!" It was a way of saying: observe and listen before you comment, and has served as good advice over the years. The second expression is from the well-loved, St. Francis of Assisi, who told his followers, "Preach the Gospel always, when necessary, use words!"

Over the years, I have come to see this as the way we are to lead our lives, as messengers of the Gospel by our Christ-like actions. We should be like transparent lamps, so that the light of Christ can shine through us by what we say and do. By this, we can be instruments of the Lord's peace, mercy and compassion to others and walk together faithfully in this life, in the friendship of the Lord, with our eyes fixed on the goal to be with Him forever in the kingdom of heaven.

# Mary

The letter "M" in the heading that we students learned stands for Mary, the Blessed Mother of Jesus Christ. She is our spiritual mother through our Baptism, since we become members of the Mystical Body of Christ. Some of my earliest recollections of the Blessed Mother in my early life come from my grammar school days. I recall that when the month of May was nearing, Sr. Mary Strazzieri, M.P.F., my first grade teacher, prepared a special table with light blue crepe paper and this fabric that looked like clouds. I later learned it was called tulle, a lightweight and very fine netting. On May first, the statue of Mary was placed on the table, and we students had all been asked to bring flowers to school that day, to decorate the altar and honor the Blessed Mother. A similar May altar was set up each year, to honor Mary in her special month, throughout my grammar school years.

Like years gone by, I still look forward to the month of May each year, knowing that it is Mary's month, the month that the spring flowers arrive after April showers, as the familiar rhyme reminds us. Although my understanding of the attributes and privileges of the Blessed Virgin Mary has developed over the years, due to my theological studies, I think it is important for us to still cultivate that childlike love for Our Lady, and have tried to do so.

In the autumn of 1977, I attended Sunday Mass at the beautiful Cathedral of the Sacred Heart in Newark, NJ, which, since then, has been elevated to the rank of a Minor Basilica. The homilist was the well-known preacher, the Servant of God, Archbishop Fulton J. Sheen, who was a brilliant man and a true genius, and whose cause for beatification was initiated in 2002. The celebrant of the Holy Mass was Bishop Joseph A. Costello, an auxiliary bishop and a man of kindness and holiness.

At the end of the Mass, prior to the dismissal, Bishop Costello addressed few remarks to the congregation, and as he concluded, directed his last comments to the guest homilist. He thanked Archbishop Sheen for his wonderful words, and then closed by telling him, "May our dear Lord bless you, and may our Blessed Mother tenderly smile upon you." Those sweet and touching words have made a lasting impression upon me, to this very day. I truly hope that this is how my own childlike and filial love for Mary should be. It is a good thing to place ourselves under her loving mantle, serve her and her Son the very best we can, and thereby please her. In this way, she may "tenderly smile" upon us as well. It has been my hope this might be the sentiment of many: to do what is pleasing to Mary, so that she can be pleased with us, and our efforts in glorifying her Son. We can best please her by being faithful to her Son, since Jesus tells us, "If you love Me, keep My commandments" (Jn. 14:15).

I once heard a talk given by, the now deceased, Jaime Cardinal Sin, (1928-2005) Archbishop of Manila. It was televised from one of the conferences that he gave to a Retreat for Priests in Rome. His topic was the Blessed Virgin Mary, and he explained Mary's role in our lives by using the five letters in the word "*Maria*," the name of Mary in Latin. Over the years, I have used the idea of these five points, when I have been asked to give a reflection on the Blessed Virgin Mary, and I believe that it would be good to reiterate them here.

The letter "M" stands for "*Mater*," Latin for Mother. Mary is Mother of Jesus Christ, True God and True man and was she named "*Theotokos*," the God-bearer at the Council of Ephesus in 431 A.D. She is the mother of all believers, given to all of us, by her Son, Jesus, as He hung upon the Cross when He said to the beloved apostle, St. John, "Behold your Mother" (Jn. 19:27). We read in the Acts of the Apostles, that after the Lord Jesus ascended to heaven, Mary supported the apostles, who were gathered in the Upper Room, "All these, with one accord, devoted themselves to prayer, together with the women and Mary, the mother of Jesus and His brethren" (Acts 1:14).

Pope Paul VI solemnly proclaimed Mary the "Mother of the Church" on November 21, 1964, during his speech at the end of the third session of the Second Vatican Council. However, the groundwork for this title was already laid by the Venerable Pope Pius XII, (1876-1958) who in the encyclical, "*Mystici Corporis Christi*" (On the Mystical Body of Christ) promulgated June 29, 1943, wrote, "Thus she who, according to the flesh was the mother of the Head, through the added title of pain and glory, became, according to the Spirit, the mother of His members" (no. 110).

There are many beautiful titles attributed to the Blessed Mother in the Litany of Loreto, which was developed in the Middle Ages, and was approved in 1587. Some of them are: Mother of our Redeemer, Mother most chaste, Mother most admirable and Mother of Good Council. The Venerable Pope John Paul II added the title, Mother of the Church to the Litany of Loreto in 1980.

The letter "A" is for "*Advocate*" in Latin. An advocate pleads our cause before the judge, and makes the case to help us. Mary is nearby Her Son Jesus in the kingdom of heaven, and she intercedes on our behalf. Some medieval paintings show Mary standing next to her Son with one of her hands on her breast, as a reminder to Him, that she was the person who brought Him into this world, and nursed Him. We then see her other hand placed on the shoulder of the patron, who is devotedly kneeling, huddled under the loving protection of her mantle. The observer understands that the person depicted, is asking help from Lord Jesus through Mary. The Blessed Mother is making the presentation of the devotee to her Son, and interceding for them.

We see the compassion and intervention of Mary at the Wedding of Cana in Galilee, where her Son performed His first Miracle at her behest (Jn. 2:1-12). This was the miracle by which "His glory was manifested and His disciples believed in Him." There was no more wine, and it would have been an embarrassment to the bride and groom and their families, to send the guests home. So Mary approached Jesus, and simply stated, "They have no more wine" as we read in the account in the Gospel. After this, she told the waiters "Do whatever He tells you."

I have often considered these words the valedictory words of Mary, her farewell address, since throughout the Gospels from that point forward, there will not be another spoken word of Mary recorded, nor would any other words ever be needed. It is almost as if she is saying: "Listen to Him now, as I do." Even her apparitions over the centuries, have reiterated this message: "Listen to my Son." As our advocate or helper, Mary has encouraged us to pray, make sacrifices for sinners, and to not offend God any more, as she told the children in Fatima, Portugal in 1917.

The letter "R" in the word Maria stands for "*Regina*," which is Latin for Queen. We honor Mary as Queen of heaven and earth, of angels, saints and the entire human race. Over the millennia, Mary has been depicted in art, music and devotion as a queen, since her Son is the King, then His mother shares in this royal status, as the Queen Mother. We think of the prayer that begins, "Hail Holy Queen." This gave doctrinal substance to an idea that recurred frequently in biblical foundations, church teaching and testimony of the Fathers, as well as popular devotion and iconography. References beginning from the Council of Ephesus in 431 were mentioned to testify to the royal dignity of Mary.

The Venerable Pope Pius XII, who was instrumental in establishing the Feast of Mary's Queenship, actually made this simple thinking official. The liturgical feast of Christ the King honors the kingly dignity of Jesus Christ, and was established in 1925 by Pope Pius XI (1857-1939). Mary's royal dignity is parallel, although subordinate, and Pope Pius XII instituted the Feast of the Queenship of Mary and her queenship was proclaimed, with the encyclical letter, "*Ad coeli Reginam*," (To the Queen of Heaven) promulgated on October 11, 1954, as the Marian Year was drawing to a close.

In a prayer composed by Pius XII, "To Mary, Our Queen" we are reminded that the gentle reign of Mary can help each of us in the way we live our lives, "Reign over the minds of men, that they may seek what is true; over their wills, that they may follow only what is good; over their hearts, that they may love only what you yourself love." This feast was originally designated to be celebrated on May 31, but with the liturgical reforms of the Second Vatican Council, is now celebrated on August 22, as a festive prolongation of the Feast of Mary's Assumption.

The letter "I" in the name Maria stands for "*Immaculata*," and represents the privilege of the Immaculate Conception of the Blessed Virgin Mary. From the early centuries, the Church's attention about Mary focused on her maternity, virginity and sinlessness. In 1830, St. Catherine Labouré, (1806-1876) received a series of apparitions from Our Lady, during which she received a medal, that came to be known as the "Miraculous Medal." Engraved on the medal were the words, "O Mary, conceived without sin, pray for us, who have recourse to thee." After consulting theologians, Blessed Pius IX, questioned the 603 bishops of the universal church, as to whether he should define the Immaculate Conception. The Pope made the declaration in his papal bull, *"Ineffabilis Deus,"* (Ineffable God) on December 8, 1854. It stated,

> "We declare, pronounce and define that the doctrine which holds that the Blessed Virgin Mary, at the first instant of her conception, by a singular privilege and grace of the Omnipotent God, in virtue of the merits of Jesus Christ, the Savior of mankind, was preserved immaculate from all stain of original sin, has been revealed by God, and therefore should firmly and constantly be believed by all the faithful."

The Liturgy for the feast of the Immaculate Conception uses the story of the fall of our first parents, Adam and Eve in the first reading. This is called the Proto-Gospel where the Mercy of God is revealed. Verse 15 states, "I will put enmity between you and the woman, and between your offspring and hers; He will strike at your head, while you strike at his heel" (Gn. 3:9-15, 20). He promises victory over the serpent, by the offspring of the woman. That woman is Mary. She is depicted, in the image of the Immaculate Conception, as crushing the head of the serpent with her feet.

The last letter, "A" in the name of Maria, stands for the Latin word *"Assumpta"* and refers to the Assumption. We believe that the body and soul of Mary were taken up into heaven at the end of her earthly life. On May 1, 1946, the Venerable Pope Pius XII sent an encyclical letter entitled *"Deiparae Virginis Mariae,"* (On the Possibility of Defining the Assumption) to the bishops of the world, to ask their prudent advice whether to propose the Assumption of the Blessed Virgin as a doctrine. After assuring himself of the "Universal, certain and firm consent of the Church's ordinary Magisterium" and by the Apostolic Constitution, *"Munificentissimus Deus,"* (The Most Bountiful God) on November 1, 1950, the Venerable Pope Pius XII solemnly defined the Assumption as a dogma of faith, stating that, "The ever-virgin Mary, having completed the course of her earthly life, was assumed body and soul into heavenly glory." This feast is celebrated each year on August 15.

Throughout the centuries, Mary has been depicted seated near the throne of her Son. Her Assumption can be seen in the light of the privilege of her Immaculate Conception, since she who was preserved from all sin, was also preserved from the corruption of the grave. She was the first of believers by her "Yes" at the Annunciation and was a faithful collaborator of her Son in the work of our Redemption. Her "Yes," representing her faithful commitment to doing the plan of God, was repeated many times after that first one, at the crib of Bethlehem, during the flight into Egypt, throughout the private and public life of the Lord.

The Blessed Virgin Mary was there standing by the cross of her Son on Calvary, "Where she as Queen of Martyrs, more than all the faithful 'filled up those things that are wanting of the sufferings of Christ' for His Body, which is the Church" "*Mystici Corporis*," (On the Mystical Body of Christ, no. 110). Our Blessed Mother Mary was there with the apostles in the Upper Room at Pentecost. Her "Yes," representing her fidelity, continued throughout her life. We ask her to help us, that we too, can be faithful to her Son and always say "Yes" to Him, in doing His will. Mary points the way to Him, Who is the Way, the Truth and the Life and by being faithful to Him on this earth, may we one day, like Mary, receive the crown of glory and be with Him forever in the kingdom of heaven.

# Jesus

This was the first letter in the heading J.M.J.L., and of course, the most important of all. It represents the Holy Name of Jesus. Over the years, as I grew from childhood to adulthood, my relationship with the Lord has also grown and developed. As a child, the beautiful feast of the Nativity or Christmas made a big impression upon me. It was a time filled with love and family and I came to understand, even when very young, that it was the "Birthday of Baby Jesus," as most children do.

By the time I was about eleven, and was an altar server, it made even more of an impression upon me, when all of us servers were in solemn procession at Midnight Mass. We all preceded the elderly pastor, Monsignor Samuel C. Bove, who carried the statue of the Infant Jesus through the center aisle of the church, and lovingly placed it in the crib of the Nativity scene. It was, and still remains, a beautiful memory, and I believe that the seeds of a priestly vocation, which probably had been planted even before then, received an extra push in germinating through such wonderful events.

Over the years, I came to a better understanding of the mystery of our Salvation. The Creed tells us: "For us men and our salvation, He came down from Heaven." This was the self-emptying of the Lord for us, and it takes the ultimate expression in His self-sacrificing death upon the cross. St. Paul wrote, "Our Lord Jesus Christ, though He was rich, for your sake, made Himself poor, so that by His poverty, you might become rich" (2 Cor. 8:9). Even in my youth, I realized that the sorrow of Good Friday was replaced a few days later by the joy of Easter Sunday.

In the seminary years, one of the Scripture professors, Archbishop John F. Whealon of Hartford, said it best: "The Nativity account was written by the Light of the Paschal Candle." The Lord Jesus underwent all this for love of us, for you and me. He willingly collaborated with the loving plan of His Heavenly Father, so that we could live in the love of the Trinity and in this world and in heaven, and we could also bring that love to others.

We remember the familiar quote, "For God so loved the world, that He gave His only Son, so that everyone who believes in Him, might not perish, but might have eternal life" (Jn. 3:16). The Lord tells us, "A new command I give you: Love one another. As I have loved you, so you must love one another. By this all men will know that you are My disciples, if you love one another" (Jn. 13:34-35).

As the years progressed and I grew older, I came to the understanding that the goal of my life was to try my very best to be transformed into "Another Christ," which is the meaning of the word Christian. St. Paul wrote, "I have been crucified with Christ; and it is no longer I who live, but Christ lives in me; and the life which I now live in the flesh, I live by faith in the Son of God, Who loved me and gave Himself up for me" (Gal. 2:19-20).

As a part of that interior transformation, we are to bring the love of the Lord to others. We are to be reflectors of God's Love, we can do that best by, above all things, having a fervent love for one another, for "Love will cover a multitude of sins" (1 Pet. 4:8). However, I believe that each one of us needs to set our priorities, and first work on being interiorly transformed into another Christ. Of course, it is possible to also continue our works of mercy and charity to help those in need, whenever possible. As St. Paul tells us, "Let us not grow weary while doing good, for in due season we shall reap if we do not lose heart" (Gal. 6:9).

One readily thinks of the words of St. John the Baptist who, when speaking about Jesus stated, "He must increase, and I must decrease" (Jn. 3:30). I once saw this same quote in Latin and repeated it several times to myself to remember it, *Illum Crescere, Me Minui.* This was the motto on the coat-of-arms of the retired bishop of Hamilton, Bermuda, and I saw it there, when I went to offer a prayer at the Cathedral of St. Theresa. It made me recall the fact that, in musical notation, when the music is to get louder, it is called "*Crescendo*" and when the music becomes softer, it is called "*Diminuendo*." This quote helps to remind us that our own ways are to be reduced and that the ways of the Lord in us are to speak louder.

This involves the crucified aspect that St. Paul wrote about in the quote above. We are to die to ourselves and our own sinful ways, and let the ways of the Lord take over. This happens when we surrender our own preferences and desires, and replace them with that which the Lord prefers.

Of course, this is a lifelong struggle, as my Dad told me many years ago, "This is why there are erasers at the end of the pencils." No one is perfect, we all make mistakes, some big and some small. However, the real mistake would be not to approach the Lord to seek His mercy and forgiveness. "God has a big eraser" I once heard. Until the very last breath of our lives, we can say, "My Jesus, mercy!" And that prayer will be heard before the throne of the Lord. Yes, one can get into heaven by the skin of their teeth, but why risk one's eternal salvation?

The parable of the landowner gives us this lesson. The landowner had hired workers throughout the entire day, and paid those who did just a few hours work at the end of the day, equally to those who began early. They complained saying,

> "These last ones worked only one hour, and you have made them equal to us, who bore the day's burden and the heat. He said to one of them in reply, 'My friend, I am not cheating you. Did you not agree with me for the usual daily wage? Take what is yours and go. What if I wish to give this last one the same as you? Am I not free to do as I wish with my own money? Are you envious because I am generous' " (Mt. 20:12-15)?

There is always an opportunity for change and conversion. I recall hearing the story of Pope Pius VII, (1740-1823) who was exiled from his papal residence at the Quirinal Palace in Rome. He remained in confinement during the time of Napoleon. While he was gone, the occupants had painted images of scantily clad Roman goddesses in the corridors. When the Holy Father returned in 1814, along with his entourage, the cardinals were aghast and hesitantly awaited the remarks of the pope. Undauntedly, he said, "With some beautiful clothes painted on, they will make fine saints." God always gives us the opportunity to change. He reaches out in His mercy; it is our choice to accept or reject it. We can all become "fine saints" one way or another, if we put our minds and hearts to it.

The last page of the book of our lives has not yet been written, and it does not matter where we begin, but where we end. Even the greatest sinner can become a great saint in the eyes of the Lord. St. Teresa of Avila wrote, "I do not fear God's justice, I count on it." While the world and others may think ill of one, the Lord God alone knows the truth in each person's lives. He has "Walked a mile in each person's moccasins," as the expression goes, and knows what every person has had to endure, and how many cups of suffering one has had to drink, in order to fulfill the Will of the Heavenly Father.

We recall the Lord's response to the plan of His heavenly Father, when He is praying in the garden of Gethsemane after the Last Supper,

> " 'My soul is sorrowful even to death. Remain here and keep watch with Me.' He advanced a little and fell prostrate in prayer, saying, 'My Father, if it is possible, let this cup pass from Me; yet, not as I will, but as You will' " (Mt. 26:38-39).

Over the years, I have believed that Jesus learned these words from his mother, Mary. She had told the angel at the Annunciation in the Gospel of St. Luke, ch.1, vs.38, "Behold, I am the handmaid of the Lord. May it be done to me according to your word." Dante Alighieri, who has been considered one of the greatest poets in all literature, wrote in the Divine Comedy, "*In Voluntate Eis Pax Nostra*" which means, "In His Will is our peace" (Canto III, line 185).

At the beginning of this chapter, I quoted the Creed that the Lord Jesus came here "For our salvation." This is the Holy Will of God. This is why Jesus came as our Redeemer to make of us

> "A chosen race, a royal priesthood, a holy nation, a people of his own, so that you may announce the praises of Him Who called you out of darkness into His wonderful light. Once you were 'no people' but now you are God's people; you 'had not received mercy' but now you have received mercy" (I Pet. 2:9-10).

We hear, "Christ becomes for us our wisdom, our sanctification and our redemption" (I Cor. 1:30). May we ask the Lord to help us to "Arrive at the knowledge of truth" (I Tim. 2:4) in each of our lives. We ask Jesus to daily bring us out of darkness, and help us not to get involved with the paths of error. We need His aid to walk in the paths of righteousness, so that we can live in His wonderful light each day, and be united to Him. The Lord Himself told us: "I am the Way and the Truth and the Life. No one comes to the Father, except through Me" (Jn. 14:6).

Over the years, I have frequently thought that the most important goal in our lives is to hear these words from the Lord Jesus, "Come, blessed of My Father, inherit the kingdom prepared for you from the foundation of the world" (Mt. 25:34). I have told people that I do not want to be named a Monsignor, Bishop, Cardinal or even elected the Pope! My goal, and that which is the ultimate goal of all of us, is above any earthly honor, and it is all of our choosing. This goal is to become a saint, not necessarily a canonized saint, who is officially recognized by the church. However, everyone who hears the above words of Jesus Christ at the end of their earthly pilgrimage, and thus invited into the kingdom of heaven is considered a saint. This is the desire of Jesus for each of us, that we become a saint.

The word "Saint" means "One who is holy," this is something or someone that is set apart for God or dedicated to God. All Christians are invited to become saints. St Paul regularly referred to the Christians of his times as saints. We hear "To all those in Rome, who are loved by God and called to be saints" (Rom. 1:7); "To all the saints in Christ Jesus, who are at Philippi" (Phil. 1:1); "To the church of God that is in Corinth, to those sanctified in Christ Jesus, called to be saints together" (1 Cor. 1:2).

This is why the Lord came to this world, to show us the way to become saints! One of the ancient Church Fathers, St. Athanasius, (296-373) the Bishop of Alexandria, wrote, "God became man, so that man can become like God." We ask the dear Lord to help us live in His friendship daily, and make that priority the most important thing in our lives. Sr. Carmel, O.P. taught me this prayer, which I have kept in my breviary since 1974,

*Dear Jesus, make Thyself to me*
*A living, bright reality.*
*Make present to faith's vision keen*
*Than any outward object seen.*
*More dear, more intimately nigh*
*Than even the sweetest earthly tie.*

My dear friend, Sister Carmel also told me "how-to" in aspiring to sanctity, when she said, "Life by yard is hard, but life by the inch is a cinch!" We are invited to collaborate with the Lord each day, and thereby be transformed into a saint totally dedicated to Him. This is our destiny; it is not our work, but the work of the Lord Jesus; we are asked to bow our heads in obedience to His Holy Will. Christ is the King and we are His faithful flock, who are invited to participate in His kingdom, while we are still pilgrims on this earth. The Preface for the Solemnity of Christ the King of the Universe, which is celebrated liturgically each year, on the last Sunday of the Church Year explains this best. This prayer is directed to the Heavenly Father,

*You anointed Jesus Christ, Your only Son,*
*with the oil of gladness,*
*as the eternal priest and universal king.*
*As priest, He offered His life on the altar of the cross*
*and redeemed the human race by this one perfect*
*sacrifice of peace.*
*As king, He claims dominion over all creation,*
*that He may present to You, His almighty Father,*
*an eternal and universal kingdom:*
*a kingdom of truth and life,*
*a kingdom of holiness and grace,*
*a kingdom of justice, love, and peace.*

We ask the Lord Jesus to lead us into His friendship in this world and to be, for us, the Way to His Heavenly Father. In this way, one day we can hear those all important words, "Come, blessed of My Father" that will admit us to the eternal joy that awaits us forever in the kingdom of heaven.

# Redemption

During his homily for Mercy Sunday, April 17, 2007, Pope Benedict XVI referred to his predecessor, the Venerable Pope John Paul II, when he stated, "In the word 'mercy,' he found summarized, and again interpreted for our time, the entire mystery of the Redemption" (in *L'Osserv. Rom.*, 17-18 Apr. 2007, p.10). The whole history of salvation is full of manifestations of the Lord's great mercy and love. God so loved the world that He gave "His only-begotten Son" (Jn. 3:16).

We read in the Gospel according to St. Matthew, "Behold, the virgin shall be with child and bear a Son, and they shall name Him Emmanuel which means, 'God is with us' " (Mt. 1:23). This expression "God is with us" in the New Testament, is the fulfillment of God's promise of return from exile, as given to the Prophet Jeremiah "You shall be My people, and I will be your God" (Jer. 30:22). This is fulfilled in the birth of Jesus. In Him, God the Son, the Second Person of the Most Holy Trinity, is with His people. The name Emmanuel is alluded to at the end of the same Gospel, when the Risen and Glorified Lord Jesus assured the disciples of His continued presence, "I am with you always, until the end of the age" (Mt. 28:20).

This is the Heavenly Father's greatest gift to all of us, the human race, Who He created out of love. He sent His only Son to come among us and be our Redeemer. St. Paul wrote, "But God proves His love for us, in that while we were still sinners, Christ died for us" (Rom. 5:8). An angel appeared to St. Joseph in a dream, and told him "Do not fear to take Mary as your wife, for That which is conceived in her is of the Holy Spirit" (Mt. 1:20). The angel indicated to St. Joseph the redemptive work of the Lord, saying, "You shall call Him Jesus, for He will save His people from their sins" (Mt. 1:21).

The Lord Jesus gave His ultimate gift for the Redemption of the world, by the shedding of His Precious Blood for each one of us. We hear in Sacred Scriptures, "Greater love has no one than this, than to lay down one's life for his friends" (Jn. 15:13). Jesus freely chose to lay down his life, and so to bring to completion the plan of His Heavenly Father. His redemptive suffering and death paid the debt due to our sin, and achieved our salvation. We hear the words of the Lord,

"This is why the Father loves Me, because I lay down My life in order to take it up again. No one takes it from Me, but I lay it down on My own. I have power to lay it down, and power to take it up again. This command I have received from My Father" (Jn. 10:16-17).

God the Father's love is shown by the great price of the Blood of Jesus His Son. He was the spotless Lamb of Sacrifice of the New Covenant, which was prefigured through the Paschal Lamb of the Old Covenant, during the time of the Prophet Moses. We hear the story of that first Passover in great detail throughout Book of Exodus. Moses was chosen by God, to ask the Pharaoh for the freedom of the Chosen People of Israel (ch. 5). Subsequently, the plagues that followed were the Lord's intervention, to enable that freedom from slavery to happen.

This led up to the Passover meal, which consisted of the roasted flesh of the lamb that was slain, along with the unleavened bread, which was made in haste, (ch. 12) since the Israelites needed to depart from Egypt. The homes that were marked with the blood of the lamb were spared from death, but not the Egyptians. The Lord God then brought the Chosen People to freedom through the sea that had parted for them, but then covered the chariots and charioteers of Pharaoh (ch. 14-15).

By the blood of the Passover lamb, the Israelites, who were God's chosen people, were released from slavery and oppression, and given their freedom. We, too, are released from slavery and oppression to sin, by the Blood of the new Passover Lamb of God, the Lord Jesus Christ, Who was slain for our offenses. Jesus defeated the evil one, the Devil, and we too are called to do the same. His victory is our victory, since through our own Baptism; we are partakers in His passion and death. St. Paul wrote, "For our paschal lamb, Christ, has been sacrificed. Therefore let us celebrate the feast, not with the old yeast, the yeast of malice and wickedness, but with the unleavened bread of sincerity and truth" (I Cor. 5:7-8).

The Passion of Christ can serve to help us refrain from sin, because we see the cost of sin, and we are thereby inspired to avoid it, in appreciation for all that the Lord underwent to free us from sin. "For our sake, He made Him to be sin, Who did not know sin, so that we might become the righteousness of God in Him" (2 Cor. 5:21).

Hopefully, each time that we look at the crucifix, and realize the sufferings the Lord Jesus endured for our salvation; it will be a reminder to live a renovated spiritual life. This includes a deep conversion from our sins, and to have a firm resolve never to offend the Merciful Lord again. I believe that we learn from the suffering of Christ while reading the accounts of His Passion. Hopefully, we can incorporate the attributes we see in Christ's suffering into our own lives; they are: obedience, humility, charity, forgiveness and perseverance.

Many of those who have visited there, myself included, can recall the great impression that a pilgrimage to Jerusalem makes upon a person. One visits the holy places such as the Way of the Cross, known as the *Via Dolorosa*, as well as the Basilica of the Holy Sepulchre. Those holy places help to bring to life the events of Our Lord's suffering, which brought about our Redemption.

The liturgy is the principle channel through which we receive the Lord's mercy and grace. The Document on the Liturgy of the Second Vatican Council, entitled *"Sacrosanctum Concilium"* (Constitution on the Sacred Liturgy) so beautifully tells us,

> "From the liturgy, therefore, and especially from the Eucharist, grace is channeled to us; and the sanctification of men in Christ and the glorification of God, to which all other activities of the Church are directed as toward their goal, are most powerfully achieved" (no. 10).

It is in the Sacred Liturgy, that the Lord God feeds us with His Holy Word, His mercy and forgiveness, and His very Life in Holy Communion. We participate in the Great Memorial of the Lord's suffering, death and triumph in the Eucharistic Banquet. The night before He died, the Lord Jesus instituted the Sacrament of the Holy Eucharist. It remains an unbloody and perpetual memorial, to commemorate the Sacrifice of the shedding of His Precious Blood, upon the wood of the cross, which would take place the next day.

The Lord commanded the apostles, "Do this in remembrance of Me" (Lk. 22:19). Our Faith teaches us that when an ordained priest repeats the words that Jesus Christ said at the Last Supper, over the gifts of bread and wine, they truly become the Body and Blood of the Lord, even though the appearance of the bread and wine remain. This is through the power of apostolic succession, which began at the Last Supper. It was on that very evening, that the power was given to the apostles, and through them, to other bishops and priests throughout the generations.

In this way, during the celebration of the Eucharist, the Sacrifice of Jesus Christ has been perpetuated throughout the centuries. All of those members of the Mystical Body of Christ can be united intimately and sacramentally to the Lord Jesus Christ, the Head of the Mystical Body. He is truly present, Body, Blood, Soul and Divinity. Each time that we reflect on the story of our Redemption, which the Lord Jesus won for us, it helps to deepen our appreciation for His merciful love for us. It is an opportunity to be grateful to the Heavenly Father for His mercy upon us by sending His Son,

> "Give thanks to the Father, Who has made you fit to share in the inheritance of the holy ones in light. He delivered us from the power of darkness and transferred us to the kingdom of His beloved Son, in Whom we have redemption, the forgiveness of sins" (Col. 1:12-14).

There is a famous excerpt from St. Jerome's Commentary on the Book of the Prophet Isaiah. St. Jerome wrote, "Ignorance of Scripture is ignorance of Christ" (Nn. 1.2: CCL 73, 1-3). We rejoice in the wonders the Lord has done for us. He created the human race as we read in the Book of Genesis. The Lord God saved His chosen People of Israel in the Book of Exodus. We read of the life, death and resurrection of the Lord Jesus in the Gospels and have the opportunity to participate in His life through the sacraments. The whole of salvation history has one purpose: to bring souls, yours and mine, to be with the Lord forever in the joys of the kingdom of heaven.

# Our Sure Foundation

There is a beautiful Hymn which tells us that the Lord Jesus Christ is our sure foundation, upon which His holy church rests. It was originally written in Latin, and records indicate that the words are from the Seventh Century:

> *Christ is made the sure foundation,*
> *Christ, our head and cornerstone,*
> *Chosen of the Lord and precious,*
> *Binding all the Church in one;*
> *Holy Zion's help forever*
> *And our confidence alone.*

The Lord Jesus founded the Church to perpetuate His work of salvation. Knowing all things, and that He would ascend to sit at the right hand of His Heavenly Father, He chose His successor, St. Peter to be His vicar on earth.

Both Saints Peter and Paul are seen as the two early "Pillars," firmly planted on the foundation stone, the Lord Jesus Christ. Our Lord chose them in His important work of the early building up of the kingdom of God, His Church on earth. When one looks at the imposing front façade of St. Peter's Basilica, there are two massive statues in the square, those of Sts. Peter and Paul, whom the Lord selected to be the early "Pioneers" in the work of propagating the faith.

Saints Peter and Paul share a feast day dedicated to their memory each year on June 29, the Solemnity of Sts. Peter and Paul. There is a saying in Latin that helps one to make the connection between these two great saints: *O Roma felix, quae duorum principum es consecrata glorioso sanguine.* This translates as, "O fortunate Rome, which has been consecrated by the blood of the two princes of the apostles."

The Pope is the successor to St. Peter. Simon was the name of this simple fisherman from Galilee. The Gospel of St. John relates how, at Cafarnaum, the Lord Jesus called him to become one of the apostles, "Jesus looked at him and said, 'You are Simon, son of

John, you will be called Kephas' " (Jn. 1:42), which means "Rock." St. Peter had a brother, the apostle, St. Andrew who followed the preaching of St. John the Baptist and learned about Jesus. It was he, when speaking about the Lord Jesus, who told his brother Simon, "We have found the Messiah" (Jn. 1:41). The Fathers of the Church tell us that St. Peter was a widower, and for this reason he had a mother-in-law.

The Gospel of St. Luke gives additional details in the calling of the first apostles, James and John, the sons of Zebedee, who along with Peter, were his partners as fishermen. While washing their nets by the Lake of Gennesaret, the Lord told them to put out into the deep water to lower their nets for a catch. Simon Peter replied, "Master, we have worked hard all night and caught nothing, but at Your command, I will lower the nets" (Lk. 5:5).

They were so astonished at the great number of fish that they caught, that Simon Peter fell at the knees of Jesus asking Him to depart from him since he was a sinful man. To this Jesus responded, "Do not be afraid; from now on, you will be fishers of men" (Lk. 5:11). They brought their boats to the shore, left everything and followed Him. Sts. Peter, James and John are seen as the Lord's closest friends, and were present at both the Transfiguration and in the Garden of Gethsemane. St. Peter was the first person to profess his faith in Jesus, when he said, "You are the Messiah, the Son of the living God" (Mt. 16:17). Jesus responded,

> "Blessed are you, Simon, son of Jonah, for flesh and blood have not revealed this to you but My heavenly Father. And so I say to you, you are Peter, and upon this rock I will build My church and the gates of the netherworld will not prevail against it. I will give you the keys of the kingdom of heaven. Whatever you bind on earth will be bound in heaven; whatever you loose on earth will be loosed in heaven" (Mt. 16:18-20).

At the Last Supper, the Lord Jesus told the apostles that the shepherd would be struck and the sheep dispersed. When He predicted

St. Peter's three-fold denial, St. Peter insisted, "Even if I have to die with You, I will not deny You" (Mk. 14:31). Later that night in the courtyard of Caiaphas, the high priest, St. Peter did indeed deny the Lord three times. Then the cock crowed, as the Lord had predicted, and he "Wept bitterly" (Mt. 26:75). After the crucifixion of the Lord, the women who saw the empty tomb reported it to St. Peter who "Ran to the tomb, bent down and saw the burial cloths alone" (Lk. 24:12). St. Peter made a three-fold profession of love to the Lord after the Resurrection, when Jesus asked him, "Do you love Me" (Jn. 21:15-19)?

In the Acts of the Apostles, we learn of St. Peter's rousing speech on Pentecost Sunday, explaining to those in Jerusalem that the Lord Jesus, Whom they had crucified, was the Messiah. He invited them to "Repent and be baptized and receive the gifts of the Holy Spirit" (Acts 2:38). Consequently, three thousand were baptized that same day (vs. 41). Sometime later, King Herod had St. Peter arrested. However, the night before the trial, he was freed from prison by an angel of the Lord (Acts 12:1-17).

According to sacred tradition, St. Peter was crucified in the year 64, under the persecution of the Emperor Nero. At his own request, he asked to be crucified upside down, saying that he was not worthy to die in the same way as the Lord Jesus. He was buried, not far from the place of his execution, and a shrine arose on the location, which later became St. Peter's Basilica in the Vatican. In the midst of excavations in the Vatican Grottos in 1939, during the papacy of the Venerable Pope Pius XII, the actual tomb of St. Peter was discovered. In 1953, inside a hole at the site, the inscription "Peter is here" was found, as well as human remains. After scientific studies they have been attributed as those of St. Peter, the first Vicar of Jesus Christ.

On June 28, 2007, His Holiness, Pope Benedict XVI proclaimed a year-long celebration to be dedicated to St. Paul. This announcement took place at the Basilica of St. Paul Outside the Walls, as the Holy Father was presiding at a Vespers Service on the Vigil of the Solemnity of Sts. Peter and Paul. The Pauline Year began on June 29, 2008 and marked the approximate 2,000[th] Anniversary of the birth of St. Paul.

According to church historians, St. Paul was born in Tarsus in Cilicia, in what is now Turkey, sometime between 7 and 10 A.D. We hear from St. Paul himself, in the Book of the Acts of the Apostles, 1:39, that his father was a Roman citizen (Acts 22:26-28) and his family were considered observant Jews, (Phil. 3:5-6) and descended from the tribe of Benjamin.

When he was born, he was given the name Saul, and was taught the trade of how to make tents (Acts 18:3). As a young man, he was sent to Jerusalem to receive his education there at the school of the learned Jew named Gamaliel (Acts 22:3). We hear about him at the time of the martyrdom of St. Stephen, (Acts 7:58-60) where we learn that "The witnesses laid down their garments at the feet of a young man named Saul." Paul is the name for Saul in Latin.

Also in the Acts of the Apostles, we hear three accounts of the Conversion of St. Paul on the road to Damascus, where he was planning to present letters from the High Priest to persecute the disciples of the Lord there. A light from heaven appeared to him and he fell to the ground hearing the words, "Saul, Saul, why dost thou persecute Me" (Acts 9:4)? The Lord Jesus identified Himself and told Saul, who remained blinded, to go to the city, and there he would be told what to do. Upon arrival, he met Ananias, who was told by the Lord to lay hands on him. Although Ananias at first protested the instructions of the Lord, he complied and baptized him and Saul regained his sight.

After his conversion, he began preaching to the Jews (Acts 9:19-20). After three years in Arabia, he then traveled to Jerusalem and there met St. Barnabas, who brought him to St. Peter. He spent fifteen days with the head of the apostles as well as St. James (Gal. 1:18). This is said to have occurred around the year 39 A.D. St. Barnabas later would accompany St. Paul on several of his missionary journeys.

St. Paul is principally known for his apostolic voyages, wherein he crisscrossed the cities located on the coast of the Mediterranean Sea. At first, he offered the message of the Gospel of Christ to the Jews, but was met with great resistance. He then brought the message to the Gentiles, establishing Christian communities among them, and he is called the Apostle of the Nations.

He endured beatings, shipwreck, harassment and imprisonment. St. Paul is also well-known for his fourteen Epistles or Letters which were to instruct and encourage the Christian communities that he had visited to remain faithful. He wrote to the Romans, Corinthians, Galatians, Ephesians, Philippians, Colossians, Thessalonians and Hebrews and he also wrote to individual disciples, Timothy, Titus and Philemon.

According to historians, about the year 59 A.D., when St. Paul visited Jerusalem for the fifth time since his conversion, the people there assailed him and would have killed him, but an officer took him into custody and sent him to the Roman Governor Felix, at Caesarea, where he was detained as a prisoner for two years. Having finally appealed to the Roman Emperor, according to the privilege of a Roman citizen, he was sent to Rome. On the voyage there, he suffered a shipwreck at Malta, in the spring of the year 61. At Rome, he was treated with respect; being allowed to dwell "For two whole years in his own hired house" (Acts 28:30).

The burning of Rome occurred, generally attributed to Nero, who put the blame on the Christians, and were consequently subjected to a severe persecution. Among the victims was St. Paul, who suffered death by beheading, since he was a Roman citizen, on June 29, 67 A.D., according to the historian Eusebius. This was on the Ostian Way, just outside the city limits of Rome. According to the ancient tradition of the Church, he received the crown of martyrdom on the very same day and year that St. Peter was crucified upside down, on the Vatican Hill, in Rome. St. Paul wrote: "I have fought the good fight, I have finished the course, I have kept the faith" (2 Tim. 4:7).

In church iconography, St. Paul is pictured as average in height, with piercing eyes and balding dark hair and a beard. He is pictured holding a sword, the instrument of his martyrdom, in one hand and a scroll to represent his letters in the other. Along with St. Peter, he is co-patron of Rome, and besides the Solemnity of Sts. Peter and Paul which is celebrated on June 29, the Feast of the Conversion of St. Paul is celebrated on January 25, annually.

We thank the Lord Jesus for the lives and legacy of these two great saints, whose writings and holy lives have been an inspiration to countless members of the flock throughout the centuries. St. Peter's words tell us to place our confidence in the paternal care and protection of the Lord, "Cast all your cares upon Him, for He cares for you" (I Pet. 5:7). These words so much remind me of the words, "Jesus, I trust in You," that Our Lord Jesus had revealed to St. Faustina.

Over the years, the copious writings of St. Paul have been a source of spiritual nourishment to me and countless others. These, in particular, have helped me through many a moment of perplexity and discouragement: "*Omnia possum in Eo Qui me confortat*," meaning, "I can do all things in Him, Who gives me strength" (Phil. 4:13). As well, I can sum up my philosophy of Christian living for myself and those whom I have the privilege to serve with these words of St. Paul, "Let everything you do or say, be in the name of the Lord with thanksgiving to God" (Col. 3:17). May the Lord Jesus give each of us the strength and perseverance to follow Him unreservedly, that we may give Him glory, as did Sts. Peter and Paul. We ask Him to help us to live faith-filled, committed lives in this world, so that we can dwell in the house of the Lord forever in the kingdom of heaven.

# 9

# Our Life of Grace

## Christian Living

Throughout the years, I have enjoyed the friendship of my dear priest friend, Fr. Anthony. Once we were discussing the daily ups and downs in life, and in particular our Christian vocation to be "Another Christ" day in and day out. This invitation is not just for priests alone, but for all those who have been baptized and are incorporated into the Mystical Body of Christ, the Church.

He told me that he remembered hearing that each one of our spiritual lives is like a house. The foundation of the house is the faith, hope comprises the walls and charity is the roof. The interior workings of the house are the sacraments, since they supply the plumbing, electricity and heating. That is what keeps the house going and in working order. The virtues help to brighten the house, furnish it and make it beautiful in the sight of God and others.

Our first goal as Christians is to give glory to God, and this is followed by the second goal, which is to edify others by the good lives that we lead. The Lord extends this loving invitation to participate in His life of grace to all of us, "I came so that they might have life, and have it more abundantly" (Jn. 10:10). This reminds me of a famous quote by St. Irenaeus of Lyon (2nd cent.-202) who wrote, *"Gloria Dei Homo vivens"* which means "The glory of God is man fully alive" (*Adv. Haer.* IV, 20, 1-7).

The Lord Jesus referred to the enemy, Satan and used both the words the evil one (Mt. 13:37-43, Lk. 11:14-21) and temptation (Mk. 14:38) in Sacred Scripture. St. John, the beloved disciple wrote, "The reason the Son of God appeared was to destroy the works of the devil" (I Jn. 3:8). The Psalms tell us that the Lord will be our protector against the attacks of the enemy, "Say to the Lord, my refuge and fortress, my God in whom I trust. God will rescue you from the fowler's snare" (Ps. 91:2-3).

Satan does not want us to live this abundant grace-filled life with Our Lord. He puts obstacles in the way, so as to try to diminish this vibrant life that we want to lead with the Lord. These are in the form of difficulties, challenges and temptations, that he sends our way to demoralize us and divert us off the course in following the Lord. He is the master of deceit. However, we can defeat the evil one by using challenges that he sends us as opportunities to grow ever closer to the Lord, by depending on Him and fortifying ourselves with His assistance. We hear this excellent advice from St. Peter,

> "Be sober and vigilant. Your opponent the devil is prowling around like a roaring lion looking for someone to devour. Resist him, steadfast in faith, knowing that your fellow believers throughout the world undergo the same sufferings. The God of all grace, Who called you to His eternal glory through Christ Jesus will Himself restore, confirm, strengthen, and establish you after you have suffered a little. To Him, be dominion forever. Amen" (I Pet. 5:8-11).

Over the years, I have come to the realization that the Lord Jesus tried to make things simple for us, so that we could indeed participate in His abundant life of grace. These words are the advice of the Lord Himself, and hopefully we can heed them and put them into practice. When He was asked which commandment in the law is the greatest, He said to them,

> "You shall love the Lord, your God, with all your heart, with all your soul, and with all your mind.

This is the greatest and the first commandment. The second is like it: You shall love your neighbor as yourself. The whole law and the prophets depend on these two commandments" (Mt. 22:37-40).

One of the shortest pieces of advice, from one of the saints, on how to accomplish this, was given to us by St. Augustine. He often prayed this simple prayer, *"Noscam Te, noscam me"* which means "May I know Thee and may I know myself." This helps one, as well, to put things in proper perspective and to keep things simple, not complicated. If we seek to love the Lord God above all things, and to know Him, then we put our priorities in proper order. We can hopefully, thereafter, focus on how we can faithfully respond to His goodness.

When I was in the second grade in 1964, we were preparing to receive our First Holy Communion. I can distinctly recall, as if it were just yesterday, one of the Catechism questions that we students needed to commit to memory. The question was: Why did God make you? The answer was: God made me so that I could know Him, love Him and serve Him in this world, and be happy with Him in heaven.

The first part of the answer to the Catechism question tells us that we should "Know God." It is He, Who can neither deceive, nor be deceived, and He is worthy of our total love and service. The best way that we can know the Lord is through what He has said and done. We are to be like dry sponges, which absorb the Sacred Scriptures, soaking up every drop possible. This is how, even with our limited human intelligence, we can better know the Lord God, Who "Raises up the lowly and sends away the proud" (Lk. 1:52).

These are the sentiments we find in the Song of Hannah in the Old Testament (1 Sam. 2:1-10) and were echoed by the Blessed Virgin Mary in her own Song of Praise called the *"Magnificat"* (Lk. 1:46-55). In this way, we too, can echo the sentiments in these verses, recalling that humility is preferred by the Lord over pride, and thereby live accordingly.

The second part of the Catechism question invites us to "Love God." Of course, now-a-days we can easily think of love as just emotional and sentimental. But love is not an emotion only, it is primarily a relationship. St. Paul wrote so beautifully about the attributes of love as we read,

> "Love is patient, love is kind. It is not jealous, is not pompous, it is not inflated, it is not rude, it does not seek its own interests, it is not quick-tempered, it does not brood over injury, it does not rejoice over wrongdoing but rejoices with the truth. It bears all things, believes all things, hopes all things, endures all things" (I Cor. 13:4-7).

This helps us to put love in proper perspective, and see that it is part of the good times and bad, sickness and health, just like the wedding vows. Our lifelong commitment with the Lord is just like that of spouses, who are faithful to each other, no matter what comes their way. We also have a loving Mother, the Church, who is the Bride of Christ. Through the Sacred Tradition of 2,000 years, the Church has helped to guide, teach and direct her children on the right paths. We are asked to respond to this invitation to love God wholeheartedly. This has been mandated from Jesus Christ Himself. When He sent out the first seventy-two disciples to proclaim that the Kingdom of God is upon them, His told the disciples, "He who hears you, hears Me" (Lk. 10:16).

The third part of the answer to the Catechism question invites us to "Serve God." How can we do this best, but by serving Him through our service to others? This entails acts of charity, kindness and in particular, mercy. There are innumerable ways of doing this that depends on our various circumstances and states in life. The Lord Jesus told St. Faustina,

> "I demand from you deeds of mercy, which are to arise out of love for Me. You are to show mercy to your neighbors always and everywhere. You must not shrink from this, or try to excuse or absolve yourself from it" (Diary, # 742).

A religious, priest, sister or brother has chosen a life of total service and given up the opportunity of having a spouse or family, so that they may have a "More perfect life" as it has been called. Celibacy gives us an undivided heart or attention, so that we can better dedicate ourselves to the things of the Lord, and the service of His flock.

The married man or woman, as well, has the call to live a holy, committed, Christ-centered life as their first priority. They, too, can beautify their "Spiritual homes" by living a virtuous life, and nourish and fortify themselves, through the worthy reception of the Sacraments. For both those who have chosen a life consecrated to the Lord, or the married life, these words of Jesus should help all of us focus on the goal of serving the Lord, "By their deeds you shall know them" (Mt. 7:16).

The last section of the Catechism question helps to keep all of us focused on the ultimate goal of our earthly pilgrimage, "To be happy with Him in heaven." All of our lives are directed to this goal. St. Paul spoke these words to the people of Athens, who were not yet believers while they listened to him in the Areopagus. They help us to remember the reason why we are in this world as well, "For in Him we live, and move, and have our being" (Acts 17:28).

And so, we can try to keep things as simple as possible, and remember the basics in living the Christian life: to know the Lord the best that we can, and thereby to know ourselves. Even with all our strengths and weaknesses, we can have a solid basis to continue to grow in the knowledge and love of the Lord, as the years progress. This is not our work alone, but His saving plan for each of us. We hear that, "God our Savior wills everyone to be saved, and to come to knowledge of the truth" (I Tim. 2:4).

Once, I was instructing a young man, who was planning to become a Catholic, on the fundamentals of the faith. During the first class, I used most of this same previous explanation with him. When I came to the end of the class, and told him how important it was to keep in focus our ultimate goal to get to heaven, he politely stopped me and said, "Oh, the last thing I want is to get stopped at the door by the bouncer, St. Peter." I agreed and said he was absolutely right. After all the efforts we make, we need to be faithful throughout our entire lives, so we can merit the eternal life of happiness that awaits us in the kingdom of heaven.

## Embracing the Cross

As one stands in the St. Peter's Square in the Vatican and faces the awe-inspiring façade of the Basilica, there in the center of the square, is a large ancient Egyptian obelisk, surmounted by a cross. It rests on a marble base, upon which the following prayer is chiseled: *"Ecce Crux Domini Fulgite Partes Adversae Vincit Leo de Tribu Iuda."* This means: "Behold the Cross of the Lord. Depart all evil things. The Lion of the Tribe of Judah has triumphed."

This prayer has always reminded me that there is great power in the cross of Jesus Christ. His salvific death on the cross, for each of us, is the cause for our hope and the great aid to our personal triumph of good over evil in our lives. The words of the Prophet Isaiah come to mind, "Those who put their hope in Me shall never be disappointed" (Is. 49:23). Yes, this means even amid our crosses and difficulties, in fact, it is especially at those times, that we need to put our hope firmly in the Lord.

The theme of the second encyclical of Pope Benedict XVI, dated November 30, 2007 was entitled *"Spe Salvi"* and taken from the Letter to the Romans, "In hope, we were saved" (8:24). In the encyclical, the Holy Father reminds us, "God is the foundation of our hope...Who has loved us to the end, each one of us and humanity in its entirety" (n. 31).

When we consider the cross and the painful death that the Lord Jesus endured for our salvation, it is not a picture that one thinks about with much pleasure. At times, we shrink away from looking at a crucifix, especially if there is too much blood on it, or we see the Lord depicted as being in pain. St. Augustine wrote, "The death of the Lord our God should not be a cause of shame for us; rather it should be our greatest hope, our greatest glory. We now have life in Him" (*Sermo Guelferbytarus* 3: PLS 2, 545-546).

St. Paul wrote, "Let me not boast, except in the cross of Our Lord Jesus Christ" (Gal. 6:14). He also gave testimony to his readers that he had a "Thorn in the flesh," (2 Cor. 12:7) due to human weakness, like all of us and even wrote, "With Christ I am nailed to the Cross" (Gal. 2:19). This helps to serve as a reminder to overcome our own weaknesses, when we unite them to the Lord, Who endured His sufferings and cross. St. Paul wrote, "For myself, I glory in nothing, save my infirmities… the Lord said to me, 'My grace is sufficient for you, for power is perfected in weakness'… for when I am weak, then I am strong" (2 Cor. 12:5, 9-10).

When I was a seminarian in Rome in 1987, I learned about the tradition of the Stational Churches for the Holy Season of Lent. It has been an ancient tradition that each day of Lent has a particular church assigned to it. This begins on Ash Wednesday at the Basilica of Santa Sabina, on the Aventine hill. The Stational Churches are assigned up to the Sunday after Easter, which over the centuries has been called *"Dominica in Albis"* meaning "White Sunday." This is because the catechumens who were baptized at the Easter Vigil would wear their white garments for the entire week after Easter up until that day.

Then, on that Sunday, they would place them at the tomb of Saint Pancras (d. 304) in the Basilica dedicated to him. He was a soldier who "Fought the good fight" (2 Tim 4:7) for the faith and served as an example to the newly-baptized. He was a model for all of them to do the same.

Over the years, since my Ordination to the Holy Priesthood, I have tried to make a Lenten pilgrimage to Rome every few years, to participate in the penitential procession and Holy Mass at the Stational Churches. Each time, I would choose another week during Lent, so as to not repeat any of those churches where I had already attended. One of the most memorable experiences was participating, still as a seminarian, in the Holy Week Masses with the Venerable Pope John Paul II in 1987.

Several decades later, in 2009, I chose the third week of Lent, which culminated with the Fourth Sunday of Lent called *"Laetare"* or "Rejoice," for my pilgrimage to the Stational Churches. The Basilica of *Santa Croce in Gerusalemme*, which means the Basilica of the Holy Cross of Jerusalem, is assigned to that Sunday. I arrived early and asked the Cistercian Abbot, who heads the community there, if I could con-celebrate the Holy Mass. The principal celebrant was His Eminence, Cardinal Miloslav Vlk, Archbishop of Prague in the Czech Republic, who is the titular Cardinal of the Basilica. The concelebrants learned that it was a very special occasion, since it was to celebrate the Centennial of the establishment of the Parish community at the Basilica.

This basilica enshrines the major relics of the Crucifixion of the Lord Jesus Christ. There is a large cross-shaped reliquary made of gold and has three glass sections that encase three pieces of the True Cross. The size of each piece was about the size of one's index finger, but a bit longer, and the fragments of wood came to a sharp point. This reliquary was very rarely taken out of the glass display case, which is temperature controlled, and where I had seen it over the years. Also preserved in the basilica is one of the nails that affixed Our Lord to the cross, as well as the title that hung above His head that read, " 'Jesus of Nazareth, King of the Jews' which was written in Hebrew, Latin, and Greek," (Jn. 19:19-20) as reported in the Gospel.

At the conclusion of the Holy Mass, the Cardinal blessed the faithful with the relic of the True Cross and then he, along with the concelebrants, myself included, went in procession, into the sacristy. There, the reliquary was laid on a beautiful turquoise velvet pillow, and remained there for a few minutes, before being returned to the display case. I had the opportunity to touch and kiss the reliquary, and at that moment to ask the Lord to please give me the strength to persevere in carrying my own crosses, and to be victorious as He had been.

For me, this had been a "Once-in-a-lifetime experience" and a great privilege given to me by the Lord. Several of the other people in the sacristy touched their rosaries to the reliquary, and I did the same. At that moment, I thought of the part of the Liturgy of Good Friday, when the celebrant announces three times, during the unveiling of the crucifix before its veneration, "This is the Wood of the Cross, on which hung the Savior of the world. Come, let us worship."

The way that the Lord Jesus had great humility and patience during His passion, gives all of us a lesson in those virtues, as we strive to overcome our failures and weaknesses. St. Paul reminds us, to "Lead a life worthy of the calling to which you have been chosen" (Eph. 4:1). Our call is to "Overcome Evil with Good," or in Latin

"*Vince Malum in Bono*," as so many of the victorious saints and martyrs have done, throughout the centuries.

There is another Latin expression which I saw etched in marble over the front entrance to the Church of St. Mary Magdalen in Rome, not far from the Pantheon. It reads: "*O Crux, Ave Spes Unica, Piis Adauge Gratiam*" which roughly translates as: "O hail the Cross, our only Hope, grant increase of grace to believers." It is taken from the ninth stanza of the sixth century Latin Hymn that honors the True Cross entitled the "*Vexilla Regis*" meaning "Royal Banner' and was written by Venantius Fortunatus, (530-609) and is considered one of the greatest hymns of the liturgy. We remember the words repeated during the Stations of the Cross, "We adore Thee, O Christ and we praise Thee, because by Thy holy cross, Thou hast redeemed the world."

We are invited by the Lord Himself: "If anyone would come after Me, he must deny himself and take up his cross daily and follow Me" (Lk. 9:23). These words are a daily invitation for each of us to advance on the road to our sanctification and salvation and to grow in grace. This is the church's goal for us, to have a more flourishing inner life and the church helps us to achieve this by being our loving mother, providing us the means to grow in holiness through the sacraments. The Lord will not abandon us, if we follow His instructions. He will help us along the royal road of the Cross, as He has trodden. It will lead to victory for us, as it has for Him. We are reminded by St. Paul,

> "For if we have grown into union with Him through a death like His, we shall also be united with Him in the resurrection. We know that our old self was crucified with Him, so that our sinful body might be done away with, that we might no longer be in slavery to sin" (Rom. 6:5-6).

The triumph of the Lord can be experienced by each one of us, even now, during our earthly pilgrimage, as the song that we proclaim each year at the Easter Vigil, the "*Exultet*," so wonderfully reminds us. We hear of the triumphant victory of Jesus Christ that

"Dispels all evil, washes guilt away, restores lost innocence, brings mourners joy, casts out hatred, brings us peace and humbles earthly pride." We can live, even while on earth, a sanctified life that will prepare for the victory that awaits us in the kingdom of heaven.

# The Portal

The church tells us that it is the desire of the Lord Jesus Christ that we flourish in His love, mercy and friendship. It is His will that we be united to Him, thereby to share in His life in this world and forever in heaven. This is called the "Universal Salvific Will of God." He desires our sanctification and salvation. Jesus tells us, "I came so that they might have life and have it more abundantly" (Jn. 10:10). This is the life of grace, which comes from the Latin word, *"Gratia,"* which means free. The grace of God is His gift, freely given to us, and cannot be earned. The Lord Jesus allows us to share His abundant life through the graces that we receive in the sacraments.

The sacrament of Baptism is the "Great Portal" that allows us to enter the family of God. We are washed clean of our sins, and plunged into the Paschal Mystery of Christ. We die with Him, by dying to sin, so we can live with Him in the life of grace. We are given the promise of eternal life, are made children of God and co-heirs of Heaven. From the very beginning of our spiritual journey, we are reminded of our call to keep our souls unstained in preparation for the day we see the Lord face to face. St. Peter tells us of the great dignity given to them,

> "You are a chosen race, a royal priesthood, a holy nation, a people of His own, so that you may announce the praises of Him, Who called you out of darkness into His wonderful light. Once you were 'no people' but now you are God's people; you 'had not received mercy' but now you have received mercy" (I Pet. 2:9-10).

At Baptism, when we are made a child of God, we receive the indwelling of the Most Holy Trinity in our souls. We are also given the gifts of the Holy Spirit, to help us to discern and grow in the friendship of the Lord. There is another outpouring of those gifts in our souls when we receive Confirmation. That sacrament is usually administered at the time when the person enters their teenage years, since shortly after that, adulthood will soon be arriving for them.

Each of those who are confirmed becomes a "Soldier of Christ" and so they are fortified with these Gifts of the Holy Spirit again, as they face the challenges that lie ahead of them. Those confirmed are made "True witnesses to Christ, and are more strictly bound to spread and defend the faith by word and deed" (Catechism, no. 1285). We learn of these gifts through the Prophet Isaiah, who first identified them: "The spirit of the Lord shall rest upon Him: a spirit of wisdom and of understanding, A spirit of counsel and of strength, a spirit of knowledge and of fear of the Lord, and his delight shall be the fear of the Lord" (Is. 11:2-3).

When I was a Parochial Vicar in one of the parishes, before becoming a pastor, I recall that the Director of Religious Education told me her "little secret." It was the way that she helped her students remember the Seven Gifts of the Holy Spirit: PUF – WACK,

*P: Piety*
*U: Understanding*
*F: Fortitude*
*W: Wisdom*
*A: Awe or Fear of the Lord*
*C: Counsel*
*K: Knowledge*

They are not presented in the traditional order, since the gift of Wisdom is usually listed first, and Fear of the Lord is the usually last on the list. However, the listing in this manner of PUF-WACK can be helpful in remembering them. In this way, we can recall that these Gifts of the Holy Spirit are a great assistance to us, in our attempt to grow in holiness. Just like any valuable gift, such as a new watch, they are not to be put in a drawer or on a shelf, to just collect dust, and not to be used for their goal and purpose.

Many of us have heard the expression regarding one's knowledge of a language: "If you don't use it, you lose it." We can never lose the Gifts of the Holy Spirit, since they are forever in our souls, indelible from the day of our Baptism. However, perhaps they can lie dormant, if not utilized properly. We need to be aware of them, and frequently invoke the Holy Spirit to help us to be wise in our decision making, have fortitude or strength in times of difficulty, and actively use the rest of the wonderful gifts that can indeed help us through life's pilgrimage.

Some people feel uncomfortable hearing the expression "Fear of the Lord" and it is good to realize that this too is an attribute that is found in Sacred Scripture as we hear, "Serve the Lord with fear," (Ps. 2:11) as well as "Fear the Lord, all you His holy ones" (Ps. 33:10). Even St. Paul wrote of the value of a holy fear, and used the word awe in this quote, which encourages one to be humble before the Lord, "Do not become haughty, but stand in awe" (Rom. 11:20). St. Francis de Sales tells us, "We are to fear God out of love for Him, not love Him out of fear."

The day of our Baptism is the day that the invitation of the Lord to "Pick up your cross and follow Me and deny yourself" (Mt. 16:24-25, Mk. 8:34-35, Lk. 9:23-24) also begins. This is the call to all of the baptized: that we can be immersed in the great Mystery of the Cross of Christ. In this way, we can raised up and participate in the triumphant life and victory of the Risen Lord. However, this can be accomplished only by our own dying to self.

My favorite part of the Rite of Baptism is when, after the pouring of the water, the priest presents the newly baptized children with the white baptismal garment and says,

> "Dear children, you have become a new creation, and have clothed yourself in Christ. See in this white garment the outward sign of your Christian dignity. With your family and friends to help you by word and example, bring that dignity unstained into the everlasting life of heaven."

This is followed by the presentation of the Lighted Candle when the priest says,

> "Receive the light of Christ. Parents and godparents, this light is entrusted to you to be kept burning

brightly. These children have been enlightened by Christ. They are to walk always as a child of the light. May they keep the flame of faith alive in their hearts. When the Lord comes, may they go out to meet Him with all the saints in the heavenly kingdom."

The Prophet Isaiah tells us that we are to "Walk in the light of the Lord" (Is. 2:5). This means rejecting the darkness of sin and error and choosing the path to holiness. Each year, the Church gives us, her children a season called Lent. It is a period of Forty Days that provides us with an opportunity to reflect upon our spiritual lives and resolve to do better. It is a blessed period of interior renewal, through prayer, fasting, almsgiving and penance. Lent culminates with Holy Week, in which we accompany Jesus in His suffering, death and triumph.

At the conclusion of Lent, during the Easter Vigil, we all are invited to participate in the renewal of our Baptismal Promises. We stand up and vow to reject Satan, all of his works and empty promises, and we recommit ourselves to a renewed friendship with the Lord. I always tell my parishioners to "Really mean it" and answer those questions boldly and loudly, and with all their hearts, so I can hear them.

The seed of faith, which is planted in the Sacrament of Baptism, must be nurtured to grow and flourish by the parents of the child. Collaborating with God, they gave the baby the gift of life, and they also, in cooperation with the Lord, gave them the gift of faith, by bringing them to be baptized. In the same way that the parents must take care of the physical needs of the child with food, clothing and education, so too, they must attend to the spiritual needs as well, and tell them about the goodness of the Lord. The Servant of God, Fr. Patrick Peyton, (1909-1992) who was called the "Rosary priest" said, "The family that prays together stays together."

When I was growing up, I recall the tradition that at Holy Mass, the Mass server would ring the bells, at the elevation after the Consecration. We were taught to strike our breast three times, when we heard the bells, asking the Lord's mercy. Over the years, my sister Suzanne has still maintained this tradition. During the

Christmas Season each year, our family takes a trip to New York City, to see the large Christmas tree that is displayed in Rockefeller Center. It is a joyful tradition, which we have maintained since we were all children.

Now that I am a priest and my sister is married and has children of her own, we still schedule the opportunity to do this. If my brother, who is a busy physician, has the opportunity to join us, he does so as well. Afterward, we usually go for dinner, to continue the celebration of the Christmas season.

In December 1995, our family continued this tradition as it has done. This included my parents, my sister and her husband and family and myself. And after our visit to see the beautifully decorated tree, we went to a rustic restaurant called "Luna" in the Little Italy section of Manhattan. It has always been a favorite of our family. I never realized before that night, but when the food order is ready, they let the waiter know by ringing a large bell, which was positioned near our table. When they rang the bell, I saw my four year old niece young niece, Francesca, strike her breast! Over the years, she had seen her mother do it at Mass, when the bell was rung.

That pointed out to me that children are taught by the good example of their parents. The children's early perceptions about the Lord come from their parents "who will be the first teachers of their children in the faith" as the Baptismal Ritual states. When I present the white garment and lighted candle at the Baptismal ceremony, I tell them that the newly baptized child needs "their family and friends to help you by word and example."

There is a story about St. Louis IX, King of France (1215-1270). He led an exemplary life, bearing constantly in mind the words of his mother, Blanche of Castile (1188-1252), "I would rather see you dead at my feet, than guilty of a mortal sin." He frequently signed his name "Louis de Poissy," and one day, he was questioned by those in his royal court why he signed his name that way. He was reminded that he had been crowned in Rheims, so he should instead write "Louis de Rheims." The king explained, "In Poissy I received the greatest honor of my life. Although I was crowned king in Rheims, I was made a Christian in Poissy, and there acquired my right to a throne in the kingdom of heaven."

# Reconciliation

The Lord Jesus washes us clean in the Sacrament of Confession and nourishes us with His Sacred Body and Blood. Our lives and actions are to reflect the splendor of God's glory. Even amid difficulties and struggles, we can live in a joyful peace, which is a sense of calm and delight as well as interior rest. This is possible, knowing that we have a clean and clear conscience, which, I believe, is the very best gift that we can give ourselves. One of my favorite books, *The Imitation of Christ* tells us, "The good man's glory is the testimony of a good conscience. Have a good conscience, and you will always have joy. A good conscience can bear much, and you will have joy even in the midst of adversity" (Bk. 2, ch. 6).

However, the devil wants us to live, not in the eye of the hurricane, where the tempest ceases, and where there is calm and is peace, but on the periphery, right in the midst of the storm, where there is turmoil. We have to cooperate with the Lord Jesus, Whose peace plan for us will counteract the wiles of the devil. We need to use the means available that are His instruments of grace. There are the sacraments, and in particular, the Sacrament of Reconciliation, that helps us recapture the beautiful purity and holiness that we should strive to have in our souls.

The Lord tells us, "Blessed are the pure in heart, for they shall see God" (Mt. 5:8). The desire of the Lord, for each of us, is that we strive to keep our soul pure, innocent and holy and most important, in a state of God's grace and friendship. St. Paul reminds us, "If God is for us, who can be against us" (Rom. 8:31)? We are invited to cooperate with His wonderful plan of holiness for each of us.

I once heard an anecdote that when the Second Vatican Council came to a conclusion in December 1965, the Archbishop of Sydney, Australia, Cardinal Norman Gilroy, returned home and there were many reporters to meet him at the airport. They asked him, "What is the greatest problem facing the Church today?" Most likely they were expecting a profound answer after all the labors of the Council. However, he answered without missing a heartbeat, "Mortal sin. It has always been, and will always be." The remedy to sin is to unite our wills to the Lord's and surrender ourselves in humility. When we are tempted, we invoke Jesus and say, "Lord, help me not to offend You and damage my wonderful friendship with You." We bow our heads in obedience, and ask to be led by the Lord in His ways, realizing that we are nothing in His eyes, but poor sinners, and are to do what is pleasing in His sight. This is done by our daily "Dying to self."

Blessed Mother Theresa of Calcutta would often tell her sisters, "Pray that you do not spoil the work of the Holy Spirit." The Venerable Cardinal Newman wrote, "Do not fear that your life will have an end, fear that it will not have a beginning." We need to begin again and again, especially after we have offended the Lord through sin and renew our love again.

There is a Latin expression, *"Nunc Coepit"* which means, "Now we begin anew." We struggle like a toddler, attempting to walk across the room, to step and fall and get up and fall again. The father is calling the child and the mother is behind them. Eventually the child gets across the room, to the delight of all the onlookers. This is how we get to heaven as well, stumbling along the way. However, the Lord Jesus understands this since "He was a man like us in all things but sin," (Heb. 2:17) as we hear in Sacred Scripture.

Jesus saw the limitations and weakness of those who surrounded Him and had even a preferential love for sinners such as "Tax collectors and prostitutes" (Mt. 21:32). Jesus saw that they, at least, wanted to do better, and reform their lives, after being touched by His message, as opposed to the obstinate Pharisees. Jesus spoke of the "Great delight of the angels in heaven when one sinner comes back" (Lk. 15:7) when He told the Parable of the Lost Sheep.

Living in the friendship of the Lord, in peace with Him and others, is our goal. Jesus promises us peace and tells us, "Peace I leave with you; my peace I give to you. Not as the world gives, do I give it to you. Do not let your hearts be troubled or afraid" (Jn. 14:27). St. Anthony of Padua (1195-1231) wrote, "We need exterior peace to live with others, internal peace to live with ourselves, and eternal peace to live with God."

Of course, making sacrifices to do the righteous thing is not easy. The devil wants us to give in to temptation and makes sin look very attractive. There is a Polish proverb, "The serpent dripping with honey is more dangerous than the serpent dripping with venom." We can all get tangled up with sin; the devil trips us up, and spins us in circles, so that we do not progress spiritually, but are held back by our own sinfulness. He wraps his tail around our feet to confound and confuse us, and he blinds our thinking and decision making. He comes when we are at our weakest moments and have our guard down, in particular when we are discouraged, lonely or vulnerable. It is important that we be vigilant against his wiles, as the saints often tell us.

Blessed Mother Theresa of Calcutta once said, "We think sometimes that poverty is only being hungry, naked and homeless. The poverty of being unwanted, unloved and uncared for is the greatest poverty. We must start in our own homes to remedy this kind of poverty." There is also interior poverty, when one feels empty and alone. This is when the enemy of our soul can strike.

I remember this word, "HALTS," given to me by my dear priest friend, Fr. Anthony, as a reminder that the devil comes to us in those vulnerable moments in our lives, when we are:

> *H - Hungry, emotionally, physically and*
> *psychologically*
> *A - Angry, recalling past, unforgiven hurts*
> *L - Lonely, looking for human consolation, at times*
> *in the wrong places*
> *T - Tired, worn out from all of the above*
> *S - Stressed, the modern epidemic, thanks in part to*
> *cell phones!*

One of my all-time favorite quotes, that has previously been mentioned, is "The Church is not a museum for saints, but a clinic for sinners." We all need to better ourselves and "Get cleaned up spiritually" in preparation to meet the Lord God. I recall the classic 1939 movie, "The Wizard of Oz," when Dorothy, the Scarecrow, the Tin Man and Cowardly Lion are finally allowed to have a meeting with the Wizard after their laborious walk on the Yellow Brick Road. However, they had to get prepared. Dorothy and the others all got their clothes cleaned, or in the case of the scarecrow, had his straw cleaned, in order to enter the presence of the all-important Wizard of Oz.

The Sacrament of Reconciliation acts something like that. We get cleaned up spiritually, and get our souls prepared before our beautiful encounter with the Lord. When I was a youngster, it was referred to as "Going to Confession." Later in my life, I heard this sacrament referred to as the "Sacrament of Penance." In more recent times, this important sacrament of the Lord's mercy and forgiveness is referred to as the "Sacrament of Reconciliation." I believe that the word "Reconciliation" has a great significance because it is a sense of bringing things back to normal. The calm that was present, before the storm of sin, has returned. Even in the formula for absolution, the priest says, "Through the ministry of the Church, may God give you pardon and peace..." before he bestows the actual words of absolution.

The wonderful means to heal ourselves of our spiritual defects and shortcomings are available to us through the Sacrament of Reconciliation. We need to take advantage of it as frequently as needed, and in particular, if we have consented to commit a mortal sin in thought, word or deed. The merciful Lord reaches out to all, and it is a grace-filled opportunity to grow in the love of Christ, and to reach our goal of living a holy life. There is an optional prayer that can be added by the priest after he absolves the penitent,

> "May the Passion of Our Lord Jesus Christ, the merits of the Blessed Virgin Mary and of all the saints and also whatever good you do or evil you endure merit for you the remission of your sins, the increase of grace and the reward of everlasting life. Amen."

This prayer has always been a source of inspiration for me. It helps to puts things in proper perspective. That is, we are aided with the help of the Lord Jesus, His Mother and the saints, and by means of the crosses we must carry. We can have contrition for our sins and a firm purpose to amend our lives, and be cautious not to fall into sin again. Thereby we can grow in the love of Christ.

We ask the Lord to give us the grace to see ourselves as He sees us, so that we may honestly and truly see the state of our soul, with all its imperfections. The excellent practice of the Examination of Conscience each night, for a few minutes before bed, is an opportunity to look at ourselves honestly and ask, "Have I been what God wanted me to be?" The blind and deaf Helen Keller expressed the sentiments that it is better to be impaired visually, and see with your heart, than to have one's vision and see nothing.

We do not need spiritual blindness, but, rather, awareness, so that we can correct our faults and grow closer in the love and friendship of the Lord. That will bring us to the goal of seeing the Lord face to face. St. Paul tells us, "At present we see indistinctly, as in a mirror, but then face to face. At present I know partially; then I shall know fully, as I am fully known" (1 Cor. 13:12).

We need to look at the goal that is the friendship with Jesus in this world and the next. Each one of us will have to stand before the throne of the Lord, and make an accounting for our lives, while we were in the body. If, while we still are living, we can bring our weaknesses to Christ, ask forgiveness and do penance, then there will be no surprises on the day of our judgment. I sometimes chuckle when a person tells me that they made provisions in their Last Will and Testament, and put aside money to serve as offerings for Holy Mass to be offered for their soul after they have died.

This is a serious matter, and assists the soul to be purified in purgatory, however the words that they use for the funds they set aside are called, "Fire insurance." Let us not depend on that fire insurance to get us out of purgatory quicker, but while we are still on our earthly path, use it prudently as a grace-filled opportunity to "Deny oneself" (Mt. 16:24) and live for Christ, Who invites us to the eternal home that awaits us in the kingdom of heaven.

# The Foretaste

The Lord wishes to share His abundant Life with us, through the greatest of all the Sacraments, the Holy Eucharist, which He instituted at the Last Supper. He gave us an everlasting remembrance of His great love and mercy for all of us. We share in the Body, Blood, Soul and Divinity of Christ and have an intimate and personal encounter with the Lord in Holy Communion. In the Constitution on the Church, *"Lumen Gentium,"* the Second Vatican Council rightly proclaimed that the Eucharistic Sacrifice as "The source and summit of the Christian life" (no. 26). An ancient prayer of the church tells us so beautifully, "O Sacred Banquet, in which Christ is received as food, the memory of His passion is renewed, the soul is filled with grace and a pledge of the life to come is given to us" (Catechism, no. 1323).

We need to remember to keep our souls pure, holy and without stain of sin or blemish, since we will be encountering the King of Kings at Holy Mass. Although it may sound like a truly impossible task, we hear, "Jesus looked at them and said, 'For man this is impossible, but for God all things are possible' " (Mt. 19:26).

There is an expression I heard in Latin, *"Juxta Domenicam Viventes"* which means, "Live close to the Sunday." Most people do not have the opportunity to attend daily Mass, due to their work schedules, but they can make their weekly encounter with the Lord at Sunday Mass be as meaningful as possible. If we choose to do so, it is possible to have the abundant graces and blessings of Holy Mass and Communion linger in our hearts. We can do this best by uniting ourselves with the Lord and recalling His love, goodness and mercies to us. In this way, the joy of our sweet encounter with the Eucharistic Lord on Sunday remains with us throughout the week that follows. St. Philip Neri wrote, "He who loves the Mass is already in paradise."

Over the years, I have been so saddened to hear people tell me that they only attend Holy Mass at Christmas and Easter; some of them are even my relatives. I always reply to them, explaining that "The same way you need to nourish your body; you need to nourish your soul." Your body would not be in very good condition at all if you only ate food only twice per year, even if it were the best food.

The Lord Jesus loves us more than we can even imagine and wants us to share in His Eucharistic Banquet to be nourished and renewed in heart, mind, and body and to be instruments of love toward others. The Lord tells us, "Unless you eat My body and drink My blood, you do not have My life within you" (Jn. 6:53). A few verses later, this is reiterated, "Whoever eats My flesh and drinks My blood remains in Me and I in him" (vs. 56). I recall the story of the Transfiguration, when the chosen apostles, Peter, James and John were invited by the Lord Jesus to go to the top of Mt. Tabor with Him and "He was transfigured before them and His face shone like the sun and His garments became white as light" (Mt. 17:2). They did not want to leave and Peter said, "Lord how good it is to be here" (vs. 4).

However, the apostles did have to depart from that uplifting experience on the mountaintop. They were on their way to Jerusalem to be witnesses to God's plan of redemption. It was to unfold when the Lord would be handed over to be put to death and then be raised triumphantly from the dead. To their great dismay, they heard Jesus tell them,

> "Behold, we are going up to Jerusalem, and the Son
> of Man will be handed over to the chief priests and
> the scribes, and they will condemn Him to death and
> hand Him over to the Gentiles, who will mock Him,
> spit upon Him, scourge Him, and put Him to death,
> but after three days He will rise" (Mk. 10:33-34).

For those chosen three apostles, Peter, James and John, the experience of the Transfiguration was a foretaste of the glory of heaven for them. So too, is the Holy Sacrifice of the Mass for each of us, we are given a foretaste of heaven when we receive our Eucharistic Lord in Holy Communion. We need to give our loving and active participation in it to benefit fully. After our encounter with Christ, the glorified Lord, in Holy Communion, we too must descend from the mountaintop, like it or not, and go back to the "Real world" but we have been enabled by the Lord's grace. It is given to us to persevere when we have to deal with the crosses of daily life that come our way.

During Holy Mass, we have had the opportunity to behold the Glory of God, and be changed into His likeness, through our encounter with Christ. I recall the disciples on the road to Emmaus, who recognized the Lord when "He was made known to them in the breaking of the bread" (Lk. 29:35). They did not want Him to depart and said, "Remain with us" (Lk. 29:35) "*Mane Nobiscum Domine.*"

The Lord Jesus manifests His great Love and Mercy to us. He feeds us with His Sacred Body and Blood and remains with us, hidden in the tabernacle, to be truly present with us. St. John Vianney, the patron of parish priests, would often point to the tabernacle and say, "He is there, Who loves us so much." During the concluding year of the Second Vatican Council, Pope Paul VI promulgated his encyclical on the Holy Eucharist, "*Mysterium Fidei*" (Mystery of Faith) dated September 3, 1965. He suggested that the most efficacious way of growing in holiness is time spent with Jesus in the Most Blessed Sacrament,

> "Anyone who has a special devotion to the Sacred Eucharist, and who tries to repay Christ's infinite love for us with an eager and unselfish love of his own, will experience and fully understand — and this will bring great delight and benefit to his soul — just how precious is a life hidden with Christ in God" (no. 67).

While in the presence of the Sacramental Lord, we have the opportunity to unite our own suffering with those of Jesus crucified. While united with Him, we can atone for the sins of the world. In this way, our own sacrificial suffering becomes our own personal way to transform each of our crosses and tribulations into tremendous blessings. We need only look at the headlines, whether on the television, or the newspaper, to be reminded of the secularization of our culture, and the ways that the Lord is neglected and offended by sin. We can spend time with the Lord to ask for His pardon and mercy for all the sacrileges against Him.

The great Church Father, St. Augustine, called the Eucharist a "Sign of unity and a bond of charity" (*Patrologia Latina*, vol. 35, 1613). It unites all of us, not only with the Lord, but also with each other, through our mutual love of the Lord. I think of our relationship to the Lord Jesus and each other by using the illustration of a bicycle wheel. Jesus Christ is at the center. We are all each individual spokes on the wheel. The closer we draw to the Lord, Who is at the center of the wheel, results in drawing us closer to each other. He is the connection which brings each of us closer together in fraternal love.

We hear, "God is Love" (I Jn. 4:8) and we are invited a few verses later to put this love of God that we have received into actions, "If we love one another, God abides in us and His love is perfected in us" (vs. 12). We should not feel compelled to participate, but do so out of love for the Lord, and to benefit our souls. The Lord tells us, "If you love Me, keep My commandments" (Jn. 14:15).

Perhaps you may have noticed that I frequently have used this particular saying of Our Lord. I believe that it is the perfect reminder to live a faithful life, out of our love for Him, and our desire to please Him. He invites us to be united to Him in love. Jesus is the remedy for all our weaknesses and ills, and we can unite ourselves to Him, in this Most Holy of the Sacraments. It is our "*Viaticum*" which is our "Food for the journey" that leads us on the path to the kingdom of heaven.

The Fathers of the Second Vatican Council tell us that the life of the Christian is incomplete, if it is not Eucharistic. In the document, "*Presbyterorum Ordinis*," (Ministry and Life of Priests) they wrote, "All ecclesiastical ministries and works of the apostolate are bound up with the Eucharist, and are directed toward it" (no. 5). This is reiterated in the Constitution on the Church which states, "Taking part in the Eucharistic sacrifice, which is the source and summit of Christian life, the faithful offer the Divine Victim to God and themselves along with it" (no. 11).

In the remaining Sacraments, we have additional opportunities to encounter the Lord Jesus, and grow in His love and friendship. In the Sacrament of Reconciliation, we approach the merciful Lord and ask His pardon and have the chance to begin anew, trying our best to "Do good and avoid evil." Throughout His life, Jesus showed mercy toward sinners. The Sacrament of Confirmation is a fuller outpouring of the seven gifts of the Holy Spirit that we received at our Baptism as a completion and compliment to it.

There are also two sacraments of adulthood. Holy Orders is the sacrament by which those who are called by the Lord to serve Him, are empowered to bring His love and mercy to others, both sacramentally and through their preaching. Christ the High Priest conferred His priesthood upon His apostles (Jn. 20:21-23, Mt. 28:19-20).

This is the only one of the seven sacraments that is pluralized, since there are three orders or levels in Holy Orders. They are, firstly, the Diaconate, which is a ministry of service, that we learn about in the Acts of the Apostles (Acts 6:1-7, Mt. 20:26). These men of good repute were selected to be helpers to the apostles in their duties, so that they could continue to devote themselves to "Prayer and the ministry of the Word" (vs. 4).

The Presbyterate, the second of the orders, is more frequently referred to as the Holy Priesthood, and the chapter that follows will be dedicated to it. The third order is the Episcopacy, wherein some priests are named by the Holy Father to become the "Successors of the Apostles." This title was given to those who serve as bishops by St. Cyprian of Carthage (Ep. 69, al. 66). Through their apostolic succession, they continue the saving work of Jesus Christ throughout the centuries. The Greek word *"Episcopos"* means "Overseer" (Acts 20:28, Tit. 1:7-9).

They do this by teaching, guiding and ordaining more priests and deacons, so that the sacraments and the abundant graces that they give to souls can be continued throughout the parishes in their respective dioceses. The priests work in concert with their local bishop, to whom they promised "Obedience and respect" on the day of their ordination. I learned that St. Catherine of Siena had once observed, "Religious and priests without obedience are like people in costumes." St. Ignatius of Antioch wrote, "Obey the bishop, as Jesus Christ obeyed the Father" (*Ad Smyrnaeos*, VIII, P.G. VIII, p. 714).

The Holy Father, who is a member of the order of bishops, is the Vicar of Jesus Christ, our Chief Shepherd. The pope is our visible shepherd on earth. My favorite title for the pope has always been that of *"Pontifex Maximus"* which means the Supreme Pontiff. This translates literally as the "Ultimate Bridge Builder." The goal of the pope, bishops, priests and deacon are to be bridge builders. We are to help the people of God to cross the bridge from the human to the divine. From the altar to the pew is the place that the grace of the Lord is destined. We are called to bring God to men and men to God.

The Holy Father rules, teaches and sanctifies. As the Lord Jesus gave "The power of the keys" to St. Peter, they remain with his successors. The Lord said, "Amen, I say to you, whatever you bind on earth shall be bound in heaven, and whatever you loose on earth shall be loosed in heaven" (Mt. 18:18). There is an expression, *"Roma Locuta Est, Causa Finita Est"* which is attributed to St. Augustine, (Sermon 131) and means "Rome has spoken, the case is finished." In other words, the Holy Father is the ultimate decision maker in matters of faith and morals.

Marriage is the sacrament in which a man and woman join together in a spiritual partnership, so together they can glorify the Lord with their lives and achieve their salvation. The couple helps each other on their path to heaven, by self-giving and sacrifices. During the wedding ceremony, the couple faces each other and administers the vows one to another, in the presence of the church's official representative, who accepts their vows in the name of Christ and His Holy Church. The bride and groom are, in fact, the celebrants of the sacrament, and the bishop, priest or deacon, who officiates is the official witness, and accepts their vows in the Name of Christ and His Holy Church.

Shortly thereafter, when the officiant imparts the Nuptial Blessing, the bride and groom kneel, and together face the same direction. I see this as that moment that they set forth their future, when together they face the same direction to focus on Christ. The author, Antoine de Saint-Exupéry, (1900-1944) stated that love is not so much to look at each other, but that together the couple should look in the same direction.

Especially on the day of their wedding, the married couple is reminded to stay close to the Lord Jesus Christ, Who is the Light of the World, and that He will accompany, enlighten and illuminate them in the many years ahead, with all its uncertainties. It is at the Holy Altar of the Lord Jesus Christ that they have inaugurated their married life and it is only with and through Christ, that they will be nourished and sustained in the "Good times and bad and in sickness and health" as the marriage vows state.

The day of their marriage, they begin a new family and a new "Household." I think of the passage from Sacred Scripture, "Unless the Lord builds the house, its builders labor in vain" (Ps. 127:1). Over the years, I have performed many marriages, some I have seen grow and flourish, and unfortunately, I have also seen a few end in divorce. I believe that it is integral that the married couple collaborate with the Lord throughout their married lives, from the very onset, and are wholeheartedly committed to living in His love and friendship. The Lord is to be included as a welcome guest in their hearts, lives and homes. Through our contact with married couples and families, we priests help and guide them as they grow to full maturity in the faith.

Each family is called a "Domestic Church," and the Venerable Pope John Paul II beautifully emphasized this during his Angelus Message on December 31, 1995. On that day, he also officially included the title, "Queen of Families" to the Litany of Loreto. During his message, the Holy Father invited families to "Be faithful to their vocation to be authentic domestic churches."

In the Sacrament of the Anointing of the Sick, we commend those who are suffering through illness or the weight of old age to the mercy of the Lord, as they join their own sufferings to the Lord's. In some cases, they prepare themselves to encounter Him, after their departure from this world. This sacrament is referred to in the Letter of St. James,

> Is anyone among you sick? He should summon the presbyters of the church, and they should pray over him and anoint him with oil in the name of the Lord, and the prayer of faith will save the sick person, and

the Lord will raise him up. If he has committed any
sins, he will be forgiven" (Jas. 5:1-15).

Regrettably, this sacrament has been somewhat misunderstood
over the years and seen as the "Last Rites," and has had the con-
notation that one needed to be near death to request the sacrament.
However, the emphasis now, is that this sacrament is an opportunity
to approach the healing and mercy of the Lord, to be fortified in
doing the Holy Will of God, whether it be recovery or enduring
one's suffering with magnanimity and courage. As well, if it is part
of Our Lord's plan, it may be the time when the person is to pass
from this earthly existence to eternal life, which awaits all those who
have lived faithful and grace-filled lives. This is the ultimate goal of
every one's life, to be united in the love of Our Lord each day of our
earthly lives, so that we can be united with Him for all eternity in the
kingdom of heaven.

# The Priesthood

The previous chapter, regarding the Holy Eucharist, should logically be followed by one on the Holy Priesthood. At the Last Supper, the Lord Jesus Christ instituted both of these sacraments. Our Lord gave the Eucharist to us as a means to participate in His divine life of grace, and thereby to help nourish and strengthen us. The Holy Priesthood was instituted to provide the means by which the graces of the Lord can be dispensed by means of the sacraments, throughout the centuries.

The priest stands in the person of Christ, *"In persona Christi"* at the altar, in his ministerial role; they are collaborators and assistant shepherds and are configured to Jesus Christ, Who is the "Chief Shepherd" (I Pet. 5:4). Although it is the priest who presides, it is Christ Who offers. In his important 1947 encyclical, *"Mediator Dei,"* (On the Sacred Liturgy) Venerable Pope Pius XII wrote, "Prior to acting as the representative of the community before the throne of God, the priest is the ambassador of the Divine Redeemer" (no. 40). In 1996, the Venerable Pope John Paul II wrote a book on the occasion of his Fiftieth Anniversary of Ordination and referred to the priesthood as both a "Gift and Mystery."

The patron saint of parish priests, St. John Vianney told us, "The priest continues the work of redemption on earth... the priesthood is the love of the Heart of Jesus." The priest is called the *"Cura animarum"* since he takes care of the soul, hence the usage of the old terminology "Curate." He is present during the major moments in people's lives, at birth, growth, sickness and death. I believe that these are both "Touchable" and "Teachable" moments.

In the Sacrament of Baptism, the priest represents Christ the Good Shepherd, Who welcomes the sheep into the fold. In Holy Communion, he acts as Christ at the Last Supper, Who gave the apostles His own Body and Blood in anticipation of His redemptive death. Every priest helps to nourish the flock of the Good Shepherd and fortify them for life's journey with all of its ups and downs.

In the sacrament of Marriage, the priest is like Christ, Who, by His very presence, blessed the union of the husband and wife at the Wedding in Cana. In the Sacraments of Penance and Anointing of the

Sick, the priest represents Christ the Divine Physician, Who heals both soul and body. Priests help in performing Christ's miracles, and let the spiritually blind to see and the spiritually lame to walk.

The Venerable Pope John Paul II in the Apostolic Exhortation, *"Pastores Dabo Vobis"* (I Shall give you Shepherds) dated March 25, 1992, wrote, "The priest acts as an instrument of Divine Mercy in the confessional, where his spiritual fatherhood is realized in a special way" (no. 22). On July 20, 2001 the same pope stated, "Because the priest is the minister of Christ's Sacrifice and of His mercy, the priest is indissolubly bound up with the two sacraments of the Eucharist and Reconciliation (*L'Osserv. Romano*, July 21, 2001).

Pope Benedict XVI reiterated this on March 16, 2007, when he reminded us that in the administration of the Sacrament of Pardon and of Reconciliation, the priest, as the Catechism of the Catholic Church recalls, acts as "The sign and the instrument of God's merciful love for the sinner" (no. 1465). Subsequently, when speaking to priests he told them that "Love for Jesus and His Church must become the passion of your lives!" I once read, "A priest must glow." Through a deep life of prayer, he can truly be transformed into "Another Christ" and bring the Lord's radiant presence to all those whom he has the honor to serve.

Saint Paul regarded himself as a servant of Christ and "Steward of the Mysteries of God" (1 Cor. 4:1). He also affirmed that he "Received this ministry through God's mercy" (2 Cor. 4:1). In this same vein, in 2001, the Congregation for the Clergy proclaimed to every priest: "Priest of God, you embody the Mystery of Mercy!" The priest, who is called "Another Christ," needs to live his own life based on an intimate friendship with Jesus Christ, the Eternal High Priest, Who is our model. It is He Who is, "Holy, blameless, unstained, separated from sinners, exalted above the heavens... a Minister in the sanctuary which is set up, not by man but by the Lord" (Heb. 7:26; 8:2).

St. Bernard of Clairvaux wrote that the priest must become a "Reservoir of grace, before they can become a channel of grace" (Sermon XVIII in *Cantica*). The word grace is from the Latin word *"Gratia"* which means free. It is a gift that we receive and that we give to others as well. The Lord Jesus said, "The gift you received, give as a gift" (Mt. 10:8).

The Lord Jesus calls his disciples to intimacy, to share in His very life as Jesus said to Martha, "*Unum Necessarium,*" there is "One thing that is necessary" (Lk. 10:42). Martha, the sister of Lazarus, had been distracted with serving the table, while her sister Mary sat at the feet of the Lord, listening to Him teaching. He told Martha not to be troubled by many things, the one thing that was needed was chosen by Mary, and that was to be attentive to Him.

We hear repeatedly in the gospels, particularly that of St. John, the beloved disciple, of the intimate friendship and love of the Lord Jesus for His chosen apostles. As the feast of the Passover approached, we hear that the Lord Jesus "Loved His own in the world and He loved them to the end" (Jn. 13:1). He also told them, "I have called you friends" (Jn. 15:15). At the Last Supper, the Lord told them, "Love one another as I have loved you" (Jn. 13:34). In this way, the continuing work of service and charity can be based on this love between Jesus and the disciple, which is the basis.

Jesus spoke to them of the necessity of being connected to Him, from which they can derive their strength, to continue His work. He even used the analogy of the interconnectedness of the vine and branches,

> "Just as a branch cannot bear fruit on its own unless it remains on the vine, so neither can you unless you remain in Me. I am the vine, you are the branches. Whoever remains in Me and I in him will bear much fruit, because without Me, you can do nothing" (Jn. 15:4-5).

Priests can get very involved in the administrative aspects of our ministerial work. There are so many details, but we cannot let the business of religion, such as paying bills and fixing roofs, ever to replace Jesus Christ in our lives and ministry. It is important for us priests to attend to our duties "Properly and faithfully" or in Latin, "*Recte et fideliter*" and, at the same time, try our best to "Choose the better part," keeping in mind the spiritual dimension. In other words, as I once heard, "Do not be so much involved with the work of the Lord, that you forget the Lord of the work."

We priests have an opportunity to read of this reality each year on November 4. It is the feast day of St. Charles Borromeo, (1538-1584) who was the Cardinal Archbishop of Milan, Italy. In the Liturgy of the Hours, also called the Breviary, the second reading in the Office of Readings is taken from a writing of the saint, wherein he reminds priests, "Are you the pastor of a parish? If so, do not neglect the parish of your own soul" (*Acta Eccl. Mediolani*, 1599, 1177-78).

The responsory that follows that reading has always made an impression upon me, as it gives scriptural support to the challenge that St. Charles gave to the priests of his Archdiocese those many centuries ago. It follows, "Seek after integrity and holiness, faith and love, patience and gentleness. These are the things that you must command and teach, and be an example to all who believe" (I Tim. 6:11; 4:11-12).

We hear similar words from the Letter of St. Paul to Timothy, the same cited in the responsory above. He instructed them to take great care in teaching the faith, and being people of prayer, since our goal is to be one with Christ, and to give good example. He wrote,

> "Attend to the reading, exhortation, and teaching. Do not neglect the gift you have, which was conferred on you through the prophetic word with the imposition of hands of the presbyterate. Be diligent in these matters and absorbed in them, so that your progress may be evident to everyone" (I Tim. 4:13-15).

The very best way that we can give good example to others is to practice what we preach. At the Ordination Rite, we are reminded by the bishop: "Know what you are doing, imitate the mysteries you celebrate, model your life on the mystery of the Cross."

A life of piety in the priest edifies the flock. If we are people of prayer and united to the Lord, then as St. Thomas Aquinas suggested our goal is, "To contemplate, and to give to others the fruits of contemplation" which is in Latin, "*Contemplare et contemplata aliis tradere*" (*Summa Theologiae*, II-II, Q. 188, A.7). This is the way I was taught to prepare my homilies. We students were told by the professor in the seminary to take a prayerful look at the readings for the following Sunday on the prior Monday morning, and then live with them for the week, pray about them, and meditate upon them. This way the Holy Word of God could "germinate, marinate and macerate" in our minds and hearts and the important points to be included in the homily can then be developed.

In this way, the words of the priest's homily are interiorized and flow from his heart and mind, just as the Lord tells, "For from the fullness of the heart the mouth speaks" (Lk. 6:45, Mt. 12:34). This expression is so beautiful in the Latin language, with the idea that the words come from the abundance of the heart, "*Ex abundantia cordis.*" On some occasions, there may even be some research involved, to perhaps locate the proper story or anecdote that might be used to illustrate a point relevant to the Gospel, psalm or readings. Then, when the weekend Masses arrive, the ideas and inspirations that have come to us, which have been incorporated in our prayers, all come together in our homily.

The four steps of a Holy Reading of the Gospel which is called "*Lectio Divina*" which is a praying of the Sacred Scriptures are: Reading, "*Lectio*" in which you comprehend the meaning of the scriptural passage. This is followed by Meditation, "*Meditatio*" a personal reflection on the reading. The third step is Prayer, "*Oratio*" in which one listens in the silence of their heart to the inspirations from the Lord regarding the scripture. The last step is Contemplation, "*Contemplatio*" which is an interior silent resting in the Lord and His Holy Word and allowing it to become integrated in you.

In the instruction to the candidates before Ordination to the Holy Priesthood, the bishop addresses them with these words: "Share with all mankind the Word of God you have received with joy. Meditate on the law of God, believe what you read, teach what you believe, and put into practice what you teach." The priest also unites himself to the Lord Jesus Christ, through his daily sacrifices and suffering, and in particular as he offers Holy Mass each day.

The Second Vatican Council wrote, "Celebrating Holy Mass is the summit of every day in the priest's life. It goes to the core of his being where the Trinity dwells" (*Lumen Gentium*, 25). Blessed Columba Marmion wrote that "The priest should see himself as a victim united to Christ the victim." Each of us priests are dramatically reminded of this each day at Holy Mass when we kiss the altar both at the very beginning and the very end of Mass. This is a sign of embracing the cross in our own lives as priests. It is never far away. As I had previously mentioned, Blessed Mother Theresa in her very simple way of expressing things, is quoted as saying, "The more we embrace the cross, the more we become like Jesus." This is particularly true for the priest, who is called to be "Another Christ."

We can use every circumstance in our lives as an opportunity to serve Christ and the kingdom, not just our public actions, but our quiet time of prayer in our own room. It is there, when we pray the Liturgy of the Hours, that we are united to the Church throughout the world. Many of us may remember this from our youth, since we were taught the prayer entitled the "Morning Offering." In it, we begin our day by dedicating all of the joys and sorrows of each day to the Lord, and uniting them to His Sacred Heart. The complete prayer is as follows:

### *Morning Offering*

*O Jesus, through the Immaculate Heart of Mary,*
*I offer You my prayers, works, joys and sufferings*
*of this day for all the intentions of Your Sacred Heart,*
*in union with the Holy Sacrifice of the Mass*
*throughout the world, in reparation for my sins, for*
*the intentions of all my relatives and friends, and*
*in particular for the intentions of the Holy Father.*
*Amen.*

The more that each priest becomes a man of prayer, the more that he can be transformed into another Christ, his goal. To be effective, he must be "hidden." This is in the sense that our own personalities are put in the background, and we must be a transparent image of Christ. Each of us has our very own unique and unrepeatable gifts and talents, and we use them to glorify the Lord and serve

His people. We are to put away our individual vanities, and not want to be noticed, so that Christ can shine through us. This is the call of all Christians as St. Augustine observed, "We have become not only Christians, but Christ."

It has been said that if the priest is holy, his people will learn to be holy through his good example. There is an old saying: "Christ taught the apostles by His lore, but practiced it before." The word "Lore" means beliefs and traditions, and this quote is to underline the fact that the Lord's actions spoke louder than His words and so do those of the priest to his flock. The priest is among his people, "Not to be served, but to serve," (Mk. 10:45) in imitation of the Lord Jesus, Who humbly washed the feet of His apostles at the Last Supper.

When I was in my junior year in High School in 1973, I recall a great teacher of English Literature. His enthusiasm helped to give me a wonderful introduction and life-long appreciation for so many well known works that is part of our great heritage. In particular, I recall the famous work of the author, Geoffrey Chaucer (c.1343-1400). In his well-known book, "*The Canterbury Tales*," specifically in the Parson's Tale, we hear the following quote, "If gold rust, what shall iron do? For if a priest in whom we trust be foul, it is no wonder if a common man rusts" (I, A, 500-502).

This quote considers the priest, as the Lord's representative, as gold and the laity as iron. Although this may have been written with a medieval mindset, the people of God, even today, do indeed look up to their priest and expect them to live a holy and committed life. A good religious sister once told me "The lily that festers is worse than the weed." We are not expecting a weed to smell good, even when it withers. However, it is much worse when the lily begins to wilt and smell awful, since it is a much more prized bloom, with a sweet-smelling fragrance. There is more of a dramatic extreme when it fades, since its smell then changes from sweet to foul.

We ask the Lord to help each one of the priests to continue to do their best in the ups and downs, joys and sufferings in the world, and the particular circumstances in which they live. They are invited to intimately unite themselves to Jesus Christ, the Great High Priest, Who suffered and triumphed. We hear, "But rejoice in so far as you

295

share in Christ's sufferings, that you may also be glad and rejoice when His glory is revealed" (I Pet. 4:13). The priest is invited to draw near to Mary in his prayer life. The Venerable Pope Pius XII wrote,

> "Our Lady loves everyone with a most tender love, but she has a particular predilection for priests, who are the living image of Jesus Christ. Take comfort in the thought of the love of the Divine Mother for all of you, and you will find the labors of your sanctification and priestly ministry much easier" *"Menti Nostra"* (On the Sanctity of Priestly Life, no. 142).

May the grace of the Lord sustain His priests in our work and help us to be faithful and humble servants of Jesus Christ the Eternal High Priest. May we be able to hear one day those all important words, "Well done, good and faithful servant," and thus be invited to the eternal joy of the kingdom of heaven.

## Patron Saint of Priests

As this book was being written, His Holiness, Pope Benedict XVI proclaimed a year-long celebration dedicated to St. John Vianney, the Patron of Parish Priests, to mark the 150th Anniversary of the death of the saint. The Pope's letter, dated June 16, 2009, proclaimed a "Year for Priests" and was inaugurated as he presided at Solemn Vespers for the Vigil of the Solemnity of the Sacred Heart of Jesus on June 19, 2009 and was to conclude on the same Solemnity in 2010. In his letter, the Holy Father expressed the hope that this year would "Deepen the commitment of all priests to interior renewal, for the sake of a more forceful and incisive witness to the Gospel in today's world."

St. Jean-Baptiste-Marie Vianney, known as the Curé of Ars, was born in Dardilly, near Lyon, France on May 8, 1786, the son of Matthieu Vianney and Marie Beluze. He was the third of six children, in a family of farmers, whose simple faith and childlike devotion to the Lord greatly influenced him. It was a difficult time, since the French Revolution began when he was three years old. He received his First Holy Communion in secret, since Holy Mass could not be offered in public at that time in his village.

He began his studies for the priesthood in 1806, under the direction of Abbé Balley, the parish priest in Ecully, a nearby village. Although he encountered insurmountable obstacles during his theological studies, he persevered throughout them all, including conscription into military service during the time of Napoleon. St. John Vianney was ordained to the Holy Priesthood on August 13, 1815, and three years later was made the pastor of the Church of St. Sixtus, in Ars-Sur-Formans, which had 230 souls at the time. It was considered a remote hamlet, and he would serve there for the next forty-one years. On the day that he was walking to Ars, he was unsure which road to take, and asked a young boy for directions. The boy responded that he lived there and was going home. To that, the saint responded, "If you show me the way to Ars, I will show you the way to heaven!"

Upon his arrival, he was shocked at the spiritual dryness of his flock. However, through prayer and mortification, he sought the spiritual renewal of his parish. He offered Holy Mass with reverence; his sermons were strong, yet simple, and his great love for the Blessed Sacrament and Blessed Mother shone through. His efforts included waging war against blasphemy, obscenity and profanity. Over the years, his reputation as a confessor and director of souls became well known and his parishioners claimed that he had the ability to read souls.

Soon, throughout France and beyond, his reputation as a holy priest spread, and he became known as the "Curé d'Ars." From 1830 to 1845, his daily visitors for confession and counsel averaged three hundred. In the winter, he was in the confessional twelve hours daily, and this would increase to eighteen hours during the summer months. Even the staunchest of sinners were converted at his mere word. By 1855, the number of pilgrims to Ars had reached twenty thousand per year.

Throughout his life, he retained a childlike simplicity, and he remains to this day, the living image of the priest after the heart of Christ. He labored incessantly with great humility, gentleness, patience and cheerfulness. In his homily on the occasion of the opening for the Year for Priests, Pope Benedict quoted a lovely and touching saying of his, which is also included in the Catechism of the Catholic Church, "The priesthood is the love of the heart of Jesus" (no. 1589).

He died on August 4, 1859 at the age of seventy-three and on October 3, 1874. Jean-Baptiste-Marie Vianney was proclaimed Venerable by Blessed Pope Pius IX and was beatified by St. Pope Pius X on January 8, 1905. He was canonized by Pope Pius XI on May 31, 1925, who also named him the principle patron saint of parish priests in 1929. His feast day is celebrated each year on August 4, and he is depicted wearing the violet stole, worn in the confessional.

One of the sayings of the holy patron of parish priests that has been brought to the attention of priests during the "Year for Priests" was the following, "A good shepherd, a pastor after God's heart, is the greatest treasure which the good Lord can grant a parish and one of the most precious gifts of divine mercy." May St. John Vianney be a model for the priests of today, so that all of them, myself included, can show the people of God "the way to heaven!"

**10**

# Thoughts on Christian Living

## Sorrows

Of course it is easy to speak and write touching words when all is going well, and one's life has not been touched by tragedy or sorrow. On several occasions in recent years, when I had preached on the importance of surrendering oneself to the Providential care of the Lord and His Holy Will, I have been approached and challenged. People had not been rude in any way, but they were just trying to figure out the will of a loving God, amid difficult and sorrowful moments. In particular, they referred to the events of the tragic terrorist attacks of September 11, 2001. When asked about this, I try my best to explain to them that the Lord gives all of us free will. We can choose to love Him, and do the right thing, or reject Him, and go down a dangerous path, which can lead to erroneous choices and to tragedies such as these. However, the Lord can take sorrow or tragedy, and even betrayal and bring some good out of them.

I recall the story of Joseph, who was sold into slavery, out of the jealousy, by his brothers. At first, they cast him into a cistern, and even wanted to kill him, so great was their hatred for their own brother, who was the favorite son of their father. Years later, when there was a famine in their land, and they needed to go to Egypt for food, they repented and asked Joseph's forgiveness. He responded that it was all in accordance with the plan of God,

299

"You shall say to Joseph, 'Jacob begs you to forgive the criminal wrongdoing of your brothers, who treated you so cruelly. Please, therefore, forgive the crime that we, the servants of your father's God, committed.' Joseph responded, 'Even though you meant harm to me, God meant it for good' " (Gen. 50:17, 20).

The Lord God has His own reasons why He allows tragedies to happen. We hear in the Sacred Scripture, "For My thoughts are not your thoughts, neither are your ways My ways, says the Lord" (Is. 55:9). Unfortunately, some people go to the opposite extreme, when they experience or see tragedies and even express to others their doubts that God exists.

I once heard a story about a man who went to the barber for a haircut. As he was clipping the man's hair, the barber was talking about so much trouble in the world, murders and tragedies and eventually stated, "God does not exist." The client said nothing throughout. However, at the end of the haircut, he looked out of the window and saw a gentleman who was disheveled, with his hair unkempt and a scraggly beard. The man told the barber, "Barbers do not exist!" The barber asked how that could be, since the man just got a haircut. The client said, "Well, look at that man, why is he like that, unless there are no barbers to clean up his hair?"

The conclusion is that people get into trouble, because they do not go to God and walk in His friendship. Then they choose the wrong path and bring murder and mayhem. This is when bad things can even happen to good, innocent people. It is just like the folks who choose not to look neat and clean and avoid the barber.

Perhaps the answer to try to understand that tragic day of September 11th, lies in the story of Todd Beamer, who led the counterattack on United Flight 93, which crashed in a field outside Shanksville, Pennsylvania. His young widow, Lisa wrote a book, "*Let's Roll*," where she explained that it was still possible to do something positive in the midst of a crisis, as her husband did. After the death of Todd, she came to the conclusion that she and others were able to move ahead in hope, courage and faith despite their troubles. On the occasion of the terrorist attacks, Pope John Paul II said, "Faith comes to our aid, when words seem to fail." St. Paul wrote about,

> "The Father of mercies, Who comforts us in our every affliction, so that we may be able to comfort those who are in any affliction with the comfort with which we ourselves are comforted by God. For as Christ's sufferings overflow to us, so through Christ do we share abundantly in comfort. If we are afflicted, it is for your comfort and salvation; if we are comforted, it is for your comfort, which enables you to endure the same sufferings that we suffer. Our hope for you is firm, for we know that as you share in the sufferings, you also share in the comfort (2 Cor. 1:4-7).

When I was a young seminarian, my very wise Spiritual Director, Fr. Arthur told me, "The harder the rubber ball hits the ground, the higher it rises." Our souls are like that ball. The Lord God gives us trials, and we even get knocked around, to draw us closer to Him, and to realize that we cannot do anything on our own strength. St. Padre Pio tells us: "Our suffering is God's gentle caresses, beckoning us to come back to Him, to admit that we are not in control of our lives, but He is in control and can be trusted with our lives completely."

Trials, adversities and obstacles can be overcome with the grace of the Lord. If we place our confidence in Him, the Lord Jesus can even give us "The peace of God that surpasses all understanding will guard your hearts and minds in Christ Jesus" (Phil. 4:7). The Lord can equip us with the fortitude and determination that we need. We believe that "If God is for us, who can be against us" (Rom. 8:31)? We are invited to be strong in the Lord, amid sorrows and suffering. The psalms attest to this. Even when King David felt besieged by his own son, Absalom, and those who wanted to destroy him, he overcame his worries and placed his trust in the Lord God, knowing that the Lord will see him though his troubles, "How many are my foes, Lord! How many rise against me! How many say of me, 'God will not save that one.' But You, Lord, are a shield around me; my glory, You keep my head high" (Ps. 3:2-4).

We also can turn our eyes to the loving care of Mary, the Mother of Our Lord. In particular, I recall her words to St. Juan Diego, (1474-1548) on December 9, 1531 when she appeared to him near what is now Mexico City. We now refer to the image imprinted on the "*tilma*," or cloak, of that holy man as "Our Lady of Guadalupe." He was canonized by the Venerable Pope John Paul II on July 31, 2002. The words of Mary to him, I believe, are an invitation to all of us to turn to Our Blessed Mother's maternal care in our times of difficulty,

> "Hear and let it penetrate into your heart, my dear little son: let nothing discourage you, nothing depress you: let nothing alter your heart or your countenance. Also do not fear any illness or vexation, anxiety or pain. Am I not here, who am your Mother? Are you not under my shadow and protection? Am I not your fountain of life? Are you not in the folds of my mantle, in the crossing of my arms? Is there anything else that you need?"

We hear the words of St. Paul, that remind us that it is by abandoning ourselves to the providential care and mercy of the Lord, that we realize we are weak human beings, in need of the grace of the Lord Jesus, to get us through difficulties,

> "The Lord said to me, 'My grace is sufficient for you, for power is made perfect in weakness.' I will rather boast most gladly of my weaknesses, in order that the power of Christ may dwell with me. Therefore, I am content with weaknesses, insults, hardships, persecutions, and constraints, for the sake of Christ; for when I am weak, then I am strong" (II Cor. 12: 9-10).

*The Imitation of Christ* reminds us of the following quote regarding suffering and how, although most of us tend to shy away from it at all costs, it can indeed serve to help put our lives in proper perspective, "It is good for us now and then to have some troubles and adversity; for oftentimes they make a man enter into himself, that he may know that he is in exile and place not his hopes in anything of the world" (Bk. 1, ch. 12).

When we realize our dependence upon the Lord, His care, comfort and mercy, we can have an inner peace, even amid difficulties and conflicts. We pray during the Lord's Prayer called the "Our Father" these words: "Thy kingdom come, Thy Will be done." It is not always easy to do the Holy Will of the Lord, especially when it involves pain or struggles. However, we surrender ourselves to the Lord, and serve Him here and now, by accepting the cross.

The wisdom we hear in the Book of Job, helps us to remember that into each life, some rain must fall, from time to time. "Shall we indeed accept good from God, and not accept adversity" (Job 2:10)? The solution in dealing with the adversity is to be courageous and trust in the Lord, as the psalm tells us, "Take courage and be stouthearted, all you who hope in the Lord" (Ps. 31:25). St. Teresa of Avila wrote, "To have courage for whatever comes in life – everything lies in that."

We also hear from St. Paul, "Rejoice with those who rejoice, weep with those who weep" (Rom. 12:15). If all is well with us, we can help to bring comfort and peace to others, who carry their own crosses. We hear how we can be instruments of the Lord, in the well-known prayer of the thirteenth century saint, St. Francis of Assisi.

> *Lord, make me an instrument of your Thy peace;*
> *where there is hatred, let me sow love;*
> *where there is injury, pardon;*
> *where there is doubt, faith;*
> *where there is despair, hope;*
> *where there is darkness, light;*
> *and where there is sadness, joy.*
> *O Divine Master,*
> *grant that I may not so much seek to be consoled,*
> *as to console;*
> *to be understood, as to understand;*

*to be loved, as to love;*
*for it is in giving that we receive,*
*it is in pardoning that we are pardoned,*
*and it is in dying that we are born to Eternal Life.*
*Amen.*

With the help and prayers of this saint and the company of heaven, may we truly be instruments of the healing and compassion of the Lord. It is by means of loving actions and good deeds, that we can demonstrate the love of the Lord which dwells within us. Jesus tells us,

> "By their fruits you will know them. Do people pick grapes from thorn bushes, or figs from thistles? Just so, every good tree bears good fruit, and a rotten tree bears bad fruit. A good tree cannot bear bad fruit, nor can a rotten tree bear good fruit" (Mt. 7:16-18).

May we be ever eager to be merciful in our concern for others. St. John tells us in the book of Revelation, regarding the reward that will be given to those who are charitable, "Blessed are the dead who die in the Lord, from now on... let them find rest from their labors, for their good works accompany them" (Rev. 14:13).

We ask the Lord that we may be merciful to those undergoing sorrows and pains, and be instruments of healing, peace and comfort to them amid their afflictions. May our good works of charity and compassion to others, in their time of sorrows, accompany us when we stand before the Lord and help us to enter into the eternal life that is prepared for us in the kingdom of heaven.

# Healing

The Lord invites all of us to live a holy life. This is easier to accomplish when we are "whole" and interiorly free, and not impeded or held back. Then, we embrace the Lord and more readily accept His invitation to live an intimate friendship with Him. We need to be without obstacles, such as pain or hurt, which can stand in the way of our love and commitment to the Lord. We do this by asking for His healing touch. Each of us needs to put away the pains of the past, as well as those in the present. They can be distractions to the goal of loving the Lord wholeheartedly, and living fully in His friendship. I truly believe that the best way we can deal with the problems and hurts that we have is to turn them over to Our Healing Lord Jesus, commending them to His mercy and pardon.

No one is perfect; we all make mistakes, and can say or do the wrong thing. Sometimes, they are mistakes that we have made, but other times they are mistakes that others have made in our regard, which have caused us pain. They can have long-term consequences that can be hurtful to ourselves or others.

Awareness is the beginning of healing and change for the better. We do not do this alone, and on our own strength. The Venerable Pope John Paul II wrote, "God alone heals, restores and transforms the human heart by His grace" "*Veritatis Splendor*" (Splendor of the Truth, no. 23). We can all learn from our mistakes, and put them in the past, in order not to repeat them, and we need to deal with the results of the mistakes of others. St. Paul wrote, "Just one thing: forgetting what lies behind, but straining forward to what lies ahead, I continue my pursuit toward the goal, the prize of God's upward calling, in Christ Jesus" (Phil. 3:13-14).

When others hurt us, it may take some time to get over the pain. When we refuse to forgive, forget and move on, we make ourselves prisoners to the anger that we hold inside, as a grudge, and it holds us back. Pope John Paul II said it succinctly, "If we do not forgive, we become prisoners of our past." We can become paralyzed and the pains we have experienced can destroy us, physically, mentally, and emotionally. We hear this lack of inner peace and suffering in the Psalms: "As long as I kept silent, my bones wasted away; I groaned all the day" (Ps. 32:3). The Book of Proverbs gives us this insight, "Man can sustain illness, but not a broken spirit" (Prov. 18:14).

I have now and then heard the expression, "I will forgive, but never forget." Well, this means that person is not really forgiving. The Lord God forgives us our sins and puts them in the past. "Though your sins are as scarlet, they will be made white as snow," we hear from the Prophet Isaiah (1:18). After he came to the realization of his great sin in having an affair with Bathsheba, King David asked the forgiveness of the Lord as we read,

> "Have mercy on me, God, in Your goodness; in Your abundant compassion blot out my offense. Wash away all my guilt; from my sin cleanse me. For I know my offense; my sin is always before me. Against You alone have I sinned; I have done such evil in Your sight. You are just in Your sentence, blameless when You condemn. True, I was born guilty, a sinner, even as my mother conceived me. Still, you insist on sincerity of heart; in my inmost being teach me wisdom. Cleanse me with hyssop, that I may be pure; wash me, make me whiter than snow" (Ps. 51:2-9).

When we forgive in our hearts, we truly set a prisoner free from captivity, and that prisoner is ourselves. The person who inflicted hurt and pain upon us has moved on, and in most cases, they probably even forgot about the whole matter. Perhaps they even came to the realization that they made a hurtful mistake in our regard, but it was too late. They did not have the opportunity to ask forgiveness, apologize or make amends. However, these hurts can sometimes eat away inside of us for decades.

I believe that we need to ask the Lord for a wonderful gift called "Spiritual Amnesia," so that after we forgive, we can also forget, and not be held down by unpleasant memories from past hurts. I believe this is how we are healed, only by surrendering the entire situation to the merciful Lord. And when thoughts reoccur, I have told people that we are to say, "Lord Jesus, I ask your mercy, please give me peace and healing in my heart, and purify and wash out these memories in Your Precious Blood."

When we sometimes think that it is not possible to get over some hurt and pain, it is good to recall that, "All things are possible with God" (Lk. 1:37). We heard this from the angel, who was sent to the Blessed Virgin Mary at the Annunciation, when she questioned how she could conceive a child, since she was a virgin. Our healing is possible only through Jesus Christ, the Son of God, Who took on the sins and burdens of all of us, and brought them to the cross. We share in His victory over sin, pain and suffering. We hear these words foretelling what the Lord would undergo for all of us as recorded by the prophet Isaiah,

> "Yet it was our infirmities that He bore, our sufferings that He endured, while we thought of Him as stricken, as one smitten by God and afflicted. But He was pierced for our offenses, crushed for our sins, Upon Him was the chastisement that makes us whole, by His stripes we were healed" (Is. 53:4-5).

Several years back, around 1992, someone recommended a book to me, called *"Miracles Do Happen."* It is by a religious Franciscan sister from Ireland, Sr. Briege McKenna. I read the entire book in one afternoon; it was just wonderful. Over the years, there has been one important part of her book that made a great impression upon me. Sr. Briege wrote about the healing power of the Lord Jesus and His miracles. In particular, she emphasized the miracle of the woman who has been afflicted with a hemorrhage for eighteen years and had sheepishly approached the Lord, just to have the opportunity to touch Him. There was a moving and yet dramatic interchange between the woman and the Lord,

> "She said, 'If I but touch His clothes, I shall be cured.' Immediately her flow of blood dried up. She felt in her body that she was healed of her affliction. Jesus, aware at once that power had gone out from Him, turned around in the crowd and asked, 'Who

has touched My clothes?' But his disciples said to Him, 'You see how the crowd is pressing upon You, and yet You ask, 'Who touched Me?' And He looked around to see who had done it. The woman, realizing what had happened to her, approached in fear and trembling. She fell down before Jesus and told Him the whole truth. He said to her, 'Daughter, your faith has saved you. Go in peace and be cured of your affliction' " (Mk. 5:28-34).

I believe that this is how we need to approach the good Lord, with trusting and ardent faith, in His great power to heal us. And the most wonderful thing of all, as Sister so well pointed out, is that we have very much more than just the hem of the Lord's garment to touch. He comes to us in Holy Communion, the Body, Blood, Soul and Divinity of Jesus, so that we encounter His Real Presence. How much more then, should we approach our Lord with trusting faith, asking Him to fill our emptiness, and make full our insufficiencies.

In this book, I had used the story of this miracle to illustrate trust over fear. Here, we see the Lord's healing power as a result of faith in Him. In another encounter involving a miracle, Jesus, in fact, "marveled" at the faith of the Centurion, who had asked for the healing of his servant. The Lord said, "Truly I say to you, I have not found such faith with anyone in Israel" (Mt. 8:10, Lk. 7:9).

At the first World Apostolic Congress on Mercy in Rome April 2-6, 2008, I was privileged to see a beautiful illustration of healing of oneself through forgiving others. One of the principle speakers at the Lateran Basilica on Saturday, April 5 was Immaculée Ilibagiza who gave a very moving personal testimony, which received a standing ovation. It was regarding her experience of hiding from potential killers in the genocide in Rwanda in 1994.

She, along with eight other women, hid in a 3 foot by 4 - foot bathroom in a house, and she kept her sanity through the praying of the Rosary and the Chaplet of the Divine Mercy. Her devout Catholic father had given her those rosary beads shortly before she needed to go into hiding, and just prior to his own brutal murder. She told us that she began to pray the Holy Rosary, as a way of drowning out the negativity, building up inside of her. Immaculée told us that she found solace and peace in prayer, and began to pray to ask the Lord to get her over the anger, resentment and rage about her situation, which otherwise could have destroyed her faith.

We learned that after her 91 days in hiding, she had gone from 115 pounds to 65 pounds. She eventually learned that her parents and most of her family had been murdered. One of the police officers had captured the man who murdered her family, and took Immaculée to the prison. The officer put her in the room with him, and gave her free rein to do whatever she wished in revenge to his killing her family members. When she came face to face with the killer of her mother and her brother, she said the unthinkable to him, "I forgive you." They were all astounded. Immaculée told us that it was through prayer, that she eventually found it possible, and in fact imperative, to forgive her tormentors and her family's murderers.

With prayer all things are possible. It will aid us in having inner peace and enable us to forgive others, and be forgiven by the mercy of God. Through the grace of the Lord, all of us can be elevated, and pulled up from the pains and hurts of the past that drag us down. We can live in the Lord's beautiful friendship, free from anger and resentment, a friendship on earth that is a foretaste of that eternal friendship to which we aspire in the kingdom of heaven.

# Forgiving

The Lord's Prayer, known as the "Our Father" reminds us of reciprocity in forgiving, when we pray, "Forgive us our trespasses, as we forgive those who trespass against us" (Mt. 6:9-13, Lk. 11:24). The Lord Jesus told us, "Love your enemies, and pray for those who persecute you," (Mt. 5:44) and He said that we need to "Forgive each other from your heart" (Mt. 18:35). He gave us a Parable of the Unforgiving Servant that illustrates this point clearly. In it, we hear of an act of mercy and forgiveness that needed to be returned to another, after it had been received. Unfortunately, although the servant was shown mercy, he failed to show it as well.

In this parable, the Lord Jesus told His listeners about a king, who decided to settle accounts with his servants, and a debtor was brought before him who owed him a huge amount. Since he had no way to pay it back, his master ordered him to be sold, along with his wife, children and property, to repay the debt. The servant then fell down, did him homage, and said,

> " 'Be patient with me, and I will pay you back in full.' Moved with compassion, the master of that servant let him go and forgave him the loan. However, when that servant had left, he found one of his fellow servants who owed him a much smaller amount. He seized him and started to choke him, demanding, 'Pay back what you owe.' Falling to his knees, his fellow servant begged him, 'Be patient with me, and I will pay you back.' But he refused. Instead, he had him put in prison until he paid back the debt. Now when his fellow servants saw what had happened, they were deeply disturbed, and went to their master and reported the whole affair. His master summoned him and said to him, 'You wicked servant! I forgave you your entire debt because you begged me to. Should you not have had pity on your fellow servant, as I had pity on you?' Then in anger his master handed him over to the torturers until he should pay

back the whole debt. So will my heavenly Father do to you, unless each of you forgives his brother from his heart" (Mt. 18:26-35).

In some cases, we also need to have mercy on ourselves, forgiving ourselves for our own mistakes, both big and small, that we have made over the years. That may be the most difficult thing of all to do. On occasion, our own poor choices may have done great damage to the lives of others or ourselves.

All actions have consequences, either good or bad, as most of us came to learn in Grammar School, when we were preparing for our Spelling Tests. If we studied hard the night before, then we got a good grade on the test. We got a nice shiny gold star on our test paper, and were proud to bring it home to show our parents. However, if we made a poor choice and on the night before the test, watched our favorite show on television, rather than study, then, most likely, we got a lot of corrections on our test papers, usually with a red pen. Then we were ashamed to show them to our parents. But, after all, it was our own fault, wasn't it? We had made a poor choice, but there is always next time, and hopefully we will remember that poor choice, and its consequences, and try to do better and study for next test, so we can get a better grade.

I have a second cousin whose name is Roseann. Her paternal grandmother and my maternal grandmother were sisters. I know her father, Ben, since I was a child and went to his wedding on June 29, 1974. Over the years, I watched Roseann and her family growing up. Ben is a dentist and has done well professionally, as well as financially, and they live in a beautiful house, in a great neighborhood in the suburbs.

In recent years, I got to know Roseann even better, since she moved to New Haven, Connecticut, not far from Bridgeport, where I was assigned, and teaches Grammar School there. She told me that a few years back, she had gotten addicted to pain killers, went to a rehabilitation facility and decided to "make a fresh start." She gave me her permission to use her name and tell her story. Roseann told me that she thought that Jesus was mad at her, because of what she did, and she is keeping her distance from Him, afraid to approach, embarrassed and ashamed of her blunder.

She told me that she tries to be a good person, and goes to yoga classes several times a week. I told her in a nice tone of voice that "Yoga is not a substitute for Jesus" in her life, and please do not keep her distance from the Lord, since He would not want that. I told her, "On the contrary, the Lord really loves you and wants to help you get through this time of struggle. You can do it with His grace and help." As well, I suggested the very best medicine for her to continue her recovery. That is to receive the Sacraments, and to rely on Jesus Christ for the healing that she needs. After almost two years of encouraging her, and a bit of cajoling, she told me that she located a Catholic Church just a few blocks away, and has been attending Mass regularly.

The Lord is merciful and forgiving, He wants us to approach His bounteous Mercy, be purified through the Sacrament of Reconciliation and get a fresh start. We hear these wonderful words from the Word of God, "Therefore, confess your sins to one another, and pray for one another, that you may be healed" (Jas. 5:16). We need to have great trust in the Lord's mercy and goodness, and not feel sorry for ourselves, ashamed, embarrassed or even unworthy to approach the dear Lord for those mistakes we made. By the grace of God, we can be lifted up, if we believe in His power to help us to overcome our difficulties. St. Paul wrote,

> "But God, Who is rich in mercy, because of the great love He had for us, even when we were dead in our transgressions, brought us to life with Christ and raised us up with Him... by grace you have been saved though faith; this is not our own doing, but it is a gift of God" (Eph. 2:4-5, 8).

When I first learned of Roseann's difficulties, I took the opportunity to reacquaint myself with the self-help programs, such as Alcoholics or Narcotics Anonymous, which are both based on a Twelve Step Program. The A.A. program for recovery was formulated in 1955, and many of the steps refer to the help of God in overcoming one's difficulties. It is based on spiritual principles. I went to the Public Library and looked through some of the Alcoholic Anonymous literature and found some inspiring quotes such as, "In every case, pain has been the price of admission to a new life. But this admission price had purchased more than we expected. It brought a measure of humility, which we soon discovered to be a healer of pain" (Twelve Steps and Twelve Traditions, p.75).

In reviewing the steps and advice that was given, I was pleased to see the spiritual dimension throughout. For example, "We will suddenly realize that God is doing for us, what we could not do for ourselves" (Alcoholics Anonymous, p.84). This brings to mind the Scriptural quote, "For it is God Who works in you, to will and act according to His good purpose" (Phil. 2:13). In Step Three, the person is asked to make a decision to turn over their difficulties to the care of God. Again, the Word of God comes to mind, "I urge you, brothers, in view of God's mercy, to offer your bodies as living sacrifices, holy and pleasing to God, which is your spiritual worship" (Rom. 12:1).

Both in Steps Six and Seven, the person asks God to remove their defects of character and shortcomings. As we hear in the writings of St. James, "Humble yourselves before the Lord, and He will lift you up" (Jas. 4:10). We read in Step Eleven, that prayer and meditation are recommended. This is indicated by St. Paul, "Let the Word of God dwell in you richly" (Col. 3:16). As well, the recovering person is invited to ask the help of God, in the knowledge of His Will, and the power to carry it out.

Over the years, I have always told people that in many of life's crises, the solution is to: "Grieve, forgive and live!" First, we have sorrow or have grief for a loss, injury or mistake. Next, we are to forgive ourselves or others. Lastly, put it all in the past, move on, and live our lives unencumbered by past errors. It is only by the grace of the Lord and commending all to His mercy, that this can be done. On our own strength, we would not get past "Square One." With God all is possible, we need to have faith, as the Lord Jesus often told his disciples (Mk. 11:22, Mt. 14:28-31, Mt. 16:8) and have confidence in Him, "Therefore, do not throw away your confidence; it will have great recompense. You need endurance to do the will of God, and receive what He has promised" (Heb. 10:35-36).

The solution for all of our ills is to involve the Lord in them. He has all the remedies and is the Divine Physician and Psychologist all wrapped up in one. With Him, we can find all the solutions, even if it involves suffering, that is part of His plan too, since He told us, "Whoever does not carry his own cross, and come after Me cannot be My disciple" (Lk. 14:27).

We need only approach Him for wholeness and healing and the grace to carry the cross that He has seen fit to give us. The Book of Psalms gives us several insights into this, that those who stay close to the Lord will be aided to overcome obstacles, "Though I walk in the midst of trouble, Thou dost preserve my life" (Ps. 138:7). As well as the following,

> "Because he cleaves to Me in love, I will deliver him; I will protect him because he knows My Name. When he calls to Me, I will answer him; I will be with him in trouble, I will rescue him and honor him. With long life I will satisfy him, and show him My salvation" (Ps. 91:14-16).

A few years ago, I was asked by a priest, who had just been named a bishop, to design his coat-of-arms. Each bishop has this design for usage on his official documents. When I met with the bishop-elect, we discussed the various elements to be incorporated on the shield. Most families have a shield, but if they include grotesque monsters and weapons for war, that were appropriate in battle in the Middle Ages, they are usually replaced by more spiritual elements. After we established that part of the design, we moved on to discuss the colors that he preferred to be used. When I asked if he has any particular preferences, he responded, "Use black and blue, they are the colors of my life!" We both burst out in laughter.

I thought how they surely might be the colors of everyone's life. We all have had our ups and downs, and taken little hits and punches and have our battle scars. The secret is to "Roll with the punches" as the expression goes, and things will work out better, and we will be less bruised along the way. We are not to take things too seriously, and let every bruise become a major life catastrophe. Over the years I remember reading these words by the well known First Lady, philanthropist and diplomat, Eleanor Roosevelt, (1884-1962) who gave the advice that a person gains strength, courage and confidence by those experiences in which one stops to look fear in the face and are able to say, "If I lived through this horror. I can take the next thing that comes along." Forgiving oneself, healing and moving forward does not happen overnight, but Our Lord can accompany us every step of the way, if we invite Him to do so. We can make Him an integral part of the healing process, and in fact, even better, the center of our very lives.

There is an expression, *"Ad Astra per Aspera"* which means "To the stars through difficulties." This is, by the way, the Kansas state motto. We recall the expression made famous by athletic trainers in gyms or diet specialists, "No pain, no gain." Well, the version that I prefer is "No cross, no crown." The heavier the cross, the more encrusted with sparkling gems our heavenly crown will be. That is the path the Lord trod, the Way of the Cross, if we follow and be faithful, it can help to lead us on the path to holiness. That is our goal, to live a holy life, which will prepare us for the eternal life in the kingdom of heaven.

# Providence

Each of us needs to help ourselves to progress spiritually, and to heal from past hurts and pains. We can do that best, by forgiving and moving on, and embracing each day, with its ups and downs, by the grace of God. We need to depend on the help of the Lord in all our endeavors, because, those splendid words, "Jesus, I trust in You" should so readily be on our lips, and a vital part of our daily lives. I once heard a quote, attributed to St. Augustine, "Work as if all depends on you, and pray as if all depends on God." A person who grew up in the Carolinas told me the following quote, complete with their bouncing southern accent, "We need to do the best we can with what we got." This is one of my very favorite expressions. At the same time, place ourselves under The Lord's providential care throughout our lives.

One of the very first Latin expressions that I learned, which in fact, gave me the interest in them, was, *"Deus Providebit"* which means "God Will Provide." St. Francis de Sales wrote, "The past we must abandon to God's mercy, the present to our fidelity, and the future to His providence." We cannot just sit back and let everything unfold, but need to collaborate and be faithful to Him, in all our actions, trusting with great confidence, that the Lord will be involved in our lives to help us throughout, come what may.

At the same time, we need to be astute, as a dear priest friend always says, "Use our wits," to see where the Lord is leading us, and comply positively with the grace-filled opportunities that He presents before us. I recall this poem that is attributed to St. Teresa of Avila. It was found after her death, on a prayer card in her prayer book, and speaks of the trust in the providential care of God in our lives,

> *Let nothing disturb you.*
> *Let nothing frighten you.*
> *All things are passing.*
> *God alone is changeless*
> *He who has patience wants for nothing*
> *He who has God has all things.*
> *God alone is sufficient.*

I distinctly remember the first time that I went to visit the hometown of my paternal grandparents in Southern Italy, Sant'Andrea di Conza. The date was 7-7-77 and it has been very easy to remember. My Grandma Francesca's youngest brother, *"Zio"* (Uncle) Stefano and his wife *"Zia"* (Aunt) Rosina, had invited me for the evening meal with their children, my father's first cousins. During our conversation, I mentioned that after the few days with them, I would be taking the train back to Rome, then returning home to the U.S.A.

Then, Zio Stefano stopped me immediately, and gently, but firmly, reminded that I must say, "If God wills, I will return to Rome..." He said this to me in Italian, *"Si Dio vuole..."* and he reminded me to be sure to always include that phrase, when speaking of my future plans. It serves as a reminder for me, to this very day, that all depends on God. In Latin, the expression goes like this: *"Deo adjuvante"* which means "With the help of God." Later in my life, I saw these words in Sacred Scripture that I truly relish,

> "Come now, you who say, 'Today or tomorrow we shall go into such and such a town, spend a year there doing business, and make a profit' you have no idea what your life will be like tomorrow. You are a puff of smoke that appears briefly and then disappears. Instead you should say, 'If the Lord wills it, we shall live to do this or that' " (Jas. 4:13-17).

Another Italian saying I heard in my childhood from my relatives on this side of the Atlantic Ocean was, *"Dio vede e provede,"* which means "God will see and provide." I enjoy recalling all these wonderful sayings that I heard as a youth and teenager, when most of my other school classmates were memorizing lyrics from the current popular band; I was memorizing Italian and Latin sayings! However, I guess that this is how things unfold, when a person has the desire to serve the Lord, as a priest, since the age of four, as I have.

Not long ago, I also recall hearing it said that "Luck is a coward's way of saying Providence" and I completely agree with that statement. When people have wished me "Good Luck," I sometimes tell them that I do not believe in luck, since nothing happens by chance, it is all part of God's plan and the blessings of the Lord that come to us. I try to do it as gently and sweetly as possible, not in a stern type of fraternal correction, which would not help at all. Hopefully, by educating them, they will see that luck has nothing to do with God's plans.

Over the years, I have continued a little known, but beautiful tradition, which occurs at the conclusion of the Christmas Season. I learned about this some years ago, when I was just a teenager, and thought it was wonderful and touching. Throughout the years, I have incorporated it into my preaching on the providence of the Lord. It is the tradition of the "Straw from the Crib." Every year the Nativity scene is set up in the church, complete with the figures of the Holy Family, shepherds, wise men and animals, surrounded by hay or straw. It is blessed when that scene is sprinkled with holy water on Christmas Eve. Then, when the Christmas Season comes to a close, with the Feast of the Baptism of the Lord, I always encourage the parishioners to go and see the display for the last time, before it is taken down and stored.

Each year, I tell each of them to take a piece of the straw from the manger scene, close to where the statue of the Baby Jesus lay. I suggest that they tuck the straw in their purse or wallet, and see it as a reminder that the Lord will provide for them, throughout the coming year. Just as the Heavenly Father helped the Holy Family to find a roof over their heads in the stable, He will help us in our needs as well. The straw is definitely not magical or a lucky charm, I tell them. However, it serves as a small reminder to trust in the providence of the Lord in our lives and in all our needs.

Of course, we must collaborate with the Lord in His providential care for us, and be prudent in the gifts He has given us. I believe in moderation in all things, eating, drinking and getting exercise. We are to take care of our bodies, even though we realize they are just the shell, and that on the inside is the more important part, our soul. We need to use the gift of Wisdom, asking the guidance of the Holy Spirit, so that we can be good stewards of the many gifts the Lord has given to us.

When difficulties come our way, those too are a part of God's plan, as long as they are not self-inflicted. When I was in grammar school, I saw a plaque that read, "What you are is God's gift to you, what you make of yourself is your gift to God." We are invited to use prudently all the gifts that the Lord has bestowed on us, according to His providential design, and in return, give Him glory and honor. In short, we are to put our priorities in place and put the Lord, and doing His Holy Will with all of our hearts, above all things. Jesus gives us this formula for life very succinctly, "But seek first the kingdom of God and His righteousness, and all these things will be given you besides" (Mt. 6:33, Lk. 12:31).

St. Teresa of Avila wrote that Jesus spoke to her in the depths of her soul when she was preoccupied with some important matter and the Lord told her, "You take care of My things, and I will take care of yours." One of the best ways to put our priorities in place is to be aware of our high dignity and great calling as children of God and co-heirs of heaven. St. Peter reminds us that we are, "A chosen race, a royal priesthood, a holy nation, a people of His own, so that you may announce the praises of Him, Who called you out of darkness into His wonderful light" (1 Pet. 2:9).

We are invited, since our baptism, to walk as children of the light. At first, our parents helped us along, but as adults, we now choose to walk in Christ's light one day at a time, by our own volition. This will keep us away from darkness, and all those things associated with it, such as doubt, depression and negativity. As we hear in the Baptismal Rite, we are to keep the "Flame of Faith alive in our hearts" on a daily basis. By doing so, we can live our Baptismal promises with a real and living faith in the Lord. St. Faustina wrote about turning to the Lord with confidence and trust. This is a remedy to doubt and fear. In her diary, she wrote,

> "Eternal God, in Whom mercy is endless and the treasury of Your Compassion inexhaustible, look kindly upon us and increase Your mercy in us, that in difficult moments, we might not despair or become despondent, but with great confidence submit our-

selves to Your Holy Will, which is Love and Mercy itself." (Diary, #950)

One of my favorite things about the Holy Season of Lent is the participation in the Stations of the Cross that we conduct each Friday. I am moved each time that I read these inspiring words of St. Alphonsus di Liguori, (1696-1787) that are repeated in practically all of the meditations for each station. It reminds me of the fact that we are to love the Lord above all things, trust in Him and He will take care of us,

> "I love you, Jesus, my Love, above all things. I repent of ever having offended You. Never allow me to offend You again. Grant that I may love You always; and do with me as You will."

I recall, as a child, hearing the expression, "Not a leaf moves on a tree, that God does not permit it." There is a book that I read when I was a student in the Seminary by Fr. Jean-Pierre de Caussade, S.J., (1675-1751) called, *"Abandonment to Divine Providence,"* which has been called, by many, one of the great spiritual classics of all time. In it, the author explained that God speaks to us through every moment of every day. He encourages us to have a joyous, affirming, selfless abandonment to Him. By entering into such active contemplation and facing ourselves honestly and openly, he assures us, we can achieve the comfort and fulfillment of a life filled with the grace of the Lord.

In his book, the readers are encouraged to surrender themselves totally to God, and completely cooperate with His will in everything, trusting in His providential plans. The author tells us, "Holiness consists in one thing only: complete loyalty to God's will," and "The truly faithful soul accepts all things as a manifestation of God's grace, ignores itself and thinks only of what God is doing."

I was interested to read how the author suggested that we deal with difficulties and crosses. He wrote, "All things are sent by God, and however troublesome they are, they will, if accepted gladly, lead us surely and quickly to holiness." Another great master in the spiritual life, St. Francis de Sales, spoke of the importance of relying on the providential care in all things,

> "Do not look forward to what might happen tomorrow; the same Everlasting Father, Who cares for you today, will take care of you tomorrow and every day. Either He will shield you from suffering, or He will give you unfailing strength to bear it. Be at peace then, and put aside all anxious thoughts and imaginations."

This has been the path chosen by countless saints throughout the centuries. By surrendering their own plans and desires to those of the Lord, and trusting in His providence, they grew in holiness. We see in the lives of the saints their own struggles. I consider them the heroes of the faith, and all of us can look to them and try to emulate their example. Looking at their lives helps to make us brave, and gives us the desire to do the same.

In particular, I think of the life of St. Francesca Cabrini, whose life did not turn out as she had planned, when in her youth. As a child, she dreamed of becoming a missionary to China. In 1880, she and six other sisters took religious vows, and she founded the Institute of the Missionary Sisters of the Sacred Heart of Jesus. Then, Mother Cabrini went to Rome for an audience with His Holiness, Pope Leo XIII, to ask for his blessing upon her missionary efforts in China.

During the Audience, the Holy Father surprised her by saying, "Do not go to the East, but to the West." There was a great need for assistance for the newly arrived Italian immigrants in the United States, which was brought to the attention of the Holy Father by Blessed Giovanni Scalabrini, (1839-1905) a bishop from Piacenza, Italy.

She arrived in New York City on March 31, 1889. From there the order established seven homes and a free school and nursery in its first five years. Although her lifelong dream was to be a missionary in China, she found peace in accepting the plan of God. She worked indefatigably, and founded 67 institutions in New York, Chicago, Seattle, New Orleans, Denver, Los Angeles, Philadelphia, and in countries throughout South America and Europe. Although she always became seasick, she crossed the Atlantic Ocean twenty-five times in her missionary efforts.

Her personal motto was "I can do all things in Christ, Who gives me strength" (Phil. 4:13). Long after her death, the Missionary Sisters would even achieve Mother Cabrini's goal of establishing a mission in China. She was naturalized as an American citizen in 1909. Mother Cabrini died at Columbus Hospital in Chicago, Illinois, of complications from malaria, which she contracted in her travels. She was canonized on July 7, 1946 by the Venerable Pope Pius XII, who in 1950 declared her the Patroness of all Immigrants.

We do not know where the Lord will lead us according to His providential plans. The last page in the book of our lives has not yet been written. Only the Lord knows where each one of our paths will lead n this earth. However, we know that the Lord is on our side throughout, as we hear in the psalm, "You are good, and do what is good, teach me Your laws" (Ps. 119:68). It is our hope that we will collaborate with His Holy Will as it unfolds, day by day, and set our eyes on the true goal of our lives, which is to live in eternal presence of the Lord God, forever in the kingdom of heaven.

## Trust

The image of Jesus Christ, as the Good Shepherd, has been very consoling for me throughout the decades of my life. The Lord tells us, "I am the Good Shepherd. A good shepherd lays down His life for the sheep" (Jn. 10:11). In His great love and mercy, the Lord tends to the flock, with great care, and seeks out the sheep that are lost, to bring them back to Himself. I often use the Twenty-third psalm at Funerals. Many of the mourners are hoping to hear it, and I am happy to accommodate their expectations.

Over the years, it had brought much inner peace and consolation to me and many others. We reflect upon the Lord as the Good Shepherd, Who brings all of us, His sheep, to repose in green pastures and restores our strength near restful waters. Both the deceased and the mourners have been through an ordeal in the last few days, weeks or even longer, and now they need that rest which the Lord alone offers. It is the Lord Jesus, the Good Shepherd, Who will lead us through the dark valley, in a time of sorrow or difficulty of any sort. As the psalm states,

> "I fear no harm for You are at my side; Your rod and staff give me courage. You set a table before me as my enemies watch, You anoint my head with oil; my cup overflows. Only goodness and kindness will follow me all the days of my life; I will dwell in the house of the Lord for years to come" (Ps. 23:4-8).

This is a psalm of confidence and trust in the care of the Lord, just as a simple sheep would unreservedly follow the shepherd, who is in charge. What a wonderful way to live our lives, by being like those sheep, with the utmost confidence, knowing that the shepherd will never lead them astray, but rather, even lay down His life for the benefit of the sheep.

Our Holy Father, Pope Benedict XVI in his first encyclical letter, *"Deus Caritas Est"* (God is Love), referred to the Lord as the Loving Shepherd in his document, and gave an example of how deep and far the love and the mercy of the Lord have gone,

323

"In Jesus Christ, it is God Himself who goes in search of the 'stray sheep'... His death on the cross is the culmination of that turning of God against Himself, in which He gives Himself in order to raise up man and save him. This is love in its most radical form" (no. 12).

Another psalm can help to remind us that the Lord is our protector, "Our soul waits for the Lord, Who is our help and our shield. For in Him our hearts rejoice; in His Holy Name we trust" (Ps. 33:20-21). We priests, as well as all those who are ordained or in religious life, pray the Liturgy of the Hours several times daily. It is a way of not just sanctifying the day, but also to keep the goodness and mercy of the Lord ever in our hearts and minds, as we go throughout our priestly ministry doing His work. Many times the psalms talk about trusting in the Lord, and they make a great impression upon me. Psalm 52 tells us, "When I fear, I will trust in You, in God, Whose word I praise. In God I trust, I shall not fear: what can mortal man do to me" (vs. 3)?

St. Paul wrote about the need to have confidence, when he expressed this to his readers, "Therefore, do not throw away your confidence; it will have great recompense. You need endurance to do the will of God, and receive what He has promised" (Heb. 10:35-36). In our lives, there may even be those times when we feel desolate or even abandoned, and echo the words of the Lord Jesus Christ, Our Savior, when He hung on the Cross for our Salvation. We make them our very own words, "My God, My God, why have You abandoned Me" (Mt. 27:46)? The Lord Jesus was quoting Psalm 22, vs. 1, in that moment of pain, desolation and anguish. Over the years, it is generally held, as an unwritten tradition, that the Lord continued to recite the rest of that psalm. It goes on to say, "But Thou, Lord are not far off! O Thou, my help, hasten to my aid" (vs. 19).

We hear, in the Prophet Isaiah, the same theme of being forsaken by the Lord, but Whose mercy and compassion will deliver them,

"For a brief moment I forsook you, but with great compassion I will gather you. In overflowing wrath for a moment I hid my face from you, but with ever-lasting love I will have compassion on you, says the Lord, your Redeemer" (Is. 54:7-8).

Even when times are difficult, we can have abiding faith, knowing that "All will be well," if we place our trust in the Lord. He has a master plan, even though, at times, we beg to differ with His timing and decisions. When the Lord Jesus explained to his apostles that His suffering and death was approaching, Peter took Jesus aside and said, "God forbid, Lord! No such thing shall ever happen to you" (Mt. 16:22). Jesus then turned and said to Peter, "Get behind me, Satan! You are an obstacle to me. You are thinking not as God does, but as man" (Mt. 16:23).

Yet, the Lord will give us the help we need to get through the difficulties. We need to surrender to Him in our times of pain, loss and sorrow and seek His comfort and consolation, to help us get through them. With the Lord all is possible. He can fill our emptiness and heal our pains. St. Paul wrote, "For as we share abundantly in Christ's sufferings, so through Christ, we share abundantly in comfort too" (II Cor. 1:5).

St. Thérèse of Lisieux also known as the "Little Flower" once wrote, "The foundation of Love is Trust." If you cannot trust a person, then how can you draw close to them and love them? It is not possible, unless there is a complete bond and understanding. I often remember this little quote I heard from my spiritual director in the 1980's,

*Love many,*
*Trust few,*
*Always paddle*
*Your own canoe!*

In many cases, it happens that human beings will let us down, since all of us are fallible. We need to have prudence in choosing those whom we can trust. It is recorded that one of the favorite prayers of St. Catherine of Siena was, "I trust in the Lord Jesus Christ, not in myself." I have been told that the middle verse of the entire Bible is located in Psalm 118, it reads, "Better to trust in the Lord, than to have confidence in men" (vs. 8).

We need to depend on the Lord alone, Who will never let us down. We are not even to trust in ourselves, since we are all weak, limited human beings. St. Alphonsus Maria de Liguori wrote, "He who trusts in himself is lost. He who trusts in God can do all things." I believe that this is why the Lord emphasized that trusting in Him will draw us closer to Him in love. St. Padre Pio tells us, "Place all your trust in the Heart of the most Gentle Jesus."

When Jesus appeared to St. Faustina on February 22, 1931 in Plock, Poland, and revealed to her the Divine Mercy image, Jesus explained, in a later vision, that

> "The two rays denote Blood and Water. The pale ray stands for the Water, which makes souls righteous. The red ray stands for the Blood, which is the life of souls. These two rays issued forth from the depth of My tender mercy, when My agonized Heart was opened by a lance on the Cross" (Diary, #299).

Several versions of this painting can be found. The Lord had this to say about the picture. "Not in the beauty of the color, nor of the brush lies the greatness of this image, but in My grace" (Diary, #313). The Lord continued speaking about the image when He told St. Faustina, "By means of this image, I shall grant many graces to souls. It is to be a reminder of the demands of My mercy, because even the strongest faith is of no avail without works" (Diary, # 742).

The Lord Jesus told St. Faustina to have an image painted according to the pattern that He had revealed to her, with the following words, " 'Jesus, I Trust in You.' I promise that the soul that will venerate this image will not perish" (Diary, #47). The Lord further instructed her to have the faithful pray these words at the hour of His death, three o'clock in the afternoon, invoking His mercy, "O Blood and Water that came from the heart of Jesus, I trust in You" (Diary, #187).

*The Imitation of Christ*, which was written several centuries earlier, tells us, "Put your whole trust in God, and let Him be your fear and your love" (Bk. 2, ch. 1). By fear in this sense, we mean a certain Holy Fear, which is one of the seven gifts of the Holy Spirit, in which we are in awe and reverence of the maker of heaven and earth; we recall that we are just mere creatures, who will one day be judged by the Creator.

The Lord Jesus Christ invites us to put away our anxieties, finding comfort when we trust in Him, Who will refresh and restore us. He tells us,

> "Come to Me, all you who labor and are burdened, and I will give you rest. Take My yoke upon you and learn from Me, for I am meek and humble of heart; and you will find rest for yourselves, for My yoke is easy, and My burden light" (Mt. 11:28-30).

The Lord also tells us not to be worried, fearful, anxious or concerned. We are to look at how beautifully the Lord takes care of the flowers of the field, and even more so all of us, as we hear His words of reassurance,

> "Therefore I tell you, do not worry about your life, what you will eat or about your body, what you will wear. Is not life more than food and the body more than clothing? Look at the birds in the sky; they do not sow or reap, they gather nothing into barns, yet your heavenly Father feeds them. Are not you more important than they? Can any of you by worrying add a single moment to your life-span? Why are you anxious about clothes? Learn from the way the wild flowers grow. They do not work or spin. But I tell you that not even Solomon in his entire splendor was clothed like one of them. If God so clothes the grass of the field, which grows today and is thrown into the oven tomorrow, will He not much more provide for you, O you of little faith? So do not worry and say, 'What are we to eat?' or 'What are we to drink?' or 'What are we to wear?' All these things the pagans

seek. Your heavenly Father knows that you need them all. But seek first the kingdom of God and His righteousness, and all these things will be given you besides. Do not worry about tomorrow; tomorrow will take care of itself. Sufficient for a day is its own evil" (Mt. 6:25-34).

In the Gospel of St. Luke, the Lord also speaks about the sparrows that are not forgotten before God. He said, "Fear not, you are more valuable than many sparrows" (Lk. 12:7).

Trust dispels fear. The Lord Jesus Christ told his disciples, "Do not be afraid of those who kill the body, but cannot kill the soul" (Mt. 10:28). I remember the beautiful and uplifting words of the Venerable Pope John Paul II who on many occasions during his pontificate told all of us, "Do not be afraid to open your heart to Jesus … I'm begging you, please do not be afraid."

When Pope Benedict XVI delivered his homily at the Mass of for the inauguration of the Pontificate on April 24, 2005, he continued this theme of his predecessor, and stressed that we should put our complete trust in Christ. On that occasion, he said, "Do not be afraid of Christ; He takes nothing away, and He gives everything. Open wide the doors to Christ and you will find true life."

St. Augustine of Hippo, in his Confessions, wrote, "You have made us for Yourself, O God and our hearts are restless until we find rest in You" (Book 1, chapter 1). I always take note that this does not have a stipulation that one has to rest in the Lord after they die, and have departed from this earthly life. It does not say, "Until we find rest in Thee… when we die." We are invited to rest and repose in the Lord's goodness and mercy throughout our lives. This is how we can have peace among the turbulence and storms that come with the crosses of daily life. St. Augustine wrote that peace is "*Tranquilitas Ordinis*" which means the "Tranquility of order."

We also need not to make "Mountains out of molehills" as the expression goes. What use is it to get upset and bothered over small things? It only leads to stress in our lives. Most folks have heard that stress can be a "Killer" and wreak havoc on one's body. On occasion, I am treated with a neck and back massage at an Asian acupressure center. There is a "cradle" that one's head goes in face down and the tension in the neck and shoulders are relieved by way of a massage. It lasts about thirty minutes. On one occasion, I went there in the week after Easter, and the Chinese fellow, Lee, made a comment, as he was working on my neck, "Gee, Father, your neck is as hard as a rock, it should be soft like a dumpling." To this I responded, "Lee, last week was Holy Week, with a lot of extra work and stress."

Lee's response to me was memorable, "Stress comes from fear, why do you fear, you are a priest, you are supposed to be holy, and supposed to trust, not have fear," I told Lee that he was a very wise fellow, and that I will long remember his words, and even pass them on to others. His simple statement is a good reminder to me, to this very day, to trust in the Lord, Who dispels fear and anxiety.

St. Paul soundly advises us, "Be anxious for nothing... then the peace of God, that surpasses all understanding, will guard your hearts and minds in Christ Jesus" (Phil. 4:6-7). The prophet Isaiah expressed those sentiments in this way, "You will keep him in perfect peace, whose mind is stayed on You, because he trusts in You" (Is. 26:3). There is a popular expression, "Do not sweat the small stuff." This was followed by, "And it is all small stuff." I recall a short poem I heard in the late 1970's,

> *It is the little things that get us*
> *and tend to hold us back,*
> *You can sit upon a mountain*
> *but not upon a tack!*

The Lord can get us through the big "stuff" and the small "stuff." We need to put things in perspective and think, "*Quid ad Aeternitatem?*" This means, "What is this, in relation to eternity? How important will this matter that is troubling or bothering me today, be in six months, six weeks or six days? Will I even remember it? How important is it, in relation to the salvation of my soul which the most important goal of my life?" The goal of my life and everyone's is to live in the love and friendship of the Lord daily and be with the Lord forever in the kingdom of heaven.

# Good vs. Evil

As a young boy, I very much enjoyed watching cartoons on the television. Back then, television was only in black and white, with a total of about twelve channels, and we were happy with that, to be sure. My favorite cartoon was the porcine character entitled, "Porky Pig" and the one particular cartoon episode that sticks out in my mind, is when my buddy Porky had a choice to make a good decision or a bad one. Over one of his shoulders was a small version of him, dressed as an angel, complete with a halo, white wings and robes and a harp. This angelic Porky was prompting him to be good, and do the right thing.

Over the other shoulder, was another small Porky representing an evil angel, and was dressed in red, with two horns coming out of his head. His cute little curly tail was now a big red tail, with a point on the end of it. Actually, it was more comical than scary, as I recall. He was telling Porky, who was in a quandary, not to listen to the other angelic Porky, but to do whatever he wanted. This, in a nutshell, is the story of our moral lives.

We have all been washed clean of Original Sin at our Baptism, and are made a "New Creation in Christ." However, the vestiges of Original Sin that we inherited from our first parents still remain, they are a "Darkened intellect and a weakened will." Our job, throughout our lives, is to try our very best to illuminate this intellect, which has been darkened, by means of study, prayer and the many opportunities that the Church offers to better know the Lord.

We also can strengthen our wills, by sacrifice, fasting, self-denial and the worthy reception of the Sacraments, all to reinforce us spiritually. They are the means to discipline ourselves, and make us ever stronger in the battle of good versus evil. Jesus accompanies us in our task, to choose good over evil, and is with us throughout our fight against the temptations of the evil one. As He prays to His heavenly Father for His followers, we hear, "I do not pray that You should take them out of this world, but that You should keep them from the evil one" (Jn. 17:15).

We also need to be cautious with relationships. There is an old expression, "Tell me with whom you go, and I will tell you who you are." Some friends can elevate us, while others can drag us down, and prevent us from the ever-present goal of "Illuminating our darkened intellect and strengthening our weakened will." On the contrary, they might be enablers, who help us to muddle things up even worse. This is the constant battle within us, and we do not need others to help get us off track and deviate from the paths of righteousness, which is so easy to do. Even St. Paul wrote, "I do not do the good which I want, but the evil that I do not want to do" (Rom. 7:19). A saint, however, is not someone who falls, but someone who stands up, again and again, with heroic virtue and tries to do better each time. Pope John Paul II told us, "If you do holy things, you become holy."

Our goal is: to seek Christ, to know Christ and to imitate Christ. God is the greatest good, the "*Summum Bonum*," and our desires and efforts are to be directed toward Him. Sometimes, however, we choose other gods that distract us. Our culture offers false gods to substitute for the True God of Glory. It is through following the commandments that brings life. Sin brings destruction to us, it is merely a temporary pleasure that helps to "Medicate the pain" in our lives. However, sin becomes an obstacle to the Love of the Lord, and helps serve to further separate ourselves from Him.

We can try our very best to live by the old axiom, "*Fac Bonum et Ne Fac Malo*" which means "Do good and not evil." We hear in the book of Psalms, when speaking of the Lord God, "You love righteousness and hate wickedness" (Ps. 45:7). The book of the Prophet Amos tells us, "Seek good and not evil, that you may live, and so the Lord of hosts will be with you... hate evil and love good" (Amos 5:14-15).

If this sounds a bit like the themes that we hear during the Season of Lent, it could not hurt if some of the discipline of Lent could be incorporated in our daily regiment, as a means to help us to deny ourselves, and live for Christ. This is how we can best follow St. Paul's advice, "Let us lay aside the works of darkness, and put on the armor of light" (Rom. 13:12).

It has been recorded that St. Francis of Assisi observed a strict Lenten fast three times each year. The first observance began with the opening of the Church Liturgical Year with the Season of Advent, leading up to Christmas, his next observance was the entire Season of Lent and the third Lenten-type observance began the day after June 29th which is the Solemnity of Sts. Peter and Paul, and concluded with the Solemnity of the Assumption of Mary on August 15.

We have a choice. Will we be swayed by the temptations of the evil one and the fallen angels, who have our spiritual destruction as their goal? Or will we listen to the inspirations of the good angels, who are there to light our path and guide us in the ways of holiness and righteousness? It is up to us and our own choices. In order to help us, we need to arm ourselves, be alert, aware and prepared, so when the attacks and temptations arrive, we will be strong and make the right choices. St. Paul tells us,

> "But since we are of the day, let us be sober, putting on the breastplate of faith and love, and the helmet that is hope for salvation. For God did not destine us for wrath, but to gain salvation through our Lord Jesus Christ" (I Thess. 5: 8-9).

St. James expressed this very succinctly, "Resist the devil, and he will flee you. Draw near to God, and He will draw near to you" (Jas. 3:7-8). In a radio address in 1940, the Venerable Pope Pius XII claimed that "The sin of the century is the loss of the sense of sin." Sin is putting our own way and our will, before God's way and His will.

When I was a teenager there was a song that was made popular by Frank Sinatra entitled, "I Did It My Way." Well, perhaps my way may not always be the best way. My way may not be consistent with the plan of the Lord; my own way might, in fact, disrupt the Lord's beautiful plan for me, if it is sinful. I prefer to think of a Christ-centered version of the title of that song, not "I Did It My Way" but "I Did It Thy Way." We have the choice every day, and in fact many times during each day. Of course, the evil one is always out there in the midst of things, to try to help confound us. The more we try to grow in a committed Christ-centered life, the more energy he puts toward stopping that growth.

The first president of the United States, George Washington (1732-1799), in his Farewell Address in 1796 stated, "There is an indissoluble link between virtue and happiness." He reiterated this point a second time in his remarks, "Religion and morality are the great pillars of human happiness." If we try to be good, then things will go well for us. This is the lesson that we hear about in the first Psalm,

> "Happy are they who do not follow the counsel of the wicked, nor go the way of sinners, they are like a tree, planted near streams of water, that yields its fruit in season. Its leaves never wither; whatever they do prospers. But not the wicked! They are like chaff driven by the wind. The Lord watches over the way of the just, but the way of the wicked leads to ruin" (Ps. 1:1, 3-4, 6).

A dear friend, whose wedding I performed, once told me, "Whenever I try to steer the boat on my own, I always crash on the rocks." Shortly after I heard that, I passed a church that has a pithy expression on their display case, which changes from week to week. When I drove past it, it read: "If God is your co-pilot, swap seats!" I really liked these two expressions and have told them to others as well. The best thing is to put our trust in the Lord, asking Him not just to get us through, but, in fact, to help lead our feet on the path we are to go. He will not lead us astray.

This is especially true when the circumstances of life send us a "Curve ball" from time to time. It is precisely then that we need to depend on the Lord Jesus. He tells us, "I am the Way, the Truth and the Life" (Jn. 14:6). He invites us to follow Him in the paths of righteousness whatever may come our way, since following Him is the best way to His Heavenly Father.

My own goal in life, which I have tried my best to teach to others, during my years of priesthood, and throughout my preaching, is to reinforce putting our trust in the mercy and love of the Lord. May all of us persevere in the love and friendship of the Lord Jesus Christ, and to try our best each and every day, to glorify Him by our lives and actions. With the help and grace of the Lord, may we collaborate with Him, and save our souls, so we may be able to enjoy His presence forever in the kingdom of heaven.

# Gratitude

Over the years, I have come to learn that gratitude is the secret to happiness. If we take a moment to step back from a situation and, in fact, our own lives, and see the big picture, we can see how blessed we have been. There is an expression that we all have heard, "One needs to step back from the forest to best see the trees."

Once I saw a bumper sticker that made me chuckle as I was driving. It had a picture of a dog on it, and there were only four words by the dog, "Wag more, Bark less." Of course, this referred to us humans. The dog wags his tail when he is content, excited and, oh, so happy to see the leash, knowing he will be going for a walk. We need to cultivate those moments of contentment in our lives and to bark, or complain less. This will give us inner peace and that is where we can find happiness.

I can attribute this understanding of happiness in my life to a lesser-known song that was composed by a very well-known Russian-born Jewish composer. His name was Israel Baline, who is more commonly known as Irving Berlin (1888-1989). He was known for many wonderful songs, such as "God Bless America," "I'm dreaming of a White Christmas" and "Easter Parade." He was truly a genius, and the list of his songs can go on and on.

The two main actors, Bing Crosby and Rosemary Clooney, in the movie, "White Christmas," sing the one particular song of which I am referring. In one scene, they both were sleepless and met unexpectedly in the kitchen, to get a glass of warm milk, a remedy to help them sleep. There just happened to be a piano nearby, as in many musicals, and the co-star, Bing Crosby, sang the memorable song to which I refer.

The lyrics of the song, entitled, "Count your Blessings," explains that, although one may be tired and unable to sleep, the best remedy is not to count sheep, but to count one's blessings, and that will put you to sleep. The second verse has the following sentiments: when you are worried about the low balance in your bank book, just recall when there was no balance at all, and you will find peace and fall asleep while you count your blessings.

This is the best song in the entire movie, as far as I am concerned. Gratitude is the key to happiness; in particular gratitude to the Lord God for the many blessings that He has given us throughout our lives. Even in the crosses that come into our lives, He has not abandoned us, but been there to help us, and not test us beyond our strength. His mercy and grace have been upon us. I think of St. Teresa of Avila who is depicted in early paintings, some done during her lifetime, with the words in Spanish, coming forth from her mouth, written on a ribbon, that are taken from Psalm 89, vs. 1, "Forever I will sing the mercies of the Lord." This is sometimes also translated as "Forever I will sing the goodness of the Lord."

Each year on Holy Thursday, the Church throughout the world begins the Easter Triduum, with the Evening Mass of the Lord's Supper. It is a very emotional night for us priests, since it commemorates the institution of the Sacrament of the Sacred Body and Blood of Christ, and the Sacrament of Holy Priesthood. Adding to that emotion, we, both priests and people, are reminded of the immense goodness and generosity of the Lord to us. The responsorial psalm during the Liturgy of the Word is taken from Psalm 116: "How can I repay the Lord for all the good done for me? I will raise the cup of salvation, and call on the name of the Lord; I will pay my vows to the Lord in the presence of all His people" (vs. 12-14).

When I celebrated my fiftieth birthday in 2006, I decided to have a big family-style party. I wanted to invite many of those couples that I had married over the years, along with their children, many of whom I had the honor of baptizing. It was a real fun event, held on a pleasant Sunday afternoon. My plan was to make it an enjoyable and special day for everyone invited. Besides the regular birthday cake for the adults, there was one set up for all of the children, it was on a tiered cardboard base, and each tier had cupcakes with lit candles on them.

Then all the children were asked to "Please join in singing 'Happy Birthday' and then help Fr. Matt blows out the candles." Afterward, I asked each child to take a cupcake and go back to the table with their parents. I thought that table with the cupcakes was going to turn over, since it rocked back and forth as the children practically attacked it, to get their cupcake! It was so much fun, and for me, perhaps the most memorable moment of the day.

In all truth, I really did not want to make the event "about me" and even on the invitation and on the inscription on the cake, had written, "Give thanks to the Lord with me." It was adapted from Psalm 34, vs. 3, "Glorify the Lord with me; let us exalt His name together."

When the nearly 140 guests arrived at the event, I said a few words of introduction to welcome everyone, and thanked them for being there, and for joining my family and me that afternoon. Then I told them that we were all celebrating "Thanksgiving Day" a few months early. When they all looked at me quizzically, I explained, "No, there was not going to be roasted turkey with all the trimmings, followed by pumpkin pie on the menu." They would be seeing that soon enough, toward the end of November, which would be here before we knew it.

Then, I told all the guests, that it was an opportunity to have them join me in lifting up their hearts, with me, in gratitude to God. Together, we could thank the good Lord for the many blessings that He bestowed upon me throughout the first fifty years of my life. Then I thanked the Lord for the wonderful parents, grandparents, sister, brother and relatives, some of whom had driven from New Jersey to Connecticut for the party. I went through the room, acknowledging the many people who have been so very kind to me, over the years of my priestly service in the various parishes of the Diocese of Bridgeport.

Most of all, I thanked Almighty God for the graces that He has given me to persevere, and the Blessed Mother for her love and maternal guidance over the years. I quoted the Blessed Virgin Mary, who said in her song of praise to her cousin Elizabeth at the Visitation, called the *"Magnificent,"* "The Almighty had done great things for me, Holy is His Name" (Lk. 1:49). As noted earlier, this was the same quote printed on the Holy Cards that were distributed at the time of my Priesthood Ordination. It is also the very first quote from Sacred Scripture that is cited in this book, found in the opening paragraph of the introduction.

In the Sacramentary, from which the priest reads the prayers during Holy Mass, there is a selection of various Prefaces according to the occasion. One of them, for Preface for Weekdays IV, has some beautiful words in it about our gratitude to the Lord. It states,

> "Lord, You have no need of our praise, yet our desire to thank You is itself Your gift. Our prayer of thanksgiving adds nothing to Your greatness, but makes us grow in Your grace, through Jesus Christ our Lord."

I very often think of the Gospel passage of the ten lepers, who approach the Lord Jesus for healing. This is the Gospel usually reading on Thanksgiving Day. The lepers stood at their distance, but raised their voices asking for mercy from the Lord and said, "Jesus, Master! Have pity on us" (Lk. 17:13)! Jesus told them to go show themselves to the priests, and one of them, who was a Samaritan, considered an outcast by the mainstream Jewish leaders at that time, realized that he was cleansed, and returned, giving glory to God and "He fell at the feet of Jesus and thanked Him" (vs. 16). The Lord Jesus said in reply, "Ten were cleansed, were they not? Where are the other nine? Has none but this foreigner returned to give thanks to God" (vs. 17-18)?

St. Paul tells us to give thanks to the Lord for the many blessings we have received. We hear, "In all things, give thanks" (I Thess. 5:18). As well, these sentiments are reiterated in another of his letters, "Giving thanks always, for all things" (Eph. 5:20). Our thanksgiving is to come from the firm conviction in our hearts, knowing that all good comes to us from the generosity and mercy of God. We also hear from St. Paul, "Blessed be the God and Father of Our Lord Jesus Christ, Who had blessed us, in Christ, with every spiritual blessing in the heavens" (Eph. 1:3).

When the civil observance of Thanksgiving arrives, on the fourth Thursday of November, I usually suggest to my flock that we should not have just one official "Day of Thanks" each year. Rather, we should change the word Thanksgiving to Thanks-living, and try to live in a spirit of gratitude and thankfulness to the Bounteous Lord every day of the year.

The German philosopher, theologian and mystic, Meister Eckhart (1260-1328) wrote, "The best prayer is 'thank you,' not just to pray in good times but in difficult ones too." We are to recall the goodness to the merciful Lord toward us, and to act in a grateful manner, recognizing and being mindful of the Lord's generosity. There is a quote to this effect in the work of William Shakespeare in his play, "*King Henry VI,*"

> *God's goodness hath been great to thee:*
> *Let never day nor night unhallow'd pass,*
> *But still remember what the Lord hath done*
> *(Part 2, Act 2, Scene 1).*

Over the years, I have told people who were "Down in the dumps" who have come to me, whether in the confessional or outside of it, that they need to step back and count their blessings and to "See the glass of water as not half empty, but half full" as the expression goes. They will see life in a different way, if they realize how good the Lord had been to them. This is what we are to do: sing forever the mercies of the Lord and acclaim His goodness to us, here in this life, as we hope to do so one day, with Him forever in the kingdom of heaven.

# Happiness

When I think of happiness, I recall the words of the Blessed Mother Mary, when she appeared to the young St Bernadette Soubirous, (1844-1879) at Lourdes, France, in the foothills of the Pyrenees Mountains. On February 18, 1858, Mary told her, "I cannot promise to make you happy in this world, but in the next." This is where our ultimate happiness can be found, in heaven. Here on this earth, we can get a few great glimpses and foretastes of true happiness, even as pilgrims to our heavenly destination. St. Alphonsus wrote, "He who desires nothing but God is rich and happy." True happiness can be found only in the Lord, even amid life's many challenges.

Throughout the years, I have made the observation that our lives are made up of a series of "black and white" events as I call them: sorrow and joy. Even the Sacred Scriptures gives us this insight. "For everything there is a season, and a time for every matter under heaven... a time to weep and a time to laugh; a time to mourn, and a time to dance" (Eccles. 3:1, 4).

The year 1978 was called "The year of the three popes." Many may recall it, even though it is now over thirty years ago, it seems like yesterday. On August 6, Pope Paul VI died. He had been pope for over 15 years. Later that month, the cardinals elected Pope John Paul I, but about one month later, he died suddenly. Then they elected the beloved pope, John Paul II. When Pope John Paul I had died unexpectedly, the next day, the headlines of a newspaper quoted a very holy man, Cardinal Humberto Medeiros, (1915-1983) Archbishop of Boston, who said, "We are all a little disappointed with God." This is how I feel, when I think of the story of Carol.

She was my next-door neighbor in Cranford, NJ and was her parents' only child, and about six months younger than I, so we were contemporaries and good friends. We had a great rapport over the years, and when she was preparing to graduate high school in 1975, the year after me, she asked my opinion on designing her page in her school Year Book. She went to a private school for girls, and each student in the graduating class was allowed a full page, that they could decorate as they wished. She chose a very touching poem:

*Happiness is like a butterfly,*
*If you pursue it, it will elude you*
*But if you turn your attention to other things,*
*It will gently rest on your shoulder.*

Later that summer, as a graduation gift, her parents took her with them on a two-week tour of Europe, and one of the places that they visited was Venice, Italy. Her mother, Lillian, purchased a beautiful lace butterfly appliqué there, telling Carol that she looked forward to one day sewing it on the shoulder of her wedding gown, come the morning of her marriage. Unfortunately, that never happened.

In 1982, Carol became ill with Hodgkin's disease, and after a long illness, passed away in October 1987. I learned that her mother sewed the butterfly on the shoulder of the dress that she wore when she was laid to rest. Carol had found her happiness, with the Lord for all eternity in the heavenly kingdom, after many years of illness. Certainly, it was not the way that her family and friends had been hoping or expecting, but it was in the plan of the Lord for her.

The years since her passing have been difficult for her dear parents to say the least, but from time to time they tell me that they are truly looking forward to being reunited with their daughter Carol again someday. They say that it will be a moment of great happiness for them, when they are all together again. Over the years, I have used this idea of being reunited to a loved one, when I have chosen the Gospel for funerals. I have, at times, selected a Gospel that is not traditionally found among those offered in the Lectionary for the Mass of Christian Burial. The Lord Jesus told His apostles during the Last Supper discourse,

"You will weep and mourn, while the world rejoices; you will grieve, but your grief will become joy. When a woman is in labor, she is in anguish because her hour has arrived; but when she has given birth to a child, she no longer remembers the pain because of her joy that a child has been born into the world. So you also are now in anguish. But I will see you again, and your hearts will rejoice, and no one will take your joy away from you." (Jn. 16:20-22).

The Lord was preparing the disciples, that they would be separated and it would be very painful, and even likened it to the pain of childbirth, but then, when they were to be reunited, they would forget the pain of separation, out of the joy of seeing each other again. These words can be applied to the passing of a loved one as well, and help calm the intensity of sorrow, due to the separation by death. There remains the great hope, that there will be a reunion some day in the heavenly kingdom.

This separation is only temporary, and so we do not say, "Farewell forever" to those who have passed away, but rather, we say, "Until we meet again someday." It is like the Italian word, *"Arrividerci"* or in Spanish, *"Hasta la vista."* For me over the years, this has been a great source of gratitude and happiness, knowing that for those who are faithful, the eternal glory awaits them in heaven; that the grave is not the end of the story. The book of Revelation tells us, "Remain faithful until death, and I will give you the crown of life" (ch. 2:10).

I recall a poem written by the famous American poet, Henry Wadsworth Longfellow (1807-1882):

*Life is real! Life is earnest!*
*And the grave is not the goal;*
*Dust thou art, to dust returnest,*
*Was not spoken of the soul.*

It is through the victory of the Lord Jesus over death by His triumphant Resurrection, that we can have this hope that we will someday share in eternal life. The Lord told this to Martha, when He visited her after the death of her brother Lazarus, "I am the Resurrection and the Life; whoever believes in Me, even if he dies, will live, and everyone who lives and believes in Me, will never die" (Jn. 11:25-26). This is what we are striving for, the eternal happiness that awaits us that day, when we achieve our goal, by God's grace, to live in the house of the Lord forever in the kingdom of heaven.

# J-O-Y

Many priests agree with me that one of the most difficult things to do is to preach to one's own family. Even the Lord Jesus commented, "A prophet is not without honor, except in his native place, and among his own kin, and in his own house" (Mk. 6:4). This point came home to me shortly after my Ordination to the Priesthood, when my relatives, who were very happy for me, each told me, "I remember when I changed your diapers when you were a baby, so now, how can I call you 'Father?' " Thank goodness, it is rather infrequent that the listeners are comprised of my family, as I feel more self-conscious and the words flow a bit less fluidly.

Many priests believe that reading their homilies makes them seem flat, and with less energy. By having the typed out the message in front of them, they can lose some spontaneity when they preach, since they are referring to the text. I agree with that opinion, and prefer to just write out several words, or even just a few initials, that help to serve as reminders of the outline.

The perfect example of this is when I have preached about joy. There are two occasions in the Church's Liturgical Year that this theme is particularly appropriate, and in fact, even encouraged. These are the Sundays called "*Gaudate*" and "*Laetare*," which are the Third Sunday of Advent and the Fourth Sunday of Lent, respectively. The opening Antiphons for both of these liturgical celebrations invite us to "Rejoice in the Lord always; again I say rejoice! The Lord is near" (Phil. 4:4-5) as we hear in Advent. In Lent, the Antiphon reads, "Rejoice Jerusalem! Be glad for her, you who love her; rejoice with her, you who mourned for her, and you will find contentment at her consoling breasts" (Is. 66:10-11).

These are the two Sundays when the vestments that the priest wears during Holy Mass are changed to the Rose color, as a reminder that the penitential seasons of Advent or Lent, in which we wear violet or purple, are now half way through. We can begin to anticipate the joy to come at Christmas or Easter. My homily reminder is the word "J-O-Y." It is so short that I do not even have to jot it down:

343

*J - Jesus first*
*O - Others next*
*Y - Yourself last*

We put "Jesus First," and find our source of true Joy in Him. The Lord Jesus Christ, Himself, spoke of joy. He said, "These things I have spoken to you, that My joy may remain in you, and that your joy may be full" (Jn. 15:11). One of the psalms tells us, "I may come to the altar of God, to God, my joy, my delight. Then I will praise You with the harp, O God, my God" (Ps. 43:3).

It is with the Lord that we are refreshed, restored and renewed. In Him, we can put aside all of our troubles and preoccupations, and thereby revive the joy of the Lord within us. The Book of Proverbs tells us, "A merry heart is good medicine, but a downcast spirit dries up the bones" (Prov. 17:22). St. Bernard of Clairvaux tells us that "Jesus is honey in the mouth, music in the ear and a shout of joy in the heart."

With the mercy and care of the Lord, we can be reinvigorated, even under adverse or difficult circumstances. With His help, it is possible to keep a spirit of joyful surrender to His Holy Will in our lives. Then we can show forth the joy of the Lord, that is within us, to others, by what we say and do. Blessed Columba Marmion wrote, "Joy is the echo of God's life within us." This is expressed through the prophet Isaiah:

> "The Lord is the eternal God, creator of the ends of the earth. He does not faint nor grow weary, and His knowledge is beyond scrutiny. He gives strength to the fainting; for the weak he makes vigor abound. Though young men faint and grow weary, and youths stagger and fall, they that hope in the Lord will renew their strength, they will soar as with eagles' wings; they will run and not grow weary, walk and not grow faint" (Is. 40:28-30).

We put "Others Next." This is an opportunity to be charitable and bring the love of the Lord to others. A wise person and a dear friend, Sister Carol Marie, O.P. once told me, "The patient needs a project." Sometimes when one is feeling sorry for themselves, they need to reach beyond themselves and do something positive for others. This is such a fulfilling feeling when, as a priest, I do my "hospital rounds."

Those are the days when I go to see those parishioners who are either hospitalized or in Nursing Homes, and bring them the Sacrament of the Sick or Holy Communion. It may be difficult, at times, to find a place to park in the hospital parking lot, but I receive much consolation knowing that I had the opportunity to bring them a few words of comfort and support, along with the sacraments.

Many times during my visits, I would tell some of the elderly Italian-American parishioners in the Italian language, *"Coraggio, figlio mio."* Which means, "Courage, my child," and here I was, in my mid-40's, telling this to someone in their mid-90's!" However, even though we both realized that I could be the age of a grandson, neither of us laughed at my statement of encouragement, because in that moment, I was talking as their caring and loving spiritual father, and was there to help bring the love and comfort of the Lord to them.

Each priest is called to nurture and love the people entrusted to their care as the "Leader and Guide of the Parish Community," which was the title of the August 4, 2002 Instruction of the Congregation for Clergy. We also uplift our parishioners, by encouraging them to put their Trust in the Lord, amid their illness and invite them to have courage and confidence. We remind them that the Lord will not abandon them, but draw close to them, if they trustingly call upon His Holy Name. We hear of the unity between the priest and his people in the Acts of the Apostles, where, "The community of believers was of one heart and mind" (Acts 4:32).

St. Paul tells us that those who serve the Lord in the ordained ministry are to collaborate with their flock. We are to equip and enable the faithful to do their part in the Mystical Body of Christ, the Church,

> "And He gave some as apostles, others as prophets,
> others as evangelists, others as pastors and teachers,
> to equip the holy ones for the work of ministry, for

building up the Body of Christ, until we all attain to
the unity of faith and knowledge of the Son of Man,
to mature manhood" (Eph. 4:11-13).

We are to put "Ourselves Last." St. Francis de Sales was once
asked, "Where did you find God?" And he answered, "Where I lost
myself." We can find this prescription for how to attain joy, through
an interior renewal in the writing of St. Paul, who tells us, "Do not
conform yourselves to this age, but be transformed by the renewal
of your mind, that you may discern what is the will of God, what is
good and pleasing and perfect" (Rom. 12:2).

Joy is one of the fruits of the Holy Spirit as we read, "But the
fruit of the Spirit is love, joy, peace, longsuffering, kindness, goodness, faithfulness, gentleness, self-control" (Gal. 5:22). Our goal is
to conform ourselves to Christ, and if we try our best to do that
which is pleasing and perfect in the sight of the Lord, then we will
be living a grace-filled, dynamic and joyful life.

As previously mentioned, I believe that "A clean conscience is
the best gift that we can give to ourselves." By doing the right thing
in God's eyes, we can have interior joy. The Lord offers us, "Peace,
not as the world gives do I give it to you. Do not let your hearts be
troubled or afraid" (Jn. 14:27). To help guide me in making the right
choices, I recall the expression, "When you are at the Crossroads,
look to the Cross." We are to involve the Lord in our choices, asking
Him for the graces we need, to glorify Him in all we say and do.

A few years ago, I went to visit a priest classmate at his rectory
in Fargo, North Dakota. It was right after the time when there were
heavy rains, and flooding and the Red River had risen to its highest
level ever. Something that I recall about the visit was that another
priest there had a wonderful quote posted on the door to his office,
so I asked him if I could please have a photocopy of it. It was by the
English medieval mystic, Juliana of Norwich, (ca. 1342-1416). She
wrote, "The greatest honor you can give Almighty God, greater than
all your sacrifices and mortifications, is to live joyfully, because of
the knowledge of His love."

St. Bonaventure wrote, "A spiritual joy is the greatest sign of
the divine grace dwelling in a soul." In many ways, I believe this

may be one of the best reminders for the source of our Christian joy, which is the love of the Lord for us. When we aspire to live in that love of the Lord, and correspond accordingly in our actions, then we can also continue to grow in the love and joy of the Lord. If we try our best to live in the friendship of God, the abundant graces of the Lord will grow and flourish in us. We hear this when the Lord uses the analogy of the Vine and the Branches,

> "Remain in Me, as I remain in you. Just as a branch cannot bear fruit on its own, unless it remains on the vine, so neither can you unless you remain in Me. I am the vine, you are the branches. Whoever remains in Me and I in him will bear much fruit, because without Me you can do nothing" (Jn. 15:4-5).

This is the invitation of the Lord, to remain united to Him as the branch is intimately united to the vine, for its very life source. This is how we remain in His love and partake in His joy. The Lord even instructs us how to remain in His love and be joyful, and that is by being faithful,

> "As the Father loves me, so I also love you. Remain in My love. If you keep My commandments, you will remain in My love, just as I have kept My Father's commandments and remain in His love. I have told you this so that My joy may be in you and your joy may be complete" (Jn. 15:9-11).

There is a complimentarily with being faithful to the commandments, and having joy. When Jesus was asked which was the greatest of the commandments, He told the listeners, "You shall love the Lord your God with all your heart, with all your soul and with all your strength and with all your mind; and your neighbor as yourself" (Lk. 10:27).

The joy that we can experience on earth by putting Jesus first, others next and yourself last, is just a mere foreshadowing of the eternal joy that awaits all those who have been faithful.

347

Of course, in our lives we have the ups and downs, sorrows as well as joys. Each of us knows that not every morning of our lives we are in the mindset to say, "This is the day the Lord had made; let us rejoice in it and be glad" (Ps. 118:24). There are days we spring out of bed cheerfully and say, "Good morning, Lord!" On other days, we are not too thrilled when the alarm goes off and say, "Good Lord, morning!"

However, we need to try our very best, day in and day out, to cultivate the sense of Christian joy and delight in the goodness and bountiful blessings of the Lord. We hear, "Take delight in the Lord, and He shall give you your heart's desire" (Ps. 37:4). This is not a magical formula or promise, wherein He will give us all our worldly needs. Rather, we ask for that burning desire for an intimate friendship with Our Lord. We believe and trust, that if we seek Him above all things, all will be well, as St. Paul tells us, "We know that all things work for good for those who love God" (Rom. 8:28).

Christian joy is to be part of our personalities. How wonderful things would be, and what good example we could give to others, if we could live by these wonderful words of St. Paul, "Be joyful always, pray constantly, give thanks in all circumstances; for this is the Will of God in Christ Jesus for you" (I Thess. 5:17-18). We can look to the example of the many saints who have gone before us, who, even amid their sufferings and difficulties, had an interior joy that showed forth to others.

St. Philip Neri (1515-1595) has been called the "Second Apostle of Rome," and lived during the time of the Counter-Reformation. He stressed that a Christian should have a cheerful temperament, rather than a melancholic one, and that we are to carry this spirit throughout our whole lives. He said, "A joyful heart is more easily made perfect than a downcast one." St. Teresa of Avila had a short prayer, "Lord, save us from solemn saints." It is our goal to keep the commandments, and do so with joy, not grudgingly. There is no merit in that. When we fall short, the mercy of the Lord is always there to heal and strengthen us, so that we can persevere in joyfully living each day, even with its struggles, with our eyes fixed on achieving our goal, to participate in the eternal joy that awaits us in the kingdom of heaven.

# 11

# Closing Reflections

## Arriving in Greenwich

The story of my transfer to a new pastorate at the Church of St. Roch in Greenwich, CT on July 1, 2009, actually begins about two years earlier. One of my parishioners at Holy Rosary Church had invited me to her home in the spring of 2007, for an afternoon visit. We had a nice chat, along with a cup of coffee and a few tasty home-made biscotti. Her lovely granddaughter, Jackie, was also there. She was a student teacher, and finishing her Master's degree in special education. She was about 28 at the time, and a cheerful person, with beautiful dimples in her cheeks. I always enjoyed seeing her accompany her grandmother, Theresa, to Mass on Sundays.

After we had our visit and I was about to leave, Theresa mentioned to me that Jackie had not yet found a good man for her husband. She asked me to please pray that she might find "Mr. Right." With that, I recalled the words of the Lord, "All that you ask the Father in My Name, He will grant you" (Jn. 16:23). I told them both that Jesus said, "Where two or three of you are gathered in My name, I am there among them" (Mt. 18:20). With that, I suggested that the three of us might pray together to the Lord, and join our hearts and voices as one, in asking Him to grant Jackie her heart's desire, to find a suitable husband. And so, we held hands and did just that. We lifted our voices together to Our Lord in petition.

Within a few weeks, Jackie met Todd, and they hit it off nicely. They were engaged on Sunday, Jan. 13, 2008, just two days after the 20th anniversary of my ordination. The wedding was planned for June 20, 2009, and I was honored to offer the Nuptial Mass and accept their exchange of vows in the name of the Church.

Around spring 2009, I realized that it was time for a change in my own life. A priest friend, Fr. Tommaso, mentioned to me that, "Change is a good thing, lest we become stagnant, as it brings new challenges, new experiences, and new opportunities to grow." Shortly before Christmas in 2007, my mother took seriously ill. We learned that a gallstone had lodged in her pancreatic duct, and had wrecked havoc with her entire system. She was on morphine for pain, heavy-duty antibiotics for the infection, and they even needed to wait several days before they could operate, just to stabilize her.

Due to my mother's illness, I was going from the parish in Bridgeport to the hospital in New Jersey every few days. However on one occasion, when returning to the parish, after a long few days surrounding Christmas, I began to doze while driving the car. This was on December 26, and I was somewhat fatigued. I thank the Good Lord that I caught myself, turned up the radio, and lowered the windows, to allow the cold air to help alert me. Within a few weeks, I came to an important realization: my parents are getting older, my sister lives in Italy, and my brother is busy with his medical profession in Pennsylvania. My folks would need my assistance more and more as the years progressed. The words of Psalm 34, which I have read so often over the years, in the Liturgy of the Hours, came to mind: "Many are the troubles of the just, but the Lord delivers from them all" (vs. 20).

Consequently, I wrote to the bishop, and asked for an opportunity to schedule a meeting. When we met, I explained the situation to him and mentioned that when I had been assigned to the Stamford area, the trip to my parents was about one-third shorter, just sixty miles from door to door, as opposed to ninety miles from Bridgeport to their home. With that, I asked him to please keep me in mind, should there be an opening for a pastorate in that area. The months passed and, although I kept in contact with the personnel office, there was no news of an opening in that greater Stamford area.

Then I remembered the prayer that Jackie, her grandmother, and I had offered, asking our Lord to locate a husband for Jackie. Her dear grandmother, Theresa had, since that time, passed away in April 2008. However, I had faith and trust that the Good Lord would come through for me, as he had for Jackie. The following Sunday, when Jackie came to Mass with her mother Terry, I asked if they would please stay for a few minutes after the Mass concluded. When the parishioners had all departed, I took them near the tabernacle, where the Lord is Truly Present in the Most Blessed Sacrament, and asked if they would please join me in praying that the Lord grant me a new assignment, as He had granted Jackie her request and she found her future husband.

Just a few Sundays prior, Jackie had told me that everything came together for her after we had prayed that day, along with her grandmother. With that in mind, I wanted to pray with them, and ask the Lord to kindly grant me His assistance, as He had for Jackie. We asked Almighty God to locate a new pastorate for me. Within a month of our prayer together, I received a phone call from the personnel director, telling me that in a few days, the bishop would be at a priests' meeting and that he would like to speak with me after it. That day, as I walked the bishop to his car, he told me that the pastorate at St. Roch Church in Greenwich was available, since the pastor was retiring early due to health issues. Bishop Lori asked me if I would be willing to go there. The Good Lord had so wonderfully come through for me, once again, and I gratefully accepted. The Town of Greenwich is even closer to my parents than Stamford, only 53 miles from door to door, and I could be at my folks' home in just over an hour, if need be.

Upon my arrival at St. Roch Church, which is the English translation for the saint more commonly known as St. Rocco, I soon learned that this is a close Italian-American community, like the one of my youth. They still celebrate, joyfully and in grand style, the annual feast day of St. Roch on August 16, with the procession of the statue in the streets preceded by a brass band.

On the day that I was moving into the Rectory, I was thinking of this story of St. John Vianney, and decided to tell it to the members of my new parish. When he arrived for his assignment at Ars, he was not sure how to proceed along the road. He asked a young boy if he knew where Ars was located, who then told the priest that he too was going there. St. John Vianney responded, "If you show me the way to Ars, I will show you the way to heaven." I told this story explaining that I arrived in their midst to show them the path to heaven. The appropriate time for this was on the occasion of my installation as the pastor, which was at the Vigil Mass for the Solemnity of All Saints, October 31, 2009. In his homily, Bishop Lori told the members of the congregation, "Priests are saint-makers." This was the perfect preparation for my first address to my new flock.

My farewell Mass at Holy Rosary Church in Bridgeport had been on the weekend following the wedding for Jackie and Todd. I feel a wonderful connection between the three of us, since the Lord came through, after together, we had elevated our hearts and voices in prayer to Him, and He mercifully opened the right path for us.

Now it will be up to us to correspond, with hearts full of gratitude, and live our own lives worthily, so as to glorify the Lord for His goodness to us. The Lord calls all of us "Out of darkness, into His marvelous light" (I Pet. 2:9). It is my job, as the pastor, to be like a "coach," and help the members of the "team" to reach the goal. That goal is, as we hear, to "Receive the end of your faith, the salvation of your souls" (I Pet. 1:9). Our fidelity to Him is how each of us can show our love and gratitude to the Lord, for the many blessings that He has shown to us. For me, it has been the blessing of a new parish, where I am to lead my flock to the best of my ability, and help them to know, love, and serve the Lord in this world so that they can be happy with Him forever in the kingdom of heaven.

## Shirley the Pianist

In the Fall of 2009, my mother had surgery to replace both knees. She had been suffering with arthritis for several years, and her physician told her that the time had come to address the situation. The day of the surgery arrived, and although our family had been a bit apprehensive, we put our trust in the Lord and followed His instructions, "Ask and you shall receive, seek and you shall find, knock and it shall be opened for you" (Lk. 11:9, Mt. 7:7). Our Lord also told us, "If you ask Me anything, in My name, I will do it" (Jn. 14:14).

The best distraction for me, to get my mind off the surgery, occurred on that day, and it was also a great life lesson as well. We had all arrived at the hospital on that mid-November morning about 5:30 a.m., to get ready for Mom's surgery. After wishing her well and giving her both a blessing and a kiss, the rest of the family hunkered down in the waiting room, until that moment when the surgeon would arrive, to tell us how the operation went. Shortly after 9:00 am, I went to the front lobby of the hospital to use my cell phone, to call the parish secretary in Greenwich, just to see how things were there. When I began my call, I noticed an elderly woman in a wheelchair, who was sitting near a piano in the lobby of the hospital. By the time I ended the call, she was at the piano playing it.

When I came back to make another phone call, about an hour later, she was still there, happily playing the piano. At first, I had thought that she was a patient, who was entertaining herself, while waiting for her medical appointment. However, it turned out that she volunteers her time, on Tuesdays and Thursdays from 9:00 to 11:30, to play the piano in the lobby. She did not have a sheet of music in front of her, since it was all played by memory. She asked me if I had a request and I told her to please play one of my favorite songs, "Because of You," which she played just delightfully.

In short time, I struck up a very pleasant conversation with her, along with her health aide, who had helped with the wheelchair. I learned that the pianist was Shirley Frances Flax, and she was born in 1915. She had written many tunes and jingles, both words and lyrics over the years. Shirley recounted that she was born in Norfolk, Virginia, and that her father, Jacob Schwartz, had a beautiful baritone voice, and became a cantor at a Synagogue in New York City on West 88ᵗʰ Street. She arrived with her family in Manhattan at the age of four.

Soon, I noticed that there was a small sign near the piano that listed her credentials, among which indicated that she had composed the theme song for a television show in the 1950's called the "Ted Steele Show" which had been on the New York station, WOR. The song was entitled, "I'm Thankful." When I inquired about that particular song, she asked if I would like to hear it, the words and simple tune were so touching. After listening to it, I asked her permission to jot down the lyrics, and share them with others, since I am a Catholic priest, and it would edify my flock. She was happy to grant her blessing and dictated them to me slowly. It goes like this,

> *I'm thankful for so many things,*
> *For a cozy home and all the joy it brings.*
> *I'm thankful that I'm able, at my dinner table,*
> *To have nourishing food with vitamins and things.*
>
> *I'm thankful that my family is at ease*
> *To worship God in just the way they please.*
> *I'm thankful for these blessings and I'm thankful too,*
> *So thankful for a caring friend like you.*

This sweet little tune was so uplifting and just what I needed at that time to cheer me up, since I was concerned about the surgery that was taking place. I have frequently told people to be thankful for their blessings, and that would dispel any dark clouds, and this was just what I needed to help brighten up my own day, one that was full of concern for my Mom's surgery.

The good Lord used this sweet old lady as His very special instrument that day. As well, I saw in Shirley a great lesson in tenacity. Perhaps another person in their mid-90's, who was wheelchair bound, would not want to go through the bother to rise early, get prepared to travel twice each week, to play the piano as a volunteer, but Shirley did. She was just thrilled to be there, and that I wanted the lyrics to her sweet song. She was glad that she could share them with me, and through me, to others. Shirley remarked, "Otherwise they would be dormant." I thanked her for the beautiful music that I very much enjoyed, and she responded with a sparkle in her eye, "Each day is a gift."

My life lesson, from my little concert, was that in the ups and downs, we need to stick with it, make the very best of the situation and even help to "Make a little beautiful music" in our own particular way, to brighten the lives of others. The Lord tells us, "I have told you this so that My joy may be in you, and that your joy may be complete" (Jn. 15:11). This quote is part of the beautiful fifteenth chapter of the Gospel of St. John, in which the Lord tells us to "Abide in Me," just as the branch needs to be attached to the vine, for "Without Me, you can do nothing" (Jn. 15:5). This is one of my favorite quotes, but perhaps, by now, you the reader, have realized that!

With this union to Christ, we know that He will see us through every situation, both good and bad, and even provide some joyful surprises along the way, more than we ever expected or deserved, but only out of His goodness and mercy. Our goal is to "Abide in Him," and not to destroy the good plan that Our Lord has in store for us: a beautiful life of grace and friendship in this world, followed by everlasting happiness in the kingdom of heaven.

# Fr. Placid

The Second World Apostolic Congress on Mercy is scheduled to be held October 1-5, 2011 at the Divine Mercy Shrine of Lagiewnicki, Poland, were St. Faustina lived, and where her tomb is located. In preparation for this Congress, I was invited, along with the other coordinators from other continents, to participate in a meeting that was held in Budapest, Hungary, on April 29 - May 2, 2010. In addition to the schedule of daily Mass and planning sessions regarding the logistics for the Congress, we also heard a powerful testimony talk regarding the Lord's Mercy.

Friday, April 30, 2010, was the ten year Anniversary of the Canonization of the great secretary of the Lord's Mercy, St. Faustina Kowalska. It was on that day, in the year 2000, that the Venerable John Paul II called "The happiest day in my life," according to his biographers. In 2010, all the members of the International Executive Committee, including myself, were assembled to prepare for the 2011 Mercy Congress.

We heard the testimony of Fr. Placid Olofsson, O.S.B., who is a ninety-four year old Benedictine priest from Budapest, who was wrongly sent to serve as a prisoner in a Russian Gulag in 1946. The "gulag," or prison camp, was in the Bryansk Forest, and was located 2,500 kilometers from his native land of Hungary, and 900 kilometers from Moscow. He along with the prisoners there spent nine hours each day, seven days each week cutting down trees in forced labor. When Stalin died in 1953, more than 2,000 Hungarian prisoners were finally released two years later, in 1955, including him.

Fr. Placid recounted that for his first two years as a prisoner there, he was unable to offer Mass, but would pray together with the prisoners and a Protestant pastor. Together, they would pray the Our Father, and at the end, Fr. Placid would add the words, "O Lord, be merciful to us, poor sinners." Over fifty years later, this same pastor had visited Fr. Placid and told him that over the years, he too would always add this phrase after praying the Our Father. The pastor had been curious why Fr. Placid had added that particular phrase.

Fr. Placid recounted the story from the Sacred Scriptures that meant so much to him. The Lord Jesus spoke about the two men who entered the Temple to pray, one of them would not raise his eyes and just prayed those words, "Lord, have mercy on me, a sinner" (Lk. 18:3).

After two years imprisonment, one day Fr. Placid noticed that one of the prisoners would not eat his bread allotment with his very thin soup. When he inquired, this fellow prisoner said that he was Jewish, and as it was a religious holiday, and he could only eat unleavened bread. It was allowed that Russian prisoners could receive packages from their families.

Fr. Placid obtained some of this unleavened bread from him, and some fresh grapes from another prisoner. He squeezed the grapes and got about three drops of juice into a small cup. He recalled that in 1942, the Venerable Pope Pius XII had decreed that Holy Mass could be offered with grape juice in extreme conditions. And so, Fr. Placid offered Mass while lying on his bed, with his fellow prisoners. He spoke to us with such happiness that he had the privilege of offering Holy Mass, even under those adverse circumstances.

He also recounted to all of us that one day he was given a bucket and a rag and told to scrub the bathrooms. After several days of doing this rather unpleasant task, he was assigned with a guard who began to sing, and so Fr. Placid began to hum Hungarian folk songs, and soon he began to sing. The guard spoke Hungarian, but did not object.

A few days later, he was with a different guard, who spoke only Russian, who also began to sing. With this, Fr. Placid began to sing Hungarian folk songs. While he was cleaning, he was passing the "death house," where the prisoners that were to be executed were kept. When singing the folk tunes, he added the following words, as he sung to the prisoners through their window, "I am a Catholic priest; I will absolve you from your sins, think of them." Then, as he continued to sing in Hungarian, and while still cleaning, he inserted the Latin words: "*Ego te absolvo a peccatis tuis,*" thereby absolving them of their sins.

He told us that a few months later, he was in the shower room along with a few of the prisoners, and one of them recognized his voice as the one who was singing. That prisoner recounted that He, too, had been in the death house, and was condemned to die, however his sentence was commuted to twenty-five years in prison. He then told Fr. Placid that among the prisoners in the death house, the atmosphere changed dramatically, from the day that he gave them absolution. There was then a spirit of peace and hope, since their souls had received the God's mercy and forgiveness, and they were now spiritually prepared to meet the Lord.

Fr. Placid spoke throughout his testimony in a voice that was very strong and enthusiastic. Although he walked with a cane, he was not a weak man, and his inner strength showed through to all of us. As he was coming to the conclusion of his testimony, he told us that he strongly believes that it was not an accident or error that he was sent there, but that it was God, Who had sent him to that place to take care of their souls. This had been his mission: to bring them God's mercy.

After Fr. Placid departed, I was talking about his awesome testimony to the secretary to the Auxiliary Bishop of Budapest, and was told that Fr. Placid is well loved by many, and known for his wonderful optimism, humor and kindness. I also learned that, although he did not share them with us in his talk, there were four rules that Fr. Placid laid down for his fellow prisoners, to help them to survive the gulag. They are:

*1 Do not complain and do not over dramatize your suffering, as it weakens us.*

*2 We need happiness to survive. Try to find the small, positive things that happened in that day, even if it was the sunshine, a flower or a butterfly that you saw. At the end of the day, everyone is to gather and share with others that which was positive to lift each other up.*

*3 We are not perfect, but we need to strive to be better than our guards, as that will give us energy.*

*4 Have faith and pray. For those who believe in God, this is easier, since we can hold on to God. We know that the Lord wants us to survive in this life and will give us the strength to do so, through faith in Him.*

Just a few days before I was to depart to attend this meeting, I had an inner ear infection and was battling a case of vertigo. It was not until the very morning I was scheduled to travel, that I finally decided to attend, packed my bag, and headed to the airport. I am so glad that I did so, since to hear the testimony of such a holy, positive and dedicated priest, such as Fr. Placid, was a wonderful gift that the merciful Lord gave me in the special Year dedicated to Priests, which would be concluding in less than two months.

Fr. Placid's message to survive the gulag can be applied to all of us, both priests and the holy People of God, who are "in the trenches" of spiritual combat. The more the evil one sees that we desire to be holy, the more he puts obstacles in our paths. St. Paul, after he was stoned and left for dead, told his disciples, "You have to overcome many obstacles to enter the kingdom of heaven" (Acts 14:22).

I hope and pray that Fr. Placid's survival aids will be of help to me, as well as those with whom I share them. Certainly, I will long remember them, and they will help me to persevere in my earthly pilgrimage. May they be a reminder to carry my crosses silently and patiently in this world, with the prize ever before me, the joys that await us in the kingdom of heaven.

# Conclusion

Each year, I greatly look forward to the beautiful Season of Advent, the time of spiritual preparation to celebrate the Solemnity of the Nativity of Our Lord Jesus Christ. For me, it is a time of great joy and reminiscing. This is due to the many Christmas cards which arrive from the various couples, whose weddings that I had the privilege to perform. Over the years, I have seen the photos of their children that have been included in their Christmas greetings, and now so many of those infants, who I baptized, are now in High School, and even College. In a few years, I will be learning that those same children are engaged or married; that will surely be a sign to me that the years have truly flown.

With the arrival of their thoughtful Christmas cards and notes, I can happily recall the wedding day of so many of them, and in particular my homily to them, on the splendid day of their Marriage in Christ. Although not a long one, it gets to the point,

> We are here today, on this very beautiful day, in the lives of our dear bride and groom. We join them with our hearts full of joy and affection for them. We are here this day, not only to witness their exchange of vows, on this the day of their wedding, but also to participate as they inaugurate the very beginning of their marriage of many years together.
>
> Today, dear bride and groom, you will receive many greetings and congratulations from your invited guests. Many will wish you a happy and healthy married life together. I wish to add another wish: that it be a holy married life as well.
>
> You begin your marriage here, in this holy place, at the sacred altar of the Lord Jesus Christ, our Savior. Remember to keep close to Our Lord Jesus, Who is the Light of the World. May He accompany you and enlighten you in the many years ahead, with all of its uncertainties. As the vows that you soon exchange reminds us: there may be good times and bad, sick-

ness and health. However, if you stay close to the Lord, He will get you through everything that will come your way.

Remember that in the same the way that we need to nourish our bodies, we need to nourish our souls. We do this through receiving the Sacrament of Holy Communion, as well as the other sacraments that offer us the graces we need to persevere through life's pilgrimage.

And so, once again, we congratulate you, and ask the Lord to bless you from this day forward. May His holy mother, Mary tenderly smile upon you. May your married life be happy, healthy, but most of all holy, and after a long married life together, may you enjoy the eternal joys awaiting us in the kingdom of heaven.

This is my also my message to the readers of my little work, that will soon come to a conclusion, that their lives be "Happy, Healthy, but most of all, Holy." It is my hope that the words contained herein will give the reader a few thoughts, which may serve, in some small way, as a help in their spiritual lives. We all have the same goal, to grow in holiness during our earthly pilgrimages. May I ask you to please keep, in your prayers, all priests, as well as those who serve the Lord? May our lives and words serve to glorify God, and may we faithfully be like bright and shining lighthouses. We are to dutifully illuminate the way, which leads through the darkness and tempests of this world, to the safe harbor at the end of life's journey. May our own hearts be aflame with the love of Jesus Christ, and bring that fire to others on earth (Lk. 12:49).

It is my hope that it can be said of me and my brother priests, the following words of my dear friend, Fr. Anthony, which he told me that he would like as his epitaph: "He did all things with faith, hope, love and apostolic zeal, for the glory of God for the salvation and sanctification of souls." May we truly earn these words, and be joined together, with those whom we have served in this world, in the eternal banquet in the kingdom of heaven.

# Index of Saints and People

# Index of Scripture Passages

For additional copies of this book, please contact:

Rev. Matthew R. Mauriello
St. Roch Church
10 St. Roch Avenue
Greenwich, CT 06830
Tel: 203.869.4176 Fax: 203.618.0341
E-mail: frmattmaurie@aol.com

Also available through:  www.amazon.com
                         www.barnesandnoble.com

CPSIA information can be obtained
at www.ICGtesting.com
Printed in the USA
FFHW02n2051010818
47623132-51194FF

9 781612 150048